How to access the supplemental web study guide

We are pleased to provide access to a web study guide that supplements your textbook, *Adapted Physical Education National Standards, Third Edition.* This resource offers practice exams that can be printed or completed online.

Accessing the web study guide is easy!
Follow these steps if you purchased a new book:

1. Visit www.HumanKinetics.com/AdaptedPhysicalEducationNationalStandards

2. Click the third edition link next to the book cover.

3. Click the Sign In link on the left or top of the page. If you do not have an account with Human Kinetics, you will be prompted to create one.

4. If the online product you purchased does not appear in the Ancillary Items box on the left of the page, click the Enter Key Code option in that box. Enter the key code that is printed at the right, including all hyphens. Click the Submit button to unlock your online product.

5. After you have entered your key code the first time, you will never have to enter it again to access this product. Once unlocked, a link to your product will permanently appear in the menu on the left. For future visits, all you need to do is sign in to the textbook's website and follow the link that appears in the left menu!

→ Click the Need Help? button on the textbook's website if you need assistance along the way.

How to access the web study guide if you purchased a used book:

You may purchase access to the web study guide by visiting the text's website, **www.HumanKinetics.com/AdaptedPhysicalEducationNationalStandards**, or by calling the following:

800-747-4457	U.S. customers
800-465-7301	Canadian customers
+44 (0) 113 255 5665	European customers
217-351-5076	International customers

For technical support, send an email to:

support@hkusa.com	U.S. and international customers
info@hkcanada.com	Canadian customers
academic@hkeurope.com	European customers

HUMAN KINETICS

1-2019

Product: Adapted Physical Education National Standards, Third Edition, web study guide

Key code: NCPEID-A47NZV-OSG

This unique code allows you access to the web study guide.

Access is provided if you have purchased a new book. Once submitted, the code may not be entered for any other user.

MW00345084

Adapted Physical Education National Standards

Third Edition

NCPEID

National Consortium for Physical Education
for Individuals with Disabilities

Luke E. Kelly, Editor

HUMAN KINETICS

Library of Congress Cataloging-in-Publication Data

Names: National Consortium for Physical Education for Individuals with Disabilities (U.S.) | Kelly, Luke E. (Luke Edward), 1952- editor.

Title: Adapted physical education national standards / NCPEID with Luke Kelly, editor.

Description: Third edition. | Champaign, IL : Human Kinetics, [2020] | Includes bibliographical references.

Identifiers: LCCN 2018046195 (print) | LCCN 2018056506 (ebook) | ISBN 9781492589716 (epub) | ISBN 9781492589709 (PDF) | ISBN 9781492589686 (print)

Subjects: LCSH: Physical education for children with disabilities--Standards--United States. | Physical education teachers--Certification--United States.

Classification: LCC GV445 (ebook) | LCC GV445 .N38 2020 (print) | DDC 796.087--dc23

LC record available at https://lccn.loc.gov/2018046195

ISBN: 978-1-4925-8968-6 (print)

The web addresses cited in this text were current as of November 2018, unless otherwise noted.

Acquisitions Editor: Ray Vallese
Managing Editor: Miranda K. Baur
Copyeditor: Janet Kiefer
Permissions Manager: Dalene Reeder
Graphic Designer: Julie L. Denzer
Cover Designer: Keri Evans
Photograph (cover): EasternLightcraft/iStockphoto/Getty Images
Photographs (interior): © Human Kinetics unless otherwise noted; photo on page 49, Getty Images/FatCamera; photo on page 177, Bold Stock/age fotostock; photo on page 247, Luke E. Kelly
Photo Asset Manager: Laura Fitch
Photo Production Coordinator: Amy M. Rose
Photo Production Manager: Jason Allen
Printer: Data Reproductions Corporation

Printed in the United States of America   10 9 8 7 6 5 4 3 2 1

The paper in this book is certified under a sustainable forestry program.

Human Kinetics
P.O. Box 5076
Champaign, IL 61825-5076
Website: www.HumanKinetics.com

In the United States, email info@hkusa.com or call 800-747-4457.
In Canada, email info@hkcanada.com.
In the United Kingdom/Europe, email hk@hkeurope.com.

For information about Human Kinetics' coverage in other areas of the world, please visit our website: **www.HumanKinetics.com**

E7781

Contents

Acknowledgments

It has been my pleasure and an honor to be able to guide the development and implementation of the Adapted Physical Education National Standards (APENS) and the national exam for the National Consortium for Physical Education for Individuals with Disabilities (NCPEID) for the past 30 years. The single most important thing I have had the privilege to experience over these years has been working with a core of highly dedicated, unselfish, hardworking professionals. These individuals have been willing to work without compensation for long hours on their own time, when they should be doing their own work, solely for the intrinsic reward of knowing they are improving the quality of their profession and increasing the probability that the physical and motor needs of students with disabilities in the United States will be fully addressed as stipulated in the Individuals With Disabilities Education Act (IDEA). Many of these dedicated professionals are recognized for their work on the various committees mentioned within this manual. I would like to acknowledge four specific members of this APENS core of professionals for their work on the 2018 revisions of the APENS and exam.

Dr. Hester Henderson—Hester started working on APENS in 1991 as one of six members of the APENS executive committee. She has since been a member of both the 2006 and 2018 APENS revisions. Hester never says no to a request for help, always goes above and beyond what is expected, and almost always gets her work done early. She is always upbeat and brings positive energy to every meeting, and all she requires is an occasional latte as a reward.

Dr. Tim Davis—At the time Tim decided to do his dissertation on the validity of APENS, little did he know the role it would play in the rest of his professional career. Tim is another tireless worker who can work on little or no sleep. He puts the needs of the profession and children with disabilities ahead of his own needs, will travel anywhere to do a workshop for parents or teachers, and requires only a promise to go fishing sometime in the future.

Dr. Suzanna Rocco Dillon—Suzanna joined APENS unknowingly when she became a CAPE. As any good professional trying to improve her profession, she got caught up doing high-quality service, which eventually resulted in her being elected the president of the NCPEID. Since any responsible president has to be on top of the major initiatives of the organization, Suzanna soon found herself spending two mornings a month on video conference calls learning more about APENS than she ever imaged. Suzanna is another one of those unique individuals who can work on little sleep, balance too many tasks at the same time, still produce high quality work, and keep a good sense of humor.

Wes Wilson—Wes technically volunteered to work on the 2018 APENS revision, but that was probably because he could not gracefully think of way to say no to his advisor. That said, Wes has provided countless hours of outstanding technical support to the APENS revision committee on top of all his normal doctoral student and teaching assistant/research assistant responsibilities. Most notably, he managed the test item revision process electronically, including the preparation, administration, and summary of the Evaluation and Review Committee (ERC) test item evaluations. In addition, he prepared and gave numerous Google tool tutorials as needed to committee members. Wes has clearly demonstrated his commitment to and an understanding of the value of professional service.

Introduction

Standards provide a guiding light in terms of the basic knowledge, skills, and attitudes of an individual within a field and those in higher education preparing such an individual for specific professions. Within the field of **adapted physical education**, the professional Adapted Physical Education National Standards (APENS) were developed in 1995 to certify professionals in adapted physical education throughout the United States. In addition, the APENS have been infused in many teacher education programs at the undergraduate and graduate levels as the foundation of the preparation programs. Further, at some universities, the completion of the APENS examination has become a graduation requirement.

As a part of keeping the national standards current, the National Consortium for Physical Education for Individuals with Disabilities (NCPEID), formerly known as the National Consortium for Physical Education and Recreation for Individuals with Disabilities, conducts a review process every several years and revises the APENS and the national exam as needed. These revisions are made by members of the profession to reflect current knowledge and practices. This manual is the third edition of the APENS.

The need for national adapted physical education standards and a national certification examination evolved over 40 years ago from the mandates of federal legislation such as the Individuals with Disabilities Education Act (IDEA). These mandates required that physical education services, specially designed if necessary, must be made available to every student with a disability receiving a free appropriate public education and that these services should be provided by highly qualified teachers (IDEIA, 2004).

Determining who was qualified to provide physical education services to students with disabilities was left to the individual state certification requirements in the federal mandates—based on the assumption that these currently existed. Unfortunately, most states still do not have defined certifications for adapted physical educators. While approximately 14 states currently define and implement some form of an endorsement or certification in adapted physical education, the vast majority of states and eight territories have not yet spelled out the qualifications teachers need to provide adapted physical education services to their students with disabilities (Cowden & Tymeson, 1984; Kelly, 1991c).

In 1991, the NCPEID, in conjunction with the National Association of State Directors of Special Education and Special Olympics International conducted an action seminar on adapted physical education for state directors of **special education** and leaders of advocacy groups for individuals with disabilities. Although numerous barriers to providing appropriate physical education services to students with disabilities were identified by the group, the most significant barriers for state education leaders were that they did not know what adapted physical education was, how individuals with disabilities could benefit from appropriate physical education programming, or what competencies teachers needed to deliver appropriate physical education services to students with disabilities. In response to these needs, it was recommended that the NCPEID develop professional standards and a means for evaluating these standards (see appendix A for background on NCPEID). These standards could then be used by state and school administrators as well as parents to communicate the need for quality adapted physical education and to evaluate who was qualified to provide physical education services to students with disabilities.

The action seminar recommendations were presented to the NCPEID board in the summer of 1991. An NCPEID committee was formed and charged with creating a plan for developing national standards and a national certification examination. To this end, a special project grant proposal (Kelly, 1992) was submitted to the United States Department of Education, Office of Special Education and Rehabilitative Services, Division of Personnel Preparation in the fall of 1991. This grant was funded in July of 1992 and provided funding for five years.

The purpose of this national standards project was to ensure that physical education instruction for students with disabilities is provided by qualified physical education instructors by (1) developing national standards for the field of adapted physical education and (2) developing a national certification examination to measure knowledge of the standards. The committees and procedures used to develop the national standards are presented in appendix B. The results of these processes culminated in the establishment of a set of national standards, which are presented in this manual.

Standards

Based on the results of a national needs **assessment** (see appendix B, Kelly & Gansneder, 1998), the content that adapted physical educators needed to know was identified and divided into 15 broad standards areas. The following are the specific standards with a brief description.

Standard 1—Human Development

The foundation of proposed goals and activities for individuals with disabilities is grounded in a basic understanding of human development and its applications to those with various needs. For the adapted physical education teacher, this implies familiarity with theories and practices related to human development. The emphasis within this standard focuses on knowledge and skills helpful in providing quality adapted physical education programs.

Standard 2—Motor Behavior

Teaching individuals with disabilities requires some knowledge of how individuals develop. In the case of adapted physical educators, it means having knowledge of typical physical and motor development as well as understanding the influence of developmental delays on these processes. It also means understanding how individuals learn motor skills and applying principles of motor learning during the planning and teaching of physical education to students with disabilities.

Standard 3—Exercise Science

As an adapted physical educator, you must understand that modifications to the scientific principles of exercise and the application of these principles may be needed when teaching individuals with disabilities to ensure that all children with disabilities enjoy similar benefits of exercise. While there is a wealth of information in the foundational sciences, the focus of this standard will be on the principles that address the physiological and biomechanical applications encountered when working with diverse populations.

Standard 4—Measurement and Evaluation

This standard is one of the foundation standards underscoring the background an adapted physical educator should have in order to comply with the mandates of legislation and to meet the needs of students. Understanding the measurement of motor performance, to a large extent, is based on a good grasp of motor development and the acquisition of motor skills covered in other standards.

Standard 5—History and Philosophy

This standard traces facts regarding legal and philosophical factors involved in current-day practices in adapted physical education. This information is important to understand the changing contribution that physical education can make in the lives of students with disabilities. Major components of each law that are related to education and physical activity are emphasized. A review of history and philosophy related to special and general education is also covered in this area.

Standard 6—Unique Attributes of Learners

This standard refers to information based on the disability areas identified in IDEIA (2004). Material is categorically organized in order to present the information in a systematic manner. This organization is not intended to advocate a categorical approach to teaching children with disabilities. All children should be treated as individuals and assessed to determine what needs they have.

Standard 7—Curriculum Theory and Development

As you are planning to teach physical education to students with disabilities, you should recognize that certain curriculum theory and development concepts, such as selecting goals based on relevant and appropriate assessments, must be understood by adapted physical educators. Curriculum theory and development are more than writing units and lesson plans; they are critical to the development of a comprehensive and **developmentally appropriate** program for a student with a disability.

Standard 8—Assessment

This standard addresses the process of assessment, one that is commonly taught as part of the basic measurement and **evaluation** course in a physical education degree curriculum. Assessment goes beyond data gathering to include measurements for the purpose of making decisions about special services and program components for individuals with disabilities (e.g., eligibility purposes, determining **present level of performance**, monitoring student progress, etc.).

Standard 9—Instructional Design and Planning

Instructional design and planning must occur before an adapted physical educator can provide services to meet legal mandates, educational goals, and most importantly, the unique needs of individuals with disabilities. Many of the principles addressed earlier in human development, motor behavior, exercise science, and curriculum theory and development are applied to this standard in order to successfully design and plan physical education programs.

Standard 10—Teaching

A major job responsibility for any adapted physical educator is teaching. Many of the principles addressed earlier in such standard areas as human development, motor behavior, and exercise science are applied to this standard in order to effectively provide quality physical education to individuals with disabilities.

Standard 11—Consultation and Staff Development

As more students with disabilities are included in the general education program, teachers will provide more **consultation** and staff development activities for colleagues. This will require sensitivity and excellent **communication** skills. The dynamics of interdisciplinary cooperation in the consultation process requires knowledge of several consultative models. This standard identifies key competencies that an adapted physical educator should understand related to consultation and staff development.

Standard 12—Student and Program Evaluation

Student evaluation can be either formative or summative and focuses on measuring individual student changes in knowledge, understanding, and physical and motor performance on the curriculum goals and objectives over time as a function of the physical education program. The importance of student evaluation for individuals with disabilities is highlighted in IDEA in the Individualized Education Program (IEP) process and procedures. **Program evaluation** is the process of using student physical education performance data to determine and communicate the degree to which the physical education program goals and objectives are being achieved among all students. Adapted physical educators must play an active role in ensuring that their students with disabilities, whether in **general physical education** or adapted physical education, are achieving their short-term annual IEP goals as well as their long-term physical education program goals.

Standard 13—Continuing Education

The goal of this standard is to focus on adapted physical educators remaining current in their field. A variety of opportunities for professional development are available with course work at the college or university level as just one avenue. Adapted physical educators can take advantage of in-service workshops, seminars, professional development podcasts and other distance learning opportunities, and presentations at conferences and conventions.

Standard 14—Ethics

A fundamental premise within the APENS is that those who seek and meet the standards to be certified as adapted physical educators will strive at all times to adhere to the highest of ethical standards in providing programs and services for children and youth with disabilities. This standard has been developed to ensure that its members not only understand the importance of sound ethical practices, but also adhere to and advance such practices.

Standard 15—Communication

In recent years, the role of the professional in adapted physical education has evolved from being a **direct service** provider to include communicating with families and other professionals in order to enhance program instruction for individuals with disabilities. This standard includes information regarding the adapted physical educator effectively communicating with families and other professionals using a team approach in order to enhance **service delivery** to individuals with disabilities.

Organization of the Text

Each of the 15 standards is presented in a separate section in this manual. Within each standard, the content adapted physical educators should know is presented in five levels (see table I.1). The first three levels represent the content that all certified physical educators should know. The fourth level represents additional content knowledge adapted physical educators should know. The fifth level contains example applications of the fourth level content that adapted physical educators should be able to demonstrate. The number and title of the standard on the opening page and at the top of the first page for each standard is the level 1 content, such as standard 10—Teaching. The level 2 information—the major components of the standard—is placed inside a rectangular box. Level 3 information, subcomponents of knowledge, is shaded in a lighter gray. Level 4 information, the unique adapted physical education content, is bolded in a darker shade of gray. The level 5 information, applications of the level 4 content knowledge, is bulleted with arrows and indented under the level 4 content (see figure I.1).

Note that standard 6, which is specific to the unique attributes of learners, is structured differently. In standard 6, level 2a contains the definitions of the disabilities as defined in IDEIA. The level 3 content divides the information that should be known about each disability into several broad categories such as etiology, classification, and psychomotor considerations. Level 4 information is still the unique content adapted physical educators should know and the level 5 content is applications of the level 4 content knowledge.

Table I.1   Example of the Five Levels of a Typical Standard

Level 1: Standard number and name	Standard 10: Teaching
Level 2: Major components of the standard	Teaching Styles: Demonstrate various teaching styles in order to promote learning in physical education
Level 3: Subcomponents, dependent pieces of knowledge of fact or principle related to the major component	Understand the command style of teaching
Level 4: Adapted physical education content— additional knowledge regarding the subcomponents that teachers working with individuals with disabilities need to know	Understand the effectiveness of using the command style of teaching with individuals with disabilities in order to promote learning in physical education
Level 5: Application of adapted physical education content knowledge from level 4 to teaching individuals with disabilities	• Provide clear, concise, and simple language when needed • Use specific, clear, concise verbal cues to highlight points • Use total communication as needed • Use visual cues to demonstrate the skill such as a colored sock to show a kicking foot

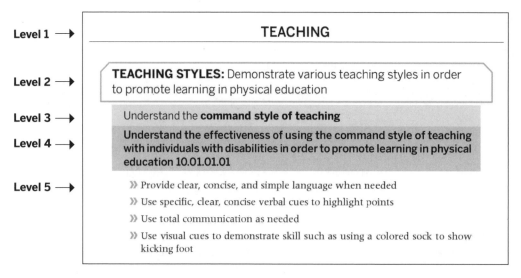

Figure I.1 Illustration of the five standards levels used in APENS.

APENS and Professional Standards for Physical Education

A basic philosophical tenet of APENS is that physical educators who teach students in integrated or segregated environments must be able to demonstrate basic instructional competencies. This is clearly reflected in the level 1 through 3 competencies, which are the foundation to the level 4 and 5 competencies specifically related to adapted physical education. As can be seen in tables I.2 and I.3, the APENS level 4 and 5 competencies are logical extensions of the Society of Health and Physical Educators (SHAPE) Initial Physical Education Teacher Education National Standards (SHAPE, 2017), the SHAPE Advanced Standards (SHAPE, 2008), and the National Board of Professional Teaching Standards for Physical Education (2014). It should be noted that the APENS, although developed *before* both the SHAPE and National Board of Professional Teaching Standards for Physical Education, clearly incorporates the content reflected in these standards.

Table I.2 Comparison of the SHAPE Initial and Advanced Physical Education Standards to APENS

SHAPE (2017) National Standards for Initial Physical Education Teacher Education	APENS (Kelly, 1996, 2006)
1. Content and Foundational Knowledge	1. Human Development 2. Motor Behavior 3. Exercise Science 4. Measurement and Evaluation 5. History and Philosophy 6. Unique Attributes of Learners 7. Curriculum Theory and Development 8. Assessment 9. Instructional Design and Planning 10. Teaching 12. Student and Program Evaluation
2. Skillfulness and Health-Related Fitness	3. Exercise Science 4. Measurement and Evaluation 6. Unique Attributes of Learners 8. Assessment
3. Planning and Implementation	4. Measurement and Evaluation 6. Unique Attributes of Learners 7. Curriculum Theory and Development 8. Assessment 9. Instructional Design and Planning
4. Instructional Delivery and Management	6. Unique Attributes of Learners 10. Teaching
5. Assessment of Student Learning	4. Measurement and Evaluation 6. Unique Attributes of Learners 8. Assessment
6. Professional Responsibility	6. Unique Attributes of Learners
ADVANCED STANDARDS	
1. Professional Knowledge	1. Human Development 2. Motor Behavior 3. Exercise Science 4. Measurement and Evaluation 5. History and Philosophy 6. Unique Attributes of Learners 7. Curriculum Theory and Development 8. Assessment 9. Instructional Design and Planning 10. Teaching 12. Student and Program Evaluation
2. Professional Practice	12. Student and Program Evaluation 13. Continuing Education 14. Ethics
3. Professional Leadership	11. Consultation and Staff Development 12. Student and Program Evaluation 13. Continuing Education 14. Ethics 15. Communication

Table I.3   Comparison of the National Board of Professional Teaching Standards for Physical Education to the APENS

National Board of Professional Teaching Standards for Physical Education (2014)	APENS (Kelly, 1995 and 2006)
1. Knowledge of students	1. Human Development 2. Motor Behavior 6. Unique Attributes of Learners
2. Knowledge of subject matter	1. Human Development 2. Motor Behavior 3. Exercise Science 4. Measurement and Evaluation 5. History and Philosophy 7. Curriculum Theory and Development 8. Assessment 9. Instructional Design and Planning 10. Teaching 12. Student and Program Evaluation
3. Curricular choices	7. Curriculum Theory and Development
4. Wellness within physical education	3. Exercise Science 7. Curriculum Theory and Development
5. Learning environment	6. Unique Attributes of Learners 7. Curriculum Theory and Development 9. Instructional Design and Planning 10. Teaching
6. Diversity and inclusion	6. Unique Attributes of Learners 7. Curriculum Theory and Development 9. Instructional Design and Planning 10. Teaching
7. Teaching practices	9. Instructional Design and Planning 10. Teaching
8. Assessment	8. Assessment 12. Student and Program Evaluation
9. Reflective practice	10. Teaching 11. Consultation and Staff Development 12. Student and Program Evaluation
10. Collaboration and partnerships	11. Consultation and Staff Development 15. Communication
11. Professional growth	13. Continuing Education
12. Advocacy	11. Consultation and Staff Development 15. Communication

How to Use This Manual

This manual can be used in different ways depending on the audience and their intended use of the standards.

Teachers Preparing for the APENS Examination

Teachers planning to take the APENS exam can use this manual to help prepare. First you need to distinguish between the content you already know and the content you need to review or learn. To start, read the level 2 and level 3 statements to understand the context. Next read the level 4 statement and its applications, which are listed in the level 5 statements. If you understand the level 4 and level 5 statements, move on to the next level 4 statement. If you do not know the level 4 statement or only vaguely remember the content, mark it. Systematically repeat this process until you have reviewed all the level 4 statements for all 15 standards.

You have now highlighted the content you should review or learn before taking the exam. If you are working by yourself, you will need to look up this content in your college or university textbooks, past class notes, or on the web. If you are studying with a group of teachers preparing to take the exam, you can divide up some of the review work. First, you can meet as a group and review the level 4 statements you each have identified. In most cases, members of the group will likely be able to teach other members of the group about unfamiliar level 4 statements. After this review, there will likely be a selected number of level 4 statements that will require additional independent or group studying efforts to learn. These can be divided among the group members. Each member looks up the content of the level 4 statements he or she is assigned and then shares this information at the next group meeting.

University Faculty

Since the APENS are based on a needs assessment of what adapted physical educators need to know to do their jobs, they can also be used by faculty members at colleges and universities to evaluate their adapted physical education preparation programs. The APENS can be used much like the National Council for Accreditation of Teacher Education, and the SHAPE standards are used to evaluate teacher preparation programs in physical education. The APENS can be distributed to the faculty, and each member can be asked to review the standards in their area and indicate which ones are addressed in their courses. A simple process like writing in the margin which course addresses each objective will suffice. Then summarize which level 3 and 4 standards are currently not being addressed in the curriculum. These can then be discussed at a future faculty meeting and distributed across the curriculum.

K to 12 Administrators

All administrators share the goal of ensuring that all students with disabilities receive physical education taught by a qualified teacher; however, many may not be able to judge who is qualified. Administrators can use the APENS and the national exam as criteria when reviewing and hiring new teachers. Since the majority of students with disabilities are educated in the general physical education setting, it would be desirable if all physical educators were certified adapted physical educators (CAPEs). If it is not feasible or realistic to employ CAPEs for all general physical education positions, adapted physical education specialists who are CAPEs should be employed to work collaboratively with general physical educators to assist them in meeting the physical education needs of the students with disabilities in their classes. The NCPEID can be contacted to identify local university faculty that can provide both credit and noncredit options for delivering these services to prepare general physical educators to appropriately address the physical education needs of the students with disabilities in their classes. The website address is www.ncpeid.org.

Parents

Parents of students with disabilities should know that if their children require specially designed instruction in physical education that it should be designed and implemented by a qualified physical educator. To this end, parents should inquire at their child's IEP meeting who will provide the adapted physical education services and what qualifies this individual for this role. If the proposed teacher is a CAPE, the parents have some assurance that this teacher has met at least the minimal national standards established by the profession. If the proposed teacher is not a CAPE, the parents should request a written explanation stating why they are not employing a teacher knowledgeable about adapted physical education for this role and indicating that the school accepts responsibility and liability for any injuries or emotional distress their child may encounter that can be attributed to not being taught by a CAPE or a state-credentialed adapted physical education teacher.

Using the Web Study Guide

This book has a companion web study guide that you can access using the key code at the front of the book when you visit www.HumanKinetics.com/AdaptedPhysical EducationNationalStandards. The web study guide provides guidance on how to prepare for the APENS exam and how to study the content for each standard. Using the web study guide, you can take multiple short practice quizzes on each standard from randomly selected questions created using the content in this manual for each standard.

Frequently Asked Questions

Based on numerous requests, an APENS frequently asked questions section has been included in this edition. To review the questions and answers, refer to appendix C.

Glossary

Given the diversity of terms and the common use of abbreviations and acronyms in the field, a glossary has been provided at the end of the manual to assist the reader. In the first appearance of each glossary term in the manual, the term is written in bold text.

Bibliography

Although not coded to each statement, a summative list of references that were used by the various committees in developing the standards is also included at the end of the manual.

HUMAN DEVELOPMENT

STANDARD 1

HUMAN DEVELOPMENT

UNDERSTAND COGNITIVE DEVELOPMENT

Explain the theory of cognitive development as proposed by Piaget

Understand the implications of Piaget's theory for the development of individuals with disabilities 1.01.01.01

» Apply Piaget's theory to the development of infants and individuals with various disabilities

» Recognize the strengths and limitations of Piaget's theory as applied to individuals with disabilities

Understand that **perception**, attention, and memory may impact the ability to effectively participate and learn in a physical education environment

Understand the impact intellectual disabilities have on perception, attention, and memory for learning in the physical education environment 1.01.02.01

» Develop programs that sequence materials appropriately for individuals with disabilities, recognizing unique attention deficits and perceptual disorders

» Create environments that enhance instruction in physical education by reducing external stimuli as needed

Understand the difference between short-term and long-term memory capacity as applied to individuals with selected disabilities (see Standard 2) 1.01.02.02

» Recognize the implications of short- and long-term memory in the learning process, specifically among individuals with disabilities

» Adapt the learning environment to compensate for short- or long-term memory deficits for individuals with disabilities such as intellectual disabilities and **traumatic brain injury**

Understand the impact of physical and sensory disability on perception, attention, and memory for learning in physical education 1.01.02.03

» Adjust programs to respond to the challenges associated with the individual's perceptual skills

» Adjust programs to respond to the challenges associated with short attention spans and decreased memory

Understand the impact of emotional disability on perception, attention, and memory for learning in physical education 1.01.02.04

» Adapt programs to respond to the needs of individuals with various forms of emotional disturbance and behavioral disorders including depression and mental illness

» Develop programs to respond to the unique needs of individuals with clinical mental disabilities including psychosis, neuroses, and **personality disorders**

» Recognize that some individuals with behavior disorders have the ability to excel in physical activity

DEMONSTRATE KNOWLEDGE OF LANGUAGE AND COGNITIVE DEVELOPMENT THROUGH THE LIFESPAN

Describe the effect of limited verbal language on participation in physical education

Understand the impact of limited expressiveness and receptive language on participation in physical education 1.02.01.01

» Develop programs that respond to the expressive and receptive language needs of individuals with selected disabilities such as autism spectrum disorder and congenital deafness

» Provide programs that respond appropriately to the needs of individuals with language disorders

» Provide programs that include visual **cues** or pictures as methods to enhance expressive and receptive language

Understand the need to use alternative/augmentative communication in physical education (see Standard 9) 1.02.01.02

» Use alternative forms of communication such as **American Sign Language** and Signing Exact English

» Apply technology so that individuals with selected disabilities, such as visual disabilities, can successfully participate in physical education activity

» Recognize that the general physical educator must not only know how to express him/herself in the mode of communication utilized by his/her students, but must also know how to receive information from augmentative communication such as sign language

UNDERSTAND ESSENTIAL CONCEPTS RELATED TO SOCIAL OR AFFECTIVE DEVELOPMENT

Understand and define important terms such as **socialization**, **social roles**, and **social norms**

Know that individuals with disabilities are often excluded and/or inappropriately portrayed in discussions of social roles and social norms 1.03.01.01

» Advocate for individuals with disabilities and their right to be included in programs of physical education and sport sponsored by schools and communities

» Include individuals with disabilities in all appropriate aspects of physical education and sport programs

» Use examples of individuals with disabilities who are role models and highlight their successes in physical education and sport activities

» Recognize individuals with and without disabilities who do well in physical education settings

» Understand that individuals with disabilities may demonstrate low self-esteem and low self-confidence

» Advocate for individuals with disabilities to demonstrate self-expression

» Provide opportunities for individuals with disabilities to know they are valued and are contributing to the activity or program

Appreciate the social influences present during infancy (e.g., attachment to objects, recognition of touch, and involvement with the environment)

Understand that some individuals with selected disabilities experience significant sensory deprivation 1.03.02.01

» Provide programs that emphasize the individual's strengths and limit situations that could cause frustration (e.g., individuals who are deaf/blind may be frustrated in large group activities)

» Utilize alternative forms of interaction to ensure that individuals with sensory disorders are not unnecessarily excluded

Recognize the role that the family plays in social development

Understand the stages of grief (denial, guilt, rejection, anger) experienced by families at birth and the early stages of development of the child with a disability 1.03.03.01

» Develop programs and opportunities for families and their infants and toddlers to participate in motor and physical activities

» Cooperate with other professionals in developing support programs and activities for families of individuals with disabilities

» Continually inform families of curricular innovations, special programs, and the progress of their child

Understand the impact of the presence of a child with a disability on the structure and function of the family 1.03.03.02

» Communicate with families about the services provided in adapted physical education and the commitment to assist the development of their child (see Standard 15)

» Listen to families, recognizing their needs to express concerns and frustrations about various issues, including the need for and value of physical activity involvement

Understand the unique needs, concerns, and worries experienced by many siblings of individuals with disabilities 1.03.03.03

» Provide opportunities for siblings to observe their brother or sister successfully participating in physical activity and sport-related movement experiences

» Share information, as appropriate, with siblings that helps to reduce anxiety and improve understanding about the long-term outlook for individuals with disabilities

Know the role that the family plays in promoting health and physical fitness throughout the lifespan of individuals with a disability 1.03.03.04

» Develop and facilitate the implementation of programs to assist families with play and interaction with an individual with a disability

» Develop lifespan physical activity programs that promote social interaction between family members and the individual with a disability

» Create opportunities where family members and/or care providers can participate with individuals with disabilities

Know the behavioral indices of an individual with a history of abuse and neglect 1.03.03.05

» Structure programs to respond to the possible special health, fitness, movement, and play needs of individuals with a history of abuse and neglect

» Accept responsibility according to state and professional standards for reporting suspected cases of abuse and neglect

Demonstrate knowledge of diversity of families in the United States including **child kinship** patterns of never-married, single-parent families, remarried, and two-parent families

Know the impact of diverse child kinship patterns on the physical activity development of the child with a disability 1.03.04.01

» Develop programs that encourage parents, care providers, and advocates to be involved in play and related movement experiences of their child without inhibition or concern for social norms

» Respect parents, care providers, advocates, and others for their willingness to actively participate in physical activities with individuals with disabilities

Demonstrate knowledge of and appreciation for cultural diversity of families in the United States

Understand the importance of culturally relevant practices, such as play, physical activity, games, and sports, toward development of the individual with a disability 1.03.05.01

» Use various forms of play and physical activity enjoyed by individuals with diverse cultural backgrounds

» Adapt games that can be enjoyed by individuals with disabilities from culturally diverse backgrounds (see Standard 10)

» Utilize knowledge of **evidence-based practices** specific to culture when developing or adapting games and/or sports

Understand the important and unique role of play in the development of the individual

Know the various stages of play such as, independent, parallel, small group, large group experienced by infants and children as they develop 1.03.06.01

» Plan programs that respond to the developmental play needs of infants, toddlers, and children

» Provide play experiences in which infants, toddlers, and children with disabilities have the opportunity to engage in positive social interaction

» Provide activities that are developmentally appropriate for individuals with disabilities

Understand the importance of group play to the process of socialization among individuals with and without disabilities 1.03.06.02

» Plan physical education programs that maximize opportunities for integrated group play

» Conduct physical education and sport programs that promote group interaction for individuals with and without disabilities

Understand the value of play interaction between and among individuals with and without disabilities 1.03.06.03

» Promote opportunities that support integrated play experiences

» Develop integrated play experiences based on the concept of **inclusion**

» Provide various activities that promote the ability of all participants

Understand the effect that various developmental delays and disabilities can have on the individual's successful participation in play activities 1.03.06.04

» Describe play behavior across the lifespan for individuals with disabilities

» Adapt programs so individuals with disabilities can be successful in play experiences

» Recognize that individuals with various disabilities may need modifications requiring teachers to individualize instruction

UNDERSTAND THEORIES OF MORAL DEVELOPMENT IN CHILDREN AND YOUTH

Understand the role and impact of social institutions on the **moral development** of individuals with disabilities

Understand the unique opportunities within the physical education curriculum to promote appropriate values for individuals with disabilities 1.04.01.01

» Provide opportunities in the physical education curriculum that allow individuals with disabilities to exercise choice

>> Use instructional strategies that emphasize the importance of fair play, sportsmanship, and teamwork

Appreciate the role of schools in the moral development of individuals with disabilities

Understand the sensitive nature of moral development and the vulnerability of some individuals with disabilities to exploitation 1.04.02.01

>> Apply moral development concepts in the teaching of sport, play, and physical activity for individuals with disabilities

>> Model acceptance of individuals with disabilities, emphasizing the individual rather than the disability

>> Emphasize that individuals with disabilities are to be treated respectfully and viewed as people rather than objects

UNDERSTAND DIFFERENT PERSONALITY THEORIES AS THEY RELATE TO HUMAN BEHAVIOR

Understand that field or **ecological theory** of personality describes the psychosocial interdependence of individuals in a community, taking into account the physical environment and the systems that operate in the environment

Understand that there is reciprocity between the actions of an individual with a disability and the actions of the other individuals participating in a physical education class 1.05.01.01

>> Model acceptance and inclusion of the individual with a disability in the physical education class

>> Develop physical education environments that emphasize the capability of the individual with a disability

>> Include individuals with disabilities in planning physical education programs and related sport experiences

Understand the ecological impact of the physical environment (where they live, what school they attend) and the subsystems (social, economic, societal, home, day care) affecting the individual 1.05.01.02

>> Review records and interview primary care providers to assist in creating successful physical education experiences

>> Accept individuals with disabilities, recognizing that their prior experience and background may require a sensitive and empathetic teacher

>> Avoid establishing predetermined limits on individuals because of background, culture, or socioeconomic status

Understand the importance of assessing individuals with disabilities by accounting for the environmental conditions under which activity

can be performed, the attributes of the performer, and the interaction of that environment and the performer 1.05.01.03

» Use an **ecological task analysis** approach in teaching physical education activities

» Change the instructional environment, as appropriate, to ensure that the relationship among the performer, task, and conditions leads to success

Know how an individual's actions affect the environment and the environment affects the individual 1.05.01.04

» Obtain desired skill level and present level of performance by utilizing various approaches, including **applied behavior analysis** and task analysis

» Structure the environment so that it responds to the needs of selected individuals such as increasing or decreasing the amount of stimuli, size of movement space, or number of cues

Understand that **self-actualization** theory emphasizes that individuals are constantly striving to realize their full inherent potential

Understand the importance of meeting basic physiological, safety and security, love and belonging, and self-esteem needs before an individual can be self-actualized 1.05.02.01

» Plan programs in cooperation with others, including related service personnel such as therapists and psychologists, as well as parents and individuals with disabilities

» Implement programs that focus on the complete individual, acknowledging the importance of incremental success

Understand the importance of unconditional positive regard of the individual with a disability 1.05.02.02

» Emphasize strengths of the individual in order to build on the needs that will generate self-actualization

» Develop a physical education environment that allows the individual with a disability to perceive the teacher and peers as supportive in the learning process

Understand that **self-efficacy** theory of personality development emphasizes the concept that belief in one's ability and personal resourcefulness will allow one to successfully achieve desired outcomes

Understand that an individual with a disability will experience a sense of personal mastery that can generalize to new situations 1.05.03.01

» Develop opportunities for individuals with disabilities to succeed using an incremental approach with **positive reinforcement**

» Encourage and facilitate individuals with disabilities to transfer skills learned during physical education class to other activities and life experiences

Understand types of cues and prompts that will foster an individual with a disability learning new behaviors 1.05.03.02

» Utilize cues and prompts that are appropriate to the instructional and/or behavioral needs of the individual with a disability

» Recognize the importance of withdrawing cues and prompts to the least intrusive level

» Recognize that the individuals are learning about their own level of competence

Understand that normalization theory emphasizes that individuals with disabilities should live and function as closely as possible to the normal living, learning, and working conditions of people in society

Understand procedures and techniques in physical education classes that enhance the image of individuals with disabilities 1.05.04.01

» Structure the learning environment to create equitable participation for individuals with and without disabilities

» Incorporate examples of successful athletes with disabilities in the physical education environment

Understand the importance of selecting appropriate services to support inclusion of individuals with disabilities in general physical education settings 1.05.04.02

» Work cooperatively with other professionals to maximize inclusive experiences for individuals with and without disabilities

» Support and advocate for other professionals who provide motor experiences for individuals with disabilities

DEMONSTRATE KNOWLEDGE OF FACTORS INFLUENCING DEVELOPMENT

Understand that many disabilities are directly attributable to genetic, medical, and environmental factors

Understand that developmental disabilities may be caused by chromosomal anomalies; gestational disorders; degenerative disorders; mineral, nutritional, endocrine, and mineral dysfunction; infections and intoxicants; and environmental factors 1.06.01.01; 1.06.01.02; 1.06.01.03

» Check medical records and be aware of current medical status and medications and their impact on motor performance

» Collaborate with the appropriate school personnel related to placement and programming in physical education

» Plan proper safety precautions during physical activity based on the unique characteristics of the disability of the individual such as modifying activities for individuals with Down syndrome who have **atlantoaxial instability**

Understand that the cause of some disabilities is not well understood 1.06.01.04

» Consult with physicians and medical experts regarding disabilities with unknown causes

» Identify local, state, and national agencies that may have information on the causes of these disabilities (see Standard 9)

Understand that development may be caused by chromosomal anomalies 1.06.01.05

» Explain the incidence of common chromosomal anomalies

» Explain the impact of common chromosomal anomalies, such as Down syndrome, on motor performance

» Collaborate with the appropriate school personnel related to placement and programming in physical education

Understand that external factors may affect development 1.06.01.06

» Explain the impact of factors such as alcohol, drugs, and other substances that can cause premature birth

» Appreciate that factors such as alcohol, drugs, and other substances can affect growth and development

MOTOR BEHAVIOR

STANDARD 2

MOTOR BEHAVIOR

STANDARD 2

UNDERSTAND MOTOR DEVELOPMENT

Understand neuromaturational/hierarchical models

Understand **sensory integration** 2.01.01.01

» Recognize the relationship between sensory integration and **ataxia**

» Identify factors in inter-sensory and intra-sensory integration related to movement control and coordination

» Select and design activities to stimulate and facilitate the development of inter-sensory and intra-sensory integration

Understand **neurodevelopmental theory** 2.01.01.02

» Structure tasks and activities to inhibit abnormal movements

» Structure tasks and activities to stimulate and facilitate normal postural responses

Understand **dynamic systems theory**

Understand the diversity and influence of rate of performance and learning constraints, such as body size and proportions, gravity, cognitive development, and biomechanical constraints, on motor experiences of individuals with disabilities 2.01.02.01

» Apply knowledge of dynamic systems theory to program planning and implementation

» Develop individual program plans that diminish and/or accommodate for the effects of rate limiters

Understand factors (including prenatal and postnatal influences) affecting motor development such as nutritional status, genetic makeup, and environmental opportunities for practice and instruction

Understand how these factors could influence the rate and sequence of development for individuals with disabilities 2.01.03.01

» Identify characteristic behaviors related to factors that impact the rate and sequence of development

» Implement a program of activities specifically designed to minimize factors affecting motor development and to maximize developmental potential

Know the importance of synthesizing information on physical, cognitive, and psychological factors and their impact on skill acquisition for individuals with disabilities 2.01.03.02

» Develop programs that maximize individuals' strengths and diminish and/or accommodate for weaknesses in specific domains of motor behavior

» Maintain an integrated programmatic approach to instruction, based on the knowledge of the individual's cognitive and social development and its relationship to motor development

Understand typical sensory development related to the visual, auditory, tactile, **vestibular**, and proprioceptive systems

Understand common deviations in the development of the visual system among individuals with disabilities 2.01.04.01

» Recognize deficits in refractive and **orthoptic vision** including accommodation and tracking abilities in individuals with disabilities

» Describe the impact of the development of visual functions, such as constancy, figure-ground perception, and depth perception, on movement control in motor activities

» Apply knowledge of visual functioning deficiencies in selecting and designing activities

» Develop and implement programs that strengthen orthoptic visual abilities such as visual fixation, pursuit, and search behaviors

» Modify activities to accommodate individuals with visual deficiencies

Understand common deviations in the development of the auditory system among individuals with disabilities 2.01.04.02

» Recognize deficits in auditory recognition, discrimination, and localization

» Describe the impact of the development of auditory functions, such as auditory figure-ground perception, on the learning of motor skills

» Select and design activities to help accommodate deficits in auditory functioning

» Modify activities to accommodate auditory deficits

Understand common deviations in the development of the tactile system among individuals with disabilities 2.01.04.03

» Recognize behaviors associated with hyper-responsive (**tactile defensive**) and hypo-responsive (tactile seeking) tactile disorders

» Select and design activities to help remediate hyper- and hypo-responsive tactile disorders

» Develop and implement programs to enhance individuals' abilities to tolerate various levels of tactile stimuli

» Develop and implement programs that enhance individuals' abilities to accurately discriminate from among various tactile stimuli and use the information effectively

Understand common deviations in the development of the vestibular system among individuals with disabilities 2.01.04.04

» Recognize behaviors associated with vestibular functioning deficiencies

» Recognize signs of vestibular overstimulation

» Conduct basic screening to assess vestibular function

» Select and design activities to help remediate balance problems related to vestibular functioning

» Develop and implement programs that stimulate the vestibular system for integration with visual, proprioceptive, and tactile inputs

Understand common deviations in the development of the proprioceptive system among individuals with disabilities 2.01.04.05

» Recognize behaviors associated with deficiencies in the proprioceptive system

» Conduct basic screening to identify possible deficiencies in proprioceptive system functioning

» Select and design activities to help remediate deficiencies in proprioceptive system functioning

» Develop and implement programs that stimulate efficient use of proprioceptive inputs and integration with vestibular, visual, and tactile input systems

Understand patterns of cognitive, perceptual, and perceptual motor development and the factors that influence those patterns

Understand the influences of perceptual **motor programs** that emphasize cognitive and perceptual abilities among individuals with disabilities 2.01.05.01

» Develop and implement programs that afford individuals opportunities to formulate and execute motor plans

» Implement opportunities for **augmented feedback** when individuals are involved in activities that enhance motor planning abilities

Understand the development of postural control and relationship to the mechanisms of balance and **equilibrium**

Understand the significance of developmental delays throughout the lifespan on balance and related tasks 2.01.06.01

» Develop and implement programs that stimulate vestibular, visual, and proprioceptive senses

» Develop and implement programs that increase the strength and **endurance** of postural muscle groups

Understand the influence of the development of **reflexes** on normal motor development and the implications on skill acquisition

Understand the relationship between persistence of **infant reflexes** (i.e., primitive and postural) and disabling conditions 2.01.07.01

» Identify the difference between primitive and postural reflexes

» Describe the influence of weak or persistent infant reflexes on the rate and sequence of motor development as well as voluntary motor control in individuals with disabilities

Understand reflexes and reactions observed in individuals developing typically and atypically 2.01.07.02

» Recognize the differing patterns of reflex behavior among individuals with disabilities such as persistent primitive reflexes in individuals with cerebral palsy

» Identify behaviors associated with persistent or weak infant residual reflexes

» Select and design activities that inhibit primitive reflexes through positioning and stimulation of voluntary responses (see Standard 9)

» Select and design activities to help stimulate the development of postural and **equilibrium reactions**

» Modify activities to accommodate persistence of infant reflexes

Understand the development and emergence of locomotion including prone progressions, assumption of an upright gait, and walking

Understand variance in achieving "motor milestones" such as typical or average age of achievement for individuals with disabilities 2.01.08.01

» Identify behaviors associated with lack of attainment of "motor milestones"

» Implement activities that stimulate upright postures and control of head, neck, and trunk

» Implement activities that strengthen postural muscles and extremities necessary for locomotion

Understand the development and emergence of manipulation skills including reaching, grasping, and releasing

Understand variance in manipulation skills associated with individuals with disabilities 2.01.09.01

» Identify the impact of developmental delays in reaching, grasping, and releasing on the ability to perform functional motor skills, sport, and lifetime recreational activities

» Select and design activities that stimulate visual fixation and enable the visual-to-motor match needed to reach-grasp-release

Understand that there are differing patterns of performance for manipulative skills among individuals with disabilities 2.01.09.02

» Modify activities to accommodate differing patterns of performance for manipulative skills

» Implement activities to reach-grasp-release through the use of supportive assistive aids to enhance voluntary controls and means-end behaviors

Understand the development of fundamental motor skills and patterns

Understand variance in the progression of fundamental motor skill performance among individuals with disabilities 2.01.10.01

» Task analyze to determine the progression of fundamental motor skill acquisition according to the area of the body (head, trunk, feet) or phase (preparation, action, and follow-through) of the skill

» Select and design activities to help stimulate fundamental motor skill development

» Modify activities to accommodate for differing patterns of performance for fundamental motor skills exhibited by some individuals with disabilities

Understand how fundamental motor skills are refined and combined to produce specialized movement skills

Understand how to adapt activities to promote development from the fundamental movement phase through the specialized movement phase for individuals with disabilities 2.01.11.01

» Task analyze the specialized movement (e.g., sport skills, outdoor pursuit skills, dance movements) according to the level of the fundamental motor skill exhibited

» Select and design activities to help stimulate the development of fundamental motor skills related to specialized movements (e.g., sport skills, outdoor pursuit skills, dance movements)

Understand the relationship between mature fundamental motor skill development and performance of sport-related skill development

Understand how appropriate modifications of the physical environment enable individuals with disabilities to perform sport skills 2.01.12.01

» Modify sport-related activities to accommodate differing patterns of fundamental skills exhibited by some individuals with disabilities

» Change the structure and organization of sports and games to include diverse skill levels and performance indicators

Understand how motor development impacts the ability to engage in lifetime recreation and sport activities

Understand the influence of sport and recreation on the overall development of individuals with disabilities 2.01.13.01

» Use a functional model of skill development

» Use equipment that has been specifically designed to enhance participation by individuals with disabilities

Know when to adapt rules to accommodate participation by individuals with a disability in a sport or recreational activity of their choice 2.01.13.02

>> Provide competitive sport opportunities for individuals with disabilities who are not currently served by an established organization

>> Develop and implement physical activities that meet the needs of individuals with disabilities who are not accommodated by existing program offerings

Know how to modify activities and programs to enhance the cognitive, affective, and psychomotor development of individuals with disabilities (see Standard 10) 2.01.13.03

>> Use knowledge about an individual's cognitive development to select tasks and activities that can be acquired, retained, and transferred to other related tasks and activities

>> Use knowledge of an individual's social development to determine which tasks and activities will provide for maximum social integration and acceptance

>> Use knowledge of an individual's psychomotor development to establish an integrated approach to program planning that includes cognitive and social development enhancement

Understand factors that contribute to positive and **negative transfer** such as the nature of the task, the goal of training, or the amount and type of practice

Understand the concepts of transfer and specificity when programming for individuals with disabilities 2.02.01.01

>> Plan practice and learning tasks that will positively transfer to the next level of skill acquisition

>> Use transfer to measure attainment of selected criterion skills

>> Apply the concept of task specificity with the understanding that it presents certain problems for some individuals with disabilities

Understand the stages of the different learning theories and models such as those of Fitts and Posner, Adams, Gentile, and Bernstein

Understand the implications of the stages of learning during skill acquisition for individuals with disabilities 2.02.02.01

>> Plan and give feedback consistent with the knowledge needed at each stage of skill acquisition

>> Structure practice and learning tasks to support individualization within a class to match different rates of skill acquisition

>> Plan for an increase in task complexity commensurate with the needs of individuals with various abilities

» Structure practice and learning tasks to move from a closed to an **open skill** such as from a ball on a batting tee to a pitched ball

» Make adjustments in teaching methods and instructions commensurate with the needs of individuals with various abilities

» Use a variety of techniques to facilitate learning during the verbal-cognitive stage

UNDERSTAND MOTOR LEARNING

Understand factors that positively and negatively affect retention such as practice schedules and failure to provide feedback

Understand the implications of overlearning on the retention of motor skills by individuals with disabilities 2.02.03.01

» Use practice variability to positively influence the retention of motor skills

» Analyze complex movements to determine which could benefit from randomly ordered practice

» Structure the duration of instructional units to facilitate retention of content

Understand pre-practice considerations (e.g., motivation and goal setting)

Know techniques and procedures that can facilitate motivation and preparation for individuals with disabilities 2.02.04.01

» Plan practice and tasks with appropriate levels of novelty and complexity

» Set and present goals that are challenging but attainable with learner input

» Use performance standards to help individuals with disabilities set goals

» Modify activities as a means of achieving success

Understand principles of practice including how and when to use **guidance** techniques, **mental practice** and imagery, and whole versus part practice

Understand how practice principles can be used for individuals with disabilities 2.02.05.01

» Analyze skills to determine the most appropriate type of practice such as whole, whole-part, and part

» Use physical and verbal guidance to avoid errors early in learning

» Emphasize the use of mental practice and imagery

» Encourage the use of a combination of mental and physical practice to increase learning efficiency

Understand how **massed and distributed practice** are used for continuous and discrete tasks

Understand the concept of practice variability when promoting skill acquisition for individuals with disabilities 2.02.06.01

>> Structure across and within practices so time spent on activities is divided into appropriate segments

>> Recognize and classify tasks according to their energy cost (see Standard 3)

>> Design practice sessions that include appropriate rest periods for **discrete** and **continuous skills**

Understand how to organize and schedule practice with emphasis on instructional efficiency

Understand how task variation complements skill acquisition in individuals with disabilities 2.02.07.01

>> Vary practice schedules along various dimensions such as distance, speed, and time

>> Use **random practice** selectively depending on the nature of the disability

>> Recognize the impact of the **contextual interference** effect on the learning of motor skills

Understand how random practice impacts learning and retention of motor skills

Know how the effect of random practice may vary for individuals with disabilities 2.02.08.01

>> Use random practice to aid task retention

>> Construct **variable practice** sessions to incorporate a wide range of movement variations

Understand the factors that affect both transfer to training and the relationship between generalizability and specificity of learning such as **automaticity**, **error detection**, and transfer and **generalization** of learning

Know how these factors (i.e., automaticity, error detection, transfer, and generalization of learning) relate to error detection and generalizability of learning of individuals with disabilities 2.02.09.01

>> Develop the ability to detect and correct errors among individuals with disabilities

>> Determine which type of feedback is most useful in correcting performance errors

Recognize characteristics of performance that accompany increased automaticity and error detection in individuals with disabilities 2.02.09.02

» Use a given stimulus pattern when practicing because it increases the probability of producing the specific response

» Design practice sessions to develop a high level of physical performance in both closed and open skills

Understand the importance of feedback to learning

Know how different types of feedback such as knowledge results, knowledge of performance, intrinsic, and augmented may be used to enhance performance of individuals with disabilities (see Standard 10) 2.02.10.01

» Use feedback to motivate individuals with disabilities

» Use feedback to reinforce appropriate movement patterns

» Use feedback to help individuals with disabilities detect and correct their own errors

Know how to vary methods of feedback delivery to enhance the performance of individuals with disabilities 2.02.10.02

» Select different types of feedback (e.g., verbal feedback, non-verbal feedback, biofeedback, video feedback, etc.) to enhance learning

» Determine which movement features are most critical for success

» Give feedback that is appropriate

» Use faded feedback and adjust schedules for **fading** to accommodate individual errors

Understand the relationship between altering the scheduling of feedback and guidance, reward, and motivation

Know how to use a system of least prompts, including when it is best to use verbal, visual, environmental, and physical prompts 2.02.11.01

» Use physical prompting to assist individuals with visual impairment

» Use appropriate visual, verbal, and physical prompts within a least-prompts instructional hierarchy

» Structure the physical environment to provide **extrinsic feedback** to individuals with disabilities

Understand how delays in **knowledge of results** affect skill acquisition

Understand how to manipulate the intertrial interval to enhance skill acquisition among individuals with disabilities 2.02.12.01

» Structure the intertrial interval to reduce the effects of delayed knowledge of results for individuals with visual disabilities

» Provide sufficient time after giving feedback for the individual with a disability to think about and understand errors

UNDERSTAND MOTOR CONTROL

Understand the stages of information processing (i.e., **stimulus identification**, **response selection**, and **response programming**)

Understand how the stages of information processing are affected by certain types of disabilities 2.03.01.01

» Modify tasks and instructions so that they are congruent with individuals' processing abilities

» Adjust strategies in game-like situations to take into account delayed response processing

Understand the importance of attention and arousal in motor performance

Understand the concept of stimulus overselectivity and its effect on motor performance in individuals with disabilities 2.03.02.01

» Manipulate the learning environment for minimum infringement on the individual's attention

» Structure and present tasks within the learning environment to elicit optimal arousal levels

» Structure activities involving tracking of objects to account for the impact of the disability on performance

Understand the parts of the central nervous system responsible for motor control processes and their function and interaction with other systems

Understand how damage to various neurological structures affect motor performance in individuals with disabilities (see Standard 3) 2.03.03.01

» Structure tasks and activities to account for damage to the basal ganglia, which will influence coordinated movements such as throwing an object by some individuals with cerebral palsy

» Structure tasks and activities to account for cerebellar problems

Distinguish among simple, choice, and **discrimination reaction time**

Understand how certain types of disabilities may affect reaction time 2.03.04.01

» Modify activities to allow more or less processing time, as needed

» Structure tasks and activities to account for greater difficulty responding to multiple-choice situations such as those experienced during dynamic game play

Distinguish among short-term sensory store, short-term memory, and long-term memory

Understand how different types of memory problems may be influenced by an individual's disability 2.03.05.01

>> Repeat previously experienced instructions or activities without negative effect

>> Evaluate the effects of different types of kinesthetic and proprioceptive deficits on the ability to retain skills such as the way a bat is held

Understand how **anticipation** affects skill acquisition

Understand how spatial and temporal uncertainty can exacerbate movement difficulties in individuals with disabilities 2.03.06.01

>> Structure tasks and activities with balls to account for difficulties with anticipation for individuals with figure-ground problems

>> Structure tasks and activities involving the flight of objects to control for problems in timing that are evident in individuals with certain types of disabilities

Differentiate between controlled and **automatic processes** with emphasis on the response selection stage

Understand controlled and automatic processes in open and closed skills with individuals with disabilities 2.03.07.01

>> Analyze skills in relation to interference resulting from the presence of infant reflex behavior such as with some individuals with cerebral palsy executing a forehand in tennis

>> Structure tasks and activities to account for reflex actions that may interfere with performance in a closed skill such as swimming the front crawl stroke for individuals with disabilities (e.g., traumatic brain injury)

Understand how feedback error and servomechanisms affect a closed loop system

Understand how positive and negative feedback systems may affect the closed motor skill performance of individuals with disabilities 2.03.08.01

>> Structure activities for success to maximize the positive feedback associated with successful execution

>> Reduce the frequency of highlighting errors in skill execution, which may adversely affect individuals with disabilities

Understand the elements in a closed loop system that may not be generated with rapid discrete actions (e.g., stages of information processing)

Understand how the stages of information processing impact the execution of a motor skill by individuals with disabilities 2.03.09.01

>> Program activities that facilitate the use of proprioceptive feedback, which may not be utilized effectively by individuals with certain types of disabilities

>> Develop short-term memory for the salient features of the task and activity to be executed

Understand the mechanisms of commonality and difference found both in open and **closed loop models**

Understand the concepts of the **open loop system** for programming activities for individuals with disabilities 2.03.10.01

>> Use an open loop system for individuals with certain types of disabilities such as autism spectrum disorder

>> Demonstrate care when programming a series of actions for individuals with certain disabilities since the instructor may be limited to certain types of adjustments or improvements

Understand the concepts of the closed loop system for programming activities for individuals with disabilities 2.03.10.02

>> Encourage individuals with disabilities to process **intrinsic feedback** through instruction and augmented feedback

>> Encourage the use of verbal rehearsal strategies to facilitate appropriate response selection

Understand the **speed–accuracy trade-off** (e.g., substituting accuracy for speed)

Understand how movement amplitude, the distance between two targets in an aiming task, is incorporated into the assessment process 2.03.11.01

>> Determine the amount of emphasis placed on the velocity of movement, such as how fast to stroke a tennis ball, and realize that it differs with various types of disabilities

>> Teach a skill with the desired movement amplitude so that the skill can be generalized to other settings

Understand how motor programs influence the execution of skilled movements

Understand individual abilities in the development of motor programs in individuals with disabilities 2.03.12.01

>> Structure tasks and activities to account for marked variations in ability relative to how an individual will learn and execute motor skills

>> Structure tasks and activities to account for deficits in short-term and long-term memory in order to combine smaller elements of a skill into longer sequences that are controlled by a single motor program

Understand the mechanisms required to change motor programs (e.g., what defines the essential details of skilled action?)

Understand the implications of open and closed loop theories such as Schmidt's schema theory and Adams' closed loop theory to skill acquisition for individuals with disabilities 2.03.13.01

» Present tasks so that the essential characteristics of the tasks are understandable

» Apply the open and closed loop theory to determine which skills or parts of skills are amenable to correction

Recognize individual differences and capabilities

Understand how to relate Henry's specificity hypothesis (tasks are composed of many unrelated abilities) to motor skill execution for individuals with disabilities 2.03.14.01

» Realize that the level of proficiency in one skill, such as underhand throwing, may be different from another similar skill, such as overhand throwing (each motor skill requires specific motor abilities for skillful performance)

» Structure activities to consider that the speed or motion of an agonistic muscle group may be faster or slower than that of the **antagonistic** muscle group

EXERCISE SCIENCE

STANDARD 3

EXERCISE SCIENCE

STANDARD 3

EXERCISE PHYSIOLOGY PRINCIPLES: Demonstrate knowledge of exercise physiology principles

Understand how to measure **metabolism** and work expenditure using indirect and direct **calorimetry**

Understand that measurement of energy expenditure may be affected by alterations in physiology or anatomy for individuals with disabilities 3.01.01.01

» Use modified protocols for measurement of energy expenditure with individuals with orthopedic disabilities such as spinal cord injury and multiple sclerosis

» Recognize that untrained individuals without disabilities who utilize upper extremities for exercise testing demonstrate lower energy expenditure levels than untrained individuals with disabilities

» Recognize that trained individuals who utilize upper extremities for exercise demonstrate higher energy expenditure levels than sedentary individuals

» Recognize that individuals with **quadriplegia** demonstrate lower levels of energy expenditure than individuals with **paraplegia**

Understand the effect of body mass on energy expenditure for individuals who are obese 3.01.01.02

» Recognize that weight-bearing activities such as running require more energy expenditure for those who are **overweight**

» Use non-weight-bearing or simplified weight-bearing activities (e.g., walking) initially

Understand **metabolic rate** at rest and during exercise

Understand that metabolic rates may be affected by various syndromes and metabolic and orthopedic disabilities 3.01.02.01

» Recognize that individuals with Down syndrome may have diminished metabolic rates, thus affecting their activity level and ability for weight management

» Recognize that individuals with Prader-Willi syndrome may have diminished metabolic rates, thus affecting their activity level and ability for weight management

Understand energy systems, sources, storage, mobilization, and roles in different activities (**power**, speed, endurance)

Understand that various disabilities may affect metabolism 3.01.03.01

» Accommodate individuals with McArdle's syndrome who are unable to utilize glycogen as a fuel source, thus limiting their ability to participate in short-term high-intensity activities

>> Recognize that individuals with spinal cord injury such as quadriplegia may have a diminished ability to utilize fat as a fuel source, thus limiting their ability to participate in long-term endurance activities

Understand neural and **endocrine control** of metabolism at rest and during exercise and its relation to exercise intensity and duration

Understand that various disabilities may affect neural and endocrine control 3.01.04.01

>> Accommodate individuals with uncontrolled diabetes who may have a diminished ability to synthesize fat and glycogen, thus limiting their ability to participate in physical activity

>> Recognize that exercise can help an individual with diabetes who is stable by reducing the amount of insulin needed

>> Appreciate that exercise can exacerbate ketosis and be deadly to an individual with diabetes whose condition is unstable

>> Realize that exercise can be deadly to an individual with diabetes whose condition is unstable by causing excessive release of growth hormone, which may contribute to blood vessel disease

NEURAL CONTROL: Demonstrate knowledge of muscular movement

Understand the neural and biomechanical control of movement from higher brain centers (anatomy and neural innervation of muscle, nerve transmission)

Understand how various disabilities may alter normal neural control of movement 3.02.01.01

>> Recognize that multiple sclerosis will have delayed nerve transmissions affecting the ability to perform activities, particularly ambulation

>> Acknowledge that spinal cord injuries have various levels of residual neural activity affecting ability to perform activities

Understand the difference between voluntary and **involuntary** movement

Understand that voluntary control of movement may be altered by various syndromes, as well as metabolic and orthopedic disabilities 3.02.02.01

>> Recognize that deficiencies in voluntary control of movement due to cerebral palsy affect an individual's ability to perform free-weight lifting

>> Acknowledge that use of upper extremities in manual wheelchair propulsion may result in extension of the lower extremities in individuals with cerebral palsy

>> Place strapping in front of the legs during manual wheelchair propulsion to prevent knee extension for individuals with extensor pattern disorders

Understand the purpose of, processes of, and how to elicit reflexes (gamma loop, muscle spindles, Golgi tendon organs)

Understand that reflexes can be affected by various disabilities 3.02.03.01

» Acknowledge that individuals with neuromuscular disorders such as muscular dystrophy will have diminished reflexes that will hinder ability to perform certain activities

» Acknowledge that individuals with spinal abnormalities may have diminished reflexes due to neural impingement

MUSCULAR CONCEPTS: Demonstrate knowledge of various muscular concepts

Understand skeletal muscle structure and function

Understand that various syndromes, as well as metabolic and orthopedic disabilities, may alter skeletal muscle structure and function 3.03.01.01

» Acknowledge that individuals with spinal cord injuries may lose strength and functional ability

» Emphasize strength training programs for hypotonic individuals

» Emphasize non-weight-bearing activities for individuals with degenerative diseases such as muscular dystrophy

» Recognize that individuals with muscular dystrophy such as Duchenne are predisposed to skeletal muscle degeneration

Understand the interaction between metabolic and **mechanical** efficiency

Understand that various syndromes, as well as metabolic and orthopedic disabilities, may alter metabolic and mechanical efficiency 3.03.02.01

» Accommodate individuals who display motor patterns resulting from mechanical inefficiency

» Accommodate individuals who display motor patterns resulting from metabolic inefficiency

Understand **muscular strength** and **muscular endurance**

Understand that various syndromes, as well as metabolic and orthopedic disabilities, may affect muscular strength and function 3.03.03.01

» Acknowledge that individuals with progressive neuromuscular conditions will lose strength

» Acknowledge that individuals with spastic cerebral palsy will have a muscular imbalance between flexor and extensor muscles

Understand the concepts of **overload**, specificity, and muscular adaptations when developing weight training programs

Understand that the overload and specificity principles apply to individuals with disabilities 3.03.04.01

» Recognize that individuals with disabilities that result in hypotonia such as Down syndrome may demonstrate a delayed response to muscular training

» Recognize that individuals with degenerative muscular diseases may not develop benefits from muscular training

Understand aspects of **flexibility**

Understand that flexibility training applies to individuals with disabilities 3.03.05.01

» Recognize that individuals with hypotonic conditions such as Down syndrome do not need flexibility emphasized in their fitness programs

» Emphasize flexibility exercise for individuals with hypertonic conditions such as cerebral palsy

CARDIORESPIRATORY FACTORS: Demonstrate knowledge of various cardiorespiratory factors

Understand the anatomy and function of the cardiorespiratory system

Understand that congenital defects or syndromes such as congenital heart defects, aortic stenosis, atrial septal defects, and Marfan syndrome may alter the anatomy and function of the cardiovascular system 3.04.01.01

» Limit the duration and intensity of exercise for individuals with impaired cardiac function

» Maintain close contact with the physician for individuals with impaired cardiac function

» Recognize the cardiovascular training limitation of individuals with heart disease

Understand the electrical and circulatory processes of the cardiac cycle, control of the heart, and basic anatomy of the circulatory system

Understand how the variability of the cardiac cycle applies to individuals with congenital defects, syndromes, or orthopedic disabilities 3.04.02.01

» Recognize that individuals with congenital heart defects may have limited aerobic capacity due to an inadequate amount of oxygenated blood or an inability to eliminate an adequate amount of carbon dioxide

» Contact a physician before engaging individuals with coronary defects in an exercise program

» Define an appropriate level of exercise intensity for individuals with congenital heart defects

Understand **oxygen consumption** ($\dot{V}O_2$) at rest and during exercise

Understand that oxygen consumption may be different between individuals with disabilities and individuals without disabilities 3.04.03.01

» Recognize that individuals with spinal cord injuries including spina bifida will have lower oxygen consumption levels due to use of small muscle mass

» Describe the differences in maximum **heart rate** (HR) between hand and/or arm **ergometry** and wheelchair ergometry

Understand the determinants and control of circulation at rest and during exercise

Understand that various orthopedic disabilities and metabolic diseases such as diabetes result in neural and vascular damage that may affect circulation 3.04.04.01

» Recognize that individuals with spinal cord injuries have impaired hemodynamic responses (such as reduced blood flow and lowered blood pressure) and **thermoregulation**

» Recognize that individuals with spinal cord injuries have impaired vasoconstriction and vasodilation

Understand cardiorespiratory dynamics (cardiac output, **stroke volume**, **contractility**, heart rate, blood pressure, synergy of contraction, distensibility of ventricles, **oxygen transport**) at rest and during exercise

Understand that congenital defects, syndromes, and orthopedic disabilities may interfere with cardiorespiratory dynamics 3.04.05.01

» Recognize that individuals with spinal cord injury, quadriplegia, and Down syndrome have reduced heart rates

» Acknowledge that the use of standard heart rate values for the determination of exercise intensity is not applicable

Understand the effects and risk factors of coronary heart disease

Understand that individuals with disabilities are often at a higher risk for cardiovascular heart disease 3.04.06.01

» Recognize that high blood pressure and high cholesterol levels are more prevalent in individuals with disabilities

» Review medical records for individuals with disabilities for elevated blood pressure and total cholesterol levels

RESPIRATORY FACTORS: Demonstrate knowledge of respiratory system

Understand the purpose of **ventilation** and respiration, oxygen exchange and transport, acid–base regulation, and partial pressures of gases

Understand that orthopedic or chronic obstructive pulmonary disease conditions can interfere with the function of the respiratory system 3.05.01.01

» Recognize that exercise may precipitate an asthma attack

» Promote desirable exercise conditions such as allergen-free and stress-free environments

» Describe techniques to control ventilation and respiration during an asthma attack

» Work with the individual and care providers on regulating medication

» Use the proper warm-up activities prior to exercise for individuals with chronic obstructive pulmonary disease

Understand the anatomy of the **pulmonary system**, dynamic and **static lung volumes**, mechanics of ventilation, ventilatory parameters (maximum voluntary ventilation, breathing frequency, tidal volume) and training adaptations

Understand that chronic obstructive pulmonary disease and orthopedic disabilities, particularly those that cause ventilatory muscle dysfunction, may interfere with the respiratory system function 3.05.02.01

» Be aware that individuals with asthma may panic because they feel they are not receiving enough air

» Practice safety precautions and relaxation techniques to control breathing

Understand the control of ventilation at rest and during exercise

Understand that chronic obstructive pulmonary disease and orthopedic disabilities may restrict ventilation 3.05.03.01

» Recognize that individuals with higher level spinal injuries often lack the muscle control for ventilation thus limiting strenuous activity

» Develop intact accessory muscles through physical activity and respiratory training

NUTRITION: Demonstrate knowledge of nutritional concepts

Understand nutritional concepts (fat, carbohydrate, **protein**), nutritional supplements (vitamins and minerals), and concept of a balanced diet

Understand that individuals with disabilities may have specific nutritional needs 3.06.01.01

» Provide guidance regarding proper nutrition for individuals with disabilities

» Monitor sugar intake for individuals with diabetes

» Monitor food intake for individuals with Prader-Willi syndrome

» Monitor aspartame intake in individuals with **phenylketonuria**

BODY COMPOSITION: Demonstrate knowledge of body composition

Understand the components of body composition

Understand the differences in the percentage of body fat in individuals with disabilities 3.07.01.01

» Utilize the **Kelly-Rimmer equation** for computing percent body fat for individuals with intellectual disability

» Recognize that lean body mass is higher in individuals with paraplegia than in those with quadriplegia

Understand the differences among **underweight**, overweight, **overfat**, and obese

Know which individuals with disabilities in general are underweight, overweight, overfat, or obese 3.07.02.01

» Demonstrate how to use height and weight tables to classify a person with a disability as overweight, using small, medium, and large frames

» Refrain from using skinfold calipers over paralyzed muscle groups and scar tissue

Understand the factors that are associated with the treatment of obesity

Understand the factors that are associated with the treatment of obesity in individuals with disabilities such as exercise, nutrition, and behavioral intervention 3.07.03.01

» Develop a weight reduction program that emphasizes exercise

» Develop a weight reduction program that emphasizes nutrition

» Develop a weight reduction program that emphasizes behavioral intervention

ENVIRONMENTAL EFFECTS: Demonstrate knowledge of environmental effects on performance

Understand the adaptations to thermal stress (hot, cold), what constitutes thermal stress, and the symptoms of thermal injury

Understand that individuals with disabilities such as asthma or orthopedic involvement may be susceptible to thermal change conditions 3.08.01.01

>> Recognize that the body's ability to thermoregulate is increasingly compromised, the higher the spinal cord injury

>> Recognize that individuals with spinal injuries, muscular dystrophy, and multiple sclerosis are particularly prone to thermal injuries and must be well hydrated and monitored when performing activity

Understand the impact of high- and low-pressure environments on individuals with disabilities 3.08.01.02

>> Monitor respiration rates of individuals with asthma at high altitudes due to reduced oxygen pressure

>> Monitor respiration rates of individuals with cystic fibrosis at high altitudes due to reduced oxygen pressure

EXERCISE PRESCRIPTION AND TRAINING: Demonstrate knowledge of exercise prescription and training

Understand the physiological benefits and adaptations of exercise (decreased blood pressure, decreased submaximal heart rate, improved endurance)

Know the benefits of exercise training for individuals with exercise-induced asthma 3.09.01.01

>> Recognize the effects of exercise response and training for individuals with exercise-induced asthma

>> Recognize the effects of medication for individuals with exercise-induced asthma

>> Design exercise programs that are safe and effective for individuals with exercise-induced asthma

>> Design conditioning programs for individuals who are wheelchair users

Understand the differences between fitness, physical activity, and rehabilitation

Know the differences between fitness, physical activity, and rehabilitation programs for individuals with disabilities 3.09.02.01

>> Assign homework for individuals with disabilities that increases activity levels

>> Develop a rehabilitation program for individuals with disabilities with the assistance of team members from allied medicine

Understand the current American College of Sports Medicine recommendations for exercise prescription

Understand that heart rate depends on the injury levels of individuals with disabilities such as spinal cord injuries 3.09.03.01

>> Use ratings of perceived exertion (RPE) to determine exercise intensity level when heart rate is difficult to obtain

» Emphasize duration of activity rather than activity intensity for individuals with obesity. After the exercise program has been ongoing, emphasize that the greater the intensity, the better

Understand the concept and use of **metabolic equivalent (MET)**

Understand the difference in maximum MET levels between individuals with and without disabilities 3.09.04.01

» Use the metabolic equivalent (MET) as a method of classifying fitness levels

» Compare and contrast METs with other methods of classifying individuals with special needs such as $\dot{V}O_2$ max, watts, etc.

Understand the **Karvonen formula** for estimation of maximal and training heart rate zone

Understand that the Karvonen formula may be ineffective for individuals with disabilities such as Down syndrome who may have chronotropic incompetence 3.09.05.01

» Calculate training heart rate using the Karvonen formula for individuals with disabilities

» Use conservative training heart rates for individuals who are severely deconditioned

Understand the concept and use of the rate of perceived exertion (RPE)

Understand the importance of RPE when gauging exercise intensity in individuals with disabilities such as type 1 diabetes mellitus and individuals on beta blockers 3.09.06.01

» Teach individuals with exercise-induced asthma how to utilize ratings of perceived exertion (RPE)

» Use prior RPEs to design new exercise programs for individuals with exercise-induced asthma

Understand the different types of maximal and submaximal methods of determining cardiovascular fitness

Understand the different testing protocols for persons with disabilities 3.09.07.01

» Use the Pacer shuttle run for individuals with disabilities such as mental retardation or partially sighted

» Use wheelchair ergometers (rollers) or arm crank ergometers (Monark) to determine submaximal test for individuals using manual wheelchairs

Understand the different types of direct and indirect determinations of muscular strength, endurance, and flexibility

Understand the types of muscular strength, endurance, and flexibility tests used for individuals with disabilities 3.09.08.01

» Use appropriate tests of muscular strength and endurance for individuals who use wheelchairs

» Use an appropriate flexibility test (goniometer) for individuals who use wheelchairs

Understand the exercise principles, such as resistance, exhaustion, overload, specificity, and reversibility and how they relate to exercise prescription

Understand the exercise principles and how they apply to individuals with disabilities when designing exercise prescriptions 3.09.09.01

» Recognize that individuals with a spinal cord injury may reach exhaustion and need more rest periods when participating in an exercise program

» Develop a strength training program for an individual with an intellectual disability applying the overload principle but increasing the resistance at a slower rate

» Design cardiorespiratory training programs utilizing the principle of specificity of exercise and include training on a wheelchair ergometer

» Accommodate for the concept of reversibility for an individual with a disability who has been removed from school for an extended period of time due to surgery

BIOMECHANICS/KINESIOLOGY: Demonstrate knowledge of basic biomechanical and kinesiological concepts and principles

Understand **kinesiology**

Understand pathokinesiology and its relationship to altered human movement patterns caused by disabilities 3.10.01.01

» Explain basic changes in movements or joint positions

» Use appropriate activities and equipment that alter movements or accommodate abnormal joint positions

Understand biomechanics

Understand pathobiomechanics and its relationship to kinesiological movement in individuals with disabilities 3.10.02.01

» Explain basic changes in biomechanical movements of joint positions

» Use appropriate activities and equipment that alter movement patterns or accommodate abnormal joint positions

Understand statics

Understand specific biomechanical and kinesiological properties such as static tension, static stretch, and equilibrium and their relationship to physical and motor performance for individuals with disabilities 3.10.03.01

» Recognize that individuals with disabilities such as deafness, developmental delays, some forms of cerebral palsy (ataxia and spasticity), and other neurological disorders have impaired static balance skills

» Accommodate individuals exhibiting exaggerated stretch reflexes with abnormally high muscle tone such as spastic cerebral palsy

Understand dynamics

Understand the mechanics of dynamic movement, equilibrium, dynamic stretch, and dynamic tension and their relationship to physical and motor performance for individuals with disabilities 3.10.04.01

» Recognize that individuals with disabilities such as deafness, developmental delays, cerebral palsy, learning disabilities, and other neurological disorders often have impaired dynamic balance

» Accommodate individuals with disabilities such as athetoid or ataxic cerebral palsy who demonstrate uncoordinated and unintegrated movements

Understand **kinematics**

Understand the relationship of time and space on motion and calculations of mechanical efficiency on physical and motor performance for individuals with disabilities 3.10.05.01

» Demonstrate an understanding of individuals with disabilities who take more time to affect a desired motor response

» Recognize that some physical impairments such as amputations change the mechanics of an activity or skill

» Recognize that individuals with disabilities may perform skills with less velocity and acceleration influencing the outcome of the skill

Understand **kinetics**

Understand **forces that affect movement and motion and their relationship to physical and motor performance for individuals with disabilities 3.10.06.01**

» Demonstrate kinetic open and closed **chains** as well as kinetic principles in instructing a variety of activities

» Recognize that individuals with neuromuscular disabilities may take longer to start or stop a movement

Understand the anatomical reference position as it is associated with body movement

Understand the anatomical positions of the body and how these positions are used for studying movement of individuals with disabilities 3.10.07.01

» Describe body and joint positions that are lateral, medial, dorsal, ventral, cephal, or caudal to each other

» Describe movements that are lateral, medial, dorsal, ventral, cephal, or caudal to each other

Understand planes associated with body movement

Understand frontal, transverse, and sagittal planes and axes as well as their relationship to movement for individuals with disabilities 3.10.08.01

» Recognize that shoulder or hip abduction and adduction take place in the frontal plane, rotation occurs in the transverse (or horizontal) plane, and flexion and extension occur in the sagittal plane

» Recognize that individuals with orthopedic disabilities may have pathokinesiological joint positions that cause excursion or placement of the joints in other planes such as varum or valgum

» Recognize that Newton's laws affect movement and how the application of forces influence the skill

Understand the relationship of the axes to corresponding planes of the human body

Understand instances where anatomical constraints of individuals with disabilities may cause movement to be in different axes of rotation 3.10.09.01

» Realize that individuals with cerebral palsy use different muscles or joints due to contractures

» Describe how individuals with joint fusion due to surgery or arthritis may need to initiate movements in different axes

Understand movement analysis

Understand the use of statics, dynamics, kinematics, kinetics, body axes, planes, balance, and equilibrium for studying and planning movement activities for individuals with disabilities 3.10.10.01

» Demonstrate ability to perform a movement analysis and plan instruction for individuals with disabilities

» Observe abnormal positions of joints or body parts and how these may affect movements

» Demonstrate ability to task analyze a skill into smaller achievable parts

» Develop a systematic observation strategy to perform a quality analysis

Understand fundamental mechanical concepts

Understand Newton's laws, levers, vectors, force, pulley system, mass/ weight, stability, gravity, inertia, momentum, torque, velocity, and acceleration and their relationship to movement for individuals with disabilities 3.10.11.01

» Accommodate individuals who are obese by providing extra time to initiate and cease their motions

» Recognize that individuals who are obese will need more strength to start and stop

» Describe the differences in wheelchair design for sports such as tennis or basketball versus track or road racing versus medical use

» Recognize that changing body position or equipment may change the mechanical advantage of a lever system

Understand balance, equilibrium, and stability

Understand the concepts of balance, equilibrium, and stability in planning activity programs for individuals with disabilities 3.10.12.01

» Demonstrate use of concepts of balance, equilibrium, and stability in planning and instructing movement activities such as teaching individuals how they can lower their center of gravity to increase their stability

» Acknowledge that individuals with cerebral palsy, amputations, and neuromuscular disorders may need special instruction in areas of balance and equilibrium

» Describe the factors that contribute to balance and stability including mass, center of gravity, line of gravity, friction, and changing the base of support

Understand force production and absorption

Understand aerodynamics, lift, drag, inertia, movement of inertia, velocity, spin/rotation, centrifugal, centripetal, lever, force arm, resistance force, and speed and their relationship to movement and motor performance for individuals with disabilities 3.10.13.01

» Describe effects of primitive reflexes in individuals with disabilities when producing too much or too little force

» Describe effects on anatomical structures in individuals with disabilities when producing too much force

» Describe mechanical differences between everyday (medical), sport, and track/racing wheelchairs

» Describe wheelchair propulsion (torque production) and recovery techniques for sport and track/racing wheelchairs

Understand basic **fluid mechanics**

Understand fluid mechanics principles of buoyancy in relation to individuals with specific disabilities 3.10.14.01

» Recognize that individuals with paralysis will have some body parts more buoyant due to atrophy of muscle tissue and increased fatty tissue

» Accommodate individuals with paralysis or contractures who cannot demonstrate a horizontal body position resulting in increased drag because lower extremities may decrease buoyancy

>> Accommodate individuals with muscular dystrophy who demonstrate increased buoyancy due to atrophy of muscle tissue and increased fatty tissue

---

BONE GROWTH AND DEVELOPMENT: Demonstrate knowledge of the biomechanics of bone growth and development

---

Understand that Wolff's law implies that bones develop and change according to mechanical loads such as compression and tension

Understand that individuals with disabilities such as scoliosis demonstrate abnormal orthopedic development 3.11.01.01

>> Recognize that unequal muscular development will result in abnormal bone growth such as limb deformities

>> Recognize that individuals who remain sedentary will undergo bone demineralization and may develop osteoporosis

Understand that processes such as cartilaginous hyperplasia, hypertrophy, and calcification may interfere with normal growth and maturation of bone

Understand that certain characteristics of disabilities associated with abnormal bone growth make individuals prone to injury 3.11.02.01

>> Recognize that contraindications such as high-impact activities and high-resistance weight training may be associated with abnormal bone growth and conditions

>> Prescribe exercises and activities that encourage healthy bone growth

Understand the effects of decreased activity or lack of exercise on bone **mineralization**

Know the effects of decreased activity or lack of exercise on bone mineralization of individuals with disabilities associated with growth problems and/or deformities 3.11.03.01

>> Realize that time spent while bedridden or immobilized results in weakened bone anatomy

>> Systematically increase an individual's physical activity time

Understand types of bone fractures

Understand common causes of various types of bone fractures such as greenstick, avulsion, longitudinal, and transverse in individuals with disabilities 3.11.04.01

>> Avoid contact sports and high-impact activities for individuals who are at risk for fractures

>> Develop a referral policy for individuals who are suspected of being at risk of a fracture

NEUROMUSCULAR FUNCTION: Demonstrate knowledge of the biomechanical aspects of neuromuscular function

Understand the basic properties of muscle tissues such as irritability, extensibility, elasticity, and contractility

Understand general deviations in basic properties of muscle tissue among individuals with disabilities 3.12.01.01

» Recognize specific deviations in basic properties of muscle tissue found with disabilities such as spasticity or contractures

» Describe specific deviations in the basic properties of muscle tissue found in individuals with disabilities such as muscular dystrophy

Understand the force–velocity relationships of muscle tissue

Understand the force–velocity relationship of muscle tissue in individuals with disabilities such as cerebral palsy, degenerative muscle conditions, and spina bifida 3.12.02.01

» Recognize that more time is needed to generate muscular force for a given movement in individuals with disabilities

» Recognize that more time is needed to generate desired motor action in individuals with disabilities such as cerebral palsy

» Recognize that it is more difficult for individuals with disabilities such as cerebral palsy and degenerative muscle conditions to generate faster purposeful movements

Understand force–length relationships with muscle tissue

Understand force–length relationship (isometric) with muscle tissue in individuals with disabilities such as cerebral palsy, degenerative muscle conditions, and spina bifida 3.12.03.01

» Recognize the optimal muscle length to generate the most force in an individual with disabilities

» Identify how power can be improved in these individuals

Understand force–time relationships with muscle tissue

Understand force–time relationship with muscle tissue in individuals with disabilities such as cerebral palsy, degenerative muscle conditions, and spina bifida 3.12.04.01

» Recognize that powerful and forceful movements will be more difficult for individuals with disabilities that include degenerative muscle conditions

» Identify how power can be improved in these individuals

Understand the concept of strength from a biomechanical perspective

Understand that improper biomechanics adversely impacts the strength of some individuals with disabilities 3.12.05.01

» Recognize that the individual may be influenced by posture and spinal deformities

» Recognize that decreased range of motion affects force production

Understand the concept of power from a biomechanical perspective

Understand that the ability of some individuals with disabilities to generate power is compromised due to improper mechanics 3.12.06.01

» Adapt activities for some individuals with disabilities to allow for additional time to effectively generate power

» Use lightweight equipment to increase strength and power

Understand the biomechanics of endurance

Understand that improper biomechanics adversely impacts the endurance of some individuals with disabilities 3.12.07.01

» Recognize that alterations in movement such as gait and range of motion may interfere with the ability of some individuals with disabilities to sustain activity

» Modify activity to recognize the endurance needs of some individuals with disabilities such as hand/arm ergometry

Understand how **sensory receptors** in muscles (muscle spindles) contribute to neuromuscular control

Understand sensory receptors in muscles (muscle spindles) for individuals with disabilities such as cerebral palsy, Down syndrome, and muscular dystrophy 3.12.08.01

» Describe **contraindicated** movements for individuals with cerebral palsy that would stimulate the stretch reflex and result in increased hypertonicity (spasticity)

» Describe exercise that stimulates the stretch reflex that helps enhance power in individuals with Down syndrome

Understand how sensory receptors in tendons (Golgi tendon organs) contribute to neuromuscular control of human movement

Understand differences in sensory receptors of tendons among individuals with disabilities such as cerebral palsy and muscular dystrophy 3.12.09.01

» Use **proprioceptive neuromuscular facilitation** exercises to enhance range of motion

» Use proprioceptive neuromuscular facilitation exercises to enhance strength

Understand how sensory receptors in other body tissues contribute to neuromuscular control of human movement

Understand structure and functions of vestibular, cutaneous, visual, and auditory receptors in individuals with disabilities 3.12.10.01

» Recognize that individuals with sensorineural hearing impairments may demonstrate balance problems or vestibular dysfunction

» Recognize that individuals with visual impairments may demonstrate diminished balance skills

» Recognize that individuals with sensory losses demonstrate impaired kinesthetic awareness

HUMAN SKELETAL ARTICULATIONS: Demonstrate knowledge of biomechanics of human skeletal articulations

Understand the characteristics of joints based on structure and movement

Understand joint anomalies in individuals with disabilities such as arthritis and cerebral palsy 3.13.01.01

» Use aquatics as a mode for physical activity

» Schedule physical education later in the day for individuals with rheumatoid arthritis

» Schedule physical education earlier in the day for individuals with osteoporosis

Understand that the three sources of joint stability are the structures of bony, ligamentous, and muscular arrangements

Understand specific disabilities associated with hyper joint flexibility, such as cerebral palsy, juvenile arthritis, osteoarthritis, rheumatoid arthritis, osteogenesis imperfecta, lax ligaments, and neuromuscular conditions 3.13.02.01

» Describe strength and muscular endurance exercises that enhance specific motor control and movement functions

» Design an activity program to ensure safe strength development

Understand the concept of joint flexibility or range of motion (ROM)

Understand specific disabilities associated with hyper joint flexibility such as cerebral palsy and Down syndrome 3.13.03.01

» Describe programming needs of individuals with hypo and hyper joint flexibility such as cerebral palsy and Down syndrome

» Describe specific proprioceptive neuromuscular facilitation exercises utilizing the stretch reflex to enhance the ROM of individuals with cerebral palsy and arthritis

Understand that individuals with specific disabilities may develop varying degrees of contractures and antagonistic stretching resulting in loss of flexibility 3.13.03.02

» Restore joint flexibility and balance by stretching contracted muscle and strengthening stretched muscle

» Use a warm-up that stretches **agonists** and strengthens antagonists in involved muscles

» Incorporate assistive stretching activities of affected musculature indicated for individuals with flaccid paralysis

» Prevent contractures using a balance training program within the tolerance of the individual

» Use **multidisciplinary approach** with the physical therapist and the occupational therapist (see Standard 15)

Understand the advantages of the different approaches such as sustained stretching and proprioceptive neuromuscular facilitation to increasing flexibility

Understand various approaches such as passive stretching, active static stretching, and proprioceptive neuromuscular facilitation to increasing flexibility of individuals with disabilities 3.13.04.01

» Apply various approaches to increasing flexibility of individuals with specific disabilities known to have low flexibility levels such as cerebral palsy

» Use rhythms as a mode for performing flexibility exercises for individuals with disabilities

Understand the benefits and harmful effects of different approaches such as dynamic or ballistic stretching

Understand how individuals with disabilities are affected by both active and passive stretching techniques 3.13.05.01

» Acknowledge that after warm-up, therapeutic stretching aids in injury prevention and relaxes joints and muscles

» Use a balanced program of activities that allows stretching of contracted muscles and strengthening of weakened (stretched) muscles

» Realize that dynamic (ballistic) stretching exercises for contracted muscles are contraindicated for all individuals

» Adapt flexibility exercise program based on therapeutic assessment performed by **multidisciplinary team**

NECK AND UPPER EXTREMITY MOVEMENT: Demonstrate knowledge of the biomechanics of neck and upper extremity movement

Understand the anatomical structure of neck and upper extremity articulations

Understand how deviations such as atlantoaxial instability, scoliosis, lordosis, kyphosis, and growth plate irregularities such as Scheuermann's disease affect anatomical structure and movement capabilities of the neck and upper extremities 3.14.01.01

» Avoid activities that compress or hyperflex the neck such as back rolls and headstands for individuals with atlantoaxial instability

» Use exercises that mobilize the spine in extension for individuals with spinal curvatures

Understand the functions of the neck and upper extremities

Understand that restrictions such as limited range of motion can affect basic functions of the neck and upper extremities 3.14.02.01

» Avoid contraindicated exercises such as neck bridges

» Seek medical advice when working with individuals with neck pain or motor limitations

Understand ways in which the spine and pelvic girdle are adapted to carry out functions such as shock absorption and ambulation

Understand neck and upper extremity function in terms of disc size, disc arrangement, compression/tensile/shear force, and structure in relation to neck and upper extremity movements in individuals with disabilities 3.14.03.01

» Recognize that individuals with fused spines will lack the mobility and shock absorption characteristic of those without fusions

» Refer individuals with herniated disc to physician for exercises that can help relieve the pain and swelling

» Prohibit activity that places stress on the neck of individuals with atlantoaxial instability

Understand the muscle groups that are active during specific neck and upper extremity movement

Understand problems such as hypertonic muscles associated with activity during neck and upper extremity movement 3.14.04.01

» Use therapeutic stretching of internal rotators and strengthening of external rotators at shoulder joints for individuals with disabilities such as spastic cerebral palsy

» Encourage individuals to utilize remaining functional capacity such as an individual with flaccid paralysis resulting from spinal cord injuries

Understand the biomechanical factors contributing to injuries of the neck and upper extremities

Understand causes and characteristics of neck and upper extremity injuries such as soft tissue injuries, ruptured/herniated disc, fractures, dislocations, and tendonitis 3.14.05.01

» Discuss structural and functional deviations with members of the multidisciplinary assessment team

» Describe the mechanical deviations of the various neuromuscular and orthopedic conditions and their effect on movement and program considerations

» Apply mechanical principles to solutions and/or modifications of movement problems

» Use orthotics such as wheelchairs, canes, and braces to improve functional movement for skill and physical fitness acquisition

» Recognize adaptations and modifications of movement patterns via mechanical principles to ambulatory individuals to increase physical fitness and skill acquisition

» Use basic mechanical principles such as low center of gravity and laws of levers and motion to minimize injury

» Use proper transfer techniques

SPINE AND PELVIS MOVEMENT: Demonstrate knowledge of the biomechanics of spine and pelvis movement

Understand how anatomical structure affects movement capabilities of the spine

Understand how deviations such as scoliosis, lordosis, anterior pelvic tilt, kyphosis, and growth plate irregularities such as Scheuermann's disease affect load-bearing and movement capabilities of the spine and pelvic girdle 3.15.01.01

» Assess movement capacity based on type and degree of deformity

» Use treatment and indicated activities for the deviations of the spine and pelvic girdle for individuals with scoliosis and lordosis

» Assess movement capacity based on type and degree of condition, and prescribe activities, including adaptations and modifications, based on evaluation

» Incorporate prescribed orthotic devices into activities based on type and degree of condition

Understand functions of the spine and pelvic girdle

Understand restrictions that can affect basic functions such as compression, flexion, extension, hyperextension, lateral flexion, and rotation of the spine and pelvic girdle for individuals with disabilities 3.15.02.01

» Recognize that individuals with upper and lower level spinal paresis lose functional support, stability, and mobility below level of lesion

» Recognize that functional and skillful movement of the trunk, pelvis, and lower extremity will be considerably diminished relative to type, degree, and location of spinal injury

» Recognize limitations to functional maintenance of posture and consequent trunk and pelvic stability, balance, and symmetry

» Use flexibility training for the lower body

Understand ways the spine and pelvic girdle are adapted to carry out functions such as vertical posture and ambulation

Understand vertebral structure in terms of size, disc, compression, shear forces, and pelvic girdle structure in relationship to spinal and lower extremity movements for individuals with disabilities 3.15.03.01

» Identify problems that can affect basic functions of the spine and pelvic girdle

» Discuss contraindications that can lead to or exacerbate disc problems

Understand the impact of the loss of muscular control on spine and pelvis movement and/or the relationship between muscle location and the effectiveness of muscle action in the trunk

Understand actions of muscles in upper and lower extremities, spine, and abdomen in trunk action for individuals with disabilities 3.15.04.01

» Describe restricted movements of upper and lower extremity muscles

» Recognize that muscle size and strength are relative to the degree of spasticity and that contracture, flaccidity, paralysis, or general paresis will cause limitations in trunk movement

» Conduct postural screening early to identify spinal curvatures to prevent further deformity

Understand the biomechanical contributors to injuries of the spine

Understand causes and characteristics of spinal injuries such as soft tissue injuries, herniated disc, and fractures 3.15.05.01

» Describe treatment for spinal injuries such as soft tissue injuries, herniated disc, and fractures

» Describe contraindicated activities for spinal injuries such as soft tissue injuries, herniated disc, and fractures

LOWER EXTREMITY MOVEMENT: Demonstrate knowledge of the biomechanics of lower extremity movement

Understand how anatomical structure affects the movement capabilities of lower extremity articulations

Understand how deviations in anatomical structure affect movement capabilities of the pelvis, hip joint, and ankle joint for individuals with disabilities 3.16.01.01

» Recognize that deviations such as coxa valga and coxa vara in anatomical structure affect the movement capabilities of the hip joint

» Recognize that deviations in anatomical structure such as genu valgum, varum, and recurvatum affect the movement capabilities of the knee joint

» Use strength and flexibility training for muscle contracture in hip and pelvic region

» Use strength and flexibility training for muscle contractures around the knee joint

» Implement flexibility training for flaccidity of muscles around the knee and compensatory strength and endurance training for involved muscles

» Implement strength and flexibility training for muscle contracture around the ankle and foot

Understand how the lower extremity is adapted to weight-bearing functions

Understand how deviations in alignment of the lower extremity can affect both lower and upper extremities for individuals with disabilities 3.16.02.01

» Describe the stance and gait of individuals with coxa valga and vara; genu valgum, varum, and recurvatum; and foot pronation and supination

» Use various methods of measurement and appraisal of postural deviation, such as plumb line, posture grids, and goniometers

» Recognize structural and functional mechanics of various postural deviations and their implications for exercise and sport

» Assess the stance and gait of individuals with postural deviations (see Standard 8)

» Accommodate structural and functional mechanics as they affect gait

» Design programs, use equipment, and modify activities for individuals with postural deviations

» Use physical fitness activities in conjunction with therapists for functional postural deviations

» Use orthotic devices for individuals with severe postural deformity

Understand muscle groups that are active during specific lower extremity movements

Understand how weight-bearing stance and gait are affected when some muscle groups are too active in individuals with disabilities 3.16.03.01

» Describe muscle groups and possible stretching exercises for hip abnormalities such as coxa valga and vara; genu valgum, varum, and recurvatum; and ankle and foot abnormalities such as pronation and supination

» Use orthotic devices for individuals with severe foot deformities

Understand the biomechanical factors contributing to injuries of the lower extremity

Understand causes and characteristics of lower extremity injuries such as soft tissue injuries, fractures, dislocations, and tendonitis for individuals with disabilities 3.16.04.01

» Describe treatment for lower extremity injuries such as soft tissue injuries, fractures, dislocations, and tendonitis

» Describe contraindicated activities, including inappropriate footwear, for lower extremity injuries, such as soft tissue injuries, fractures, dislocations, and tendonitis

MEASUREMENT AND EVALUATION

MEASUREMENT AND EVALUATION

STANDARD 4

STANDARDIZED PROCEDURES: Demonstrate knowledge of a set of conditions, equipment, and instructions to which data collection must conform to ensure validity

Demonstrate knowledge of **standardized instruments** and procedures as well as **direct measures** for use in determining current level of fitness and of motor performance such as fitness tests, motor development profiles, motor skills tests, reflex and perceptual motor inventories

Understand instruments and procedures for measuring and evaluating physical and motor fitness of individuals with disabilities 4.01.01.01

» Use standardized instruments and procedures for measuring and evaluating physical fitness such as AAHPERD Health-Related Fitness Test, Fitness-Gram®, and the Brockport Physical Fitness Test

» Evaluate physical fitness using measurement methods such as skinfold calipers for body composition and goniometers for range of motion with individuals with disabilities

Understand instruments and procedures for measuring and evaluating motor skills of individuals with disabilities 4.01.01.02

» Use standardized instruments or procedures for measuring and evaluating motor skills such as The Test of Gross Motor Development and Bruininks-Oseretsky Test of Motor Proficiency

» Measure and evaluate the acquisition of motor skills of individuals with disabilities using curriculum-based procedures such as **Everyone CAN** and the **Achievement-Based Curriculum** (ABC)

Understand instruments and procedures for measuring motor development in individuals with disabilities 4.01.01.03

» Measure motor development using instruments such as the Brigance Diagnostic Inventory of Early Development and the Denver Developmental Screening Test with individuals with disabilities

» Measure motor development using direct measures of reflexes such as reflex testing

Understand the use of instruments and procedures that have implications for aspects of performance such as components of language tests and perceptual motor tests 4.01.01.04

» Interpret the motor demands of standardized instruments measuring language and cognitive function

» Observe procedures used by other professionals to measure and evaluate movement including reflex testing, mobility, flexibility, sensory motor strengths and weaknesses, gross and fine motor skills, positioning/handling techniques, leisure skills, and postural analysis

>> Interpret the effects of culture on the motor demands made by motor performance instruments

Use instruments to determine eligibility for adapted physical education and individualized program planning in the local education agency (LEA) 4.01.01.05

>> Use measurement and evaluation procedures prescribed

>> Use specific standardized instruments or procedures for determining the need for **related services** such as checklists, **rubrics**, or observation techniques as suggested by other professionals

Demonstrate knowledge of how to locate and obtain standardized instruments and procedures for use

Access resources for measuring motor performance of individuals with disabilities in the LEA 4.01.02.01

>> Use resource centers for test instruments

>> Use resources such as professional organizations, web-based user groups, and special interest groups

>> Use the *Buros Mental Measurement Yearbook* to identify tests

Demonstrate knowledge of teachers/staff who could assist in locating resources in the LEA 4.01.02.02

>> Meet with resource specialists available in your school or online

>> Communicate with other adapted physical educators regarding the availability of resources for measurement

Evaluate the quality of available standardized instruments

Understand the test characteristics such as measures of central tendency and variability that describe the nature of the instrument/procedure as it pertains to individuals with disabilities 4.01.03.01

>> Explain the difference between the mean and median on standardized instruments

>> Explain the standard deviation and what it means in the interpretation of test scores

Know information sources for evaluating tests for individuals with disabilities 4.01.03.02

>> Use information published on standardized instruments to determine use with individuals with disabilities

>> Describe test characteristics used in the selection of standardized instruments and procedures such as validity and reliability

Recognize potential limitations and problems related to the use of standardized instruments and procedures

Understand the limitations of using standardized test instruments with different disabilities 4.01.04.01

» Determine appropriate tests for specific types of disabilities such as the *Brockport Physical Fitness Test*

» Recognize when the use of standardized instruments is inappropriate for use with individuals with disabilities

» Demonstrate appropriate use of authentic test instruments

Understand the problems of using standardized instruments with individuals with various disabilities 4.01.04.02

» Modify standardized test instructions for individuals with disabilities

» Select appropriate alternative test items

» Develop an authentic test instrument

Recognize the necessity to construct instruments and/or modify procedures to measure the current level of motor performance of individuals

Understand the effect of modifying a standardized test on the reliability and validity of the test and the results 4.01.05.01

» Modify testing procedures and/or instruments for individuals with disabilities

» Identify and utilize appropriate test items for measuring parameters of interest

Understand the process of developing a teacher-made test

Know the basis for identifying and selecting performances to be measured that are appropriate to the needs, capacities, and limitations of individuals with disabilities 4.01.06.01

» Select test items reflecting the major instructional areas identified in federal law

» Select test items reflecting school, local, or state curriculum guidelines that reflect an authentic, community-based, functional test

TYPES OF SCORES: Demonstrate knowledge of the nature of scores, which determines their use (e.g., interpretation, improvement, comparison with standards, achievement, manipulation)

Demonstrate knowledge of continuous, discrete, dichotomous, interval, ordinal, and nominal scores

Demonstrate knowledge of the types of scores generated by standardized instruments/ procedures commonly used to measure the performance of individuals with disabilities 4.02.01.01

» Use dichotomous, ordinal, and nominal scores when explaining student progress or class standing

» Use continuous, discrete, and interval scores when determining eligibility for special class placement

Understand the use of various types of scores for use in determining current levels of performance of individuals with disabilities 4.02.01.02

» Explain the characteristics of the different types of scores for determining the current level of performance

» Utilize different types of scores for determining the current level of performance

» Compare the relative values of the different types of scores for determining the current level of performance

» Explain the limitations of the different types of scores for determining the current level of performance

STANDARD SCORES: Demonstrate knowledge of scores on a scale that has been generated by transforming a set of raw scores to a common unit of measure using the mean and standard deviation

Understand the concept of conversion from raw scores to standard scores such as T and Z scores

Use standard scores in reporting current level of performance of individuals with disabilities 4.03.01.01

» Interpret T and Z scores in terms of the mean of each scale

» Interpret T and Z scores in terms of the standard deviation of each scale

Understand the value of standard scores in communicating assessment results

Know the importance of communicating assessment results to parents or guardians of individuals with disabilities and to other professionals 4.03.02.01

» Convert class raw scores on other performances to standard scores to enhance comparison and communication

» Explain standard scores used in expressing motor performance

Know the importance of being able to communicate assessment results expressed in age equivalencies or motor quotients for individuals with disabilities 4.03.02.02

» Explain developmental motor quotient and age equivalent scores of individuals with disabilities to other professionals

» Correlate developmental motor quotients and age equivalent scores to standard scores or scores expressing position in a group such as percentile ranks

Understand established standards for referring students for special services such as adapted physical education and related services

Understand eligibility criteria for adapted physical education in terms of standard scores 4.03.03.01

» Explain eligibility criteria for adapted physical education services

» Determine eligibility for adapted physical education (see Standard 8)

INDICATORS OF RELATIONSHIP BETWEEN PERFORMANCES: Demonstrate an understanding of relationships of measurements gathered on varied performances by one individual

Understand how performance on one test or test item may relate to performance on another test or test item

Understand that relationships may exist among scores gathered on individuals with disabilities 4.04.01.01

» Draw conclusions on the **present level of performance** utilizing scores expressed in different units of measure, standard score, or position in a group

» Draw conclusions on the present level of performance from multiple measures of motor performance

NORMAL CURVE: Demonstrate knowledge of a symmetrical curve centered on a point that is the mean score; also called a bell-shaped curve

Understand the concept of a normal distribution of scores

Understand that individuals with disabilities will usually obtain scores at the low end of a normal distribution of scores 4.05.01.01

» Compare a raw score on a distribution of scores obtained on individuals without disabilities with a distribution of scores obtained on individuals with disabilities

» Explain the relationship between percentile rank and the normal curve

Know that tests usually exclude individuals with disabilities 4.05.01.02

» Explain how test protocols and instructions may be difficult to understand and/or adversely impact performance

» Explain that scores for individuals with disabilities may appear lower when compared to individuals without disabilities

Understand the scores in a normal distribution cluster near the mean

Understand the meaning of obtained test scores that range two or more standard deviations below the mean as related to individuals with disabilities 4.05.02.01

>> Explain that scores two or more standard deviations below the mean are significantly outside the normal range

>> Prioritize needs of individuals with disabilities based on their deviation from the mean

Understand that a normal distribution is not always obtained unless a large number of scores are plotted including high scores obtained by individuals who are gifted as well as low scores obtained by individuals with disabilities 4.05.02.02

>> Interpret the distribution of scores obtained in a single class in terms of heterogeneity of performance

>> Interpret the distribution of scores obtained in a single class in terms of homogeneity of performance

DESCRIPTIVE VALUES: Demonstrate knowledge of results of score analysis that bring meaning to a set of scores

Understand the concepts involved in measures of central tendency such as the influence of extreme scores or a small number of scores on the mean and median

Understand when to use the median as a reference for comparing a raw score with group performance of individuals with disabilities 4.06.01.01

>> Explain an individual's score relative to the median when a few scores skew the distribution of a single class

>> Explain how the number of scores affects the differential between the median and the mean

Understand when to use the mean as a reference for comparing a raw score with group performance of individuals with disabilities 4.06.01.02

>> Explain an individual's score relative to the mean when a few scores skew the distribution of a single class

>> Explain how the number of scores affects the differential between the mean and the median

Understand the concepts involved in measures of variability such as the reflection of the homogeneity or heterogeneity of a group of scores

Understand when to use standard deviation for comparing a raw score with group performance of individuals with disabilities 4.06.02.01

>> Explain an individual's score in terms of standard deviations

>> Explain how the number of scores affects the standard deviation of a set of scores from a single class

Understand when to use variance for comparing a raw score with group performance of individuals with disabilities 4.06.02.02

» Explain the variance of a set of scores when reporting the median

» Determine the variance of a set of scores for use in determining eligibility for special services

Understand the use of measures of central tendency and variability to gain a perspective of obtained scores for individuals with disabilities 4.06.02.03

» Explain an individual's score relative to the mean and standard deviation of a set of scores

» Explain an individual's score relative to the mean and standard deviation of a standardized instrument

MEASURES OF POSITION: Demonstrate knowledge of a score that has a specified proportion of the population below it in a distribution thereby defining its position in the distribution

Understand the concept of conversion from raw scores to measures of group position such as percentile ranks, quartiles, and stanines

Know the use of percentiles, quartiles, or stanines when reporting current level of performance of individuals with disabilities 4.07.01.01

» Express an individual's scores in terms of percentiles and explain their meaning

» Express an individual's scores in terms of quartiles and explain their meaning

» Express an individual's scores in terms of stanines and explain their meaning

Recognize the relative value of percentiles, percentile ranks, quartiles, and stanines for communicating test results

Understand how measures of position compare the raw score of an individual with a disability with its position in a larger distribution 4.07.02.01

» Explain the position of an individual's raw score that converts to a given percentile

» Explain the position of an individual's raw score that converts to a given quartile

» Explain the position of an individual's raw score that converts to a given stanine

Understand that percentiles and quartiles work from a base of 10 and therefore may be easier to interpret for individuals with disabilities 4.07.02.02

>> Explain that the percentile or quartile reflects the point below which the percentage of others who took the test have scored

>> Explain that a percentile or quartile score is not the percentage correct on the test

TEST CHARACTERISTICS: Demonstrate knowledge of the qualities of a test such as reliability, validity, and objectivity that make it functional for a given purpose such as identification of unique needs and eligibility for services, placement, evaluation of achievement, prediction, or program evaluation

Understand the relationship between the purpose for assessing (e.g., screening) and the characteristics of the tests used

Understand the desirable characteristics of tests used for screening individuals with disabilities 4.08.01.01

>> Explain the **administrative feasibility** of a selected screening instrument

>> Explain the economy of a screening instrument

Understand the desirable characteristics of tests necessary for the decision-making process (e.g., identification, placement, and achievement) specific to working with individuals with disabilities 4.08.01.02

>> Describe the discrimination ability of tests used for educational decisions

>> Explain how norm-referenced standards assist with making decisions relative to eligibility, program planning, **individualized education program (IEPs)**, and placement

Understand the desirable characteristics of tests used for developing individualized educational programs, individualized family service plans, or transitional plans for individuals with disabilities 4.08.01.03

>> Explain test validity

>> Develop an authentic, community-based, functional test

Understand the most important characteristics of motor performance tests such as reliability, validity, objectivity, and **utility**

Understand standard error of measurement and its common sources especially with individuals with disabilities 4.08.02.01

>> Understand standard error of measurement and how it affects the reliability and validity of a test score

>> Understand what standard error of measurement means relative to a single test score

Understand the impact of multicultural and linguistic issues affecting the valid and reliable measurement of motor performance among individuals with disabilities 4.08.02.02

» Encourage dress codes that maximize motor performance while being sensitive to cultural practices of dress

» Limit the amount of competition during measurement as some cultural mores preclude competition

» Recognize impact of culture on prior exposure to and experiences with physical activity and sport

Understand impact of disabling conditions on the reliability, objectivity, validity and utility of motor performance test results 4.08.02.03

» Recognize the impact of disabling conditions that can adversely affect the test-retest reliability of assessment results

» Recognize the impact of disabling conditions that can adversely affect the content, concurrent, and face validity of a test

» Recognize the impact of disabling conditions that can adversely affect the objectivity (interrater reliability) of the test results

» Evaluate a test or procedure for its appropriateness for individuals with disabilities

Select appropriate tests and procedures based on intended purpose, characteristics of the instrument, as well as the attributes of the population to be assessed

Understand that federal law (IDEA) mandates that valid and non-discriminatory tests be used to evaluate the performance of individuals with disabilities in all areas including physical education 4.08.03.01

» Identify valid tests for use with various populations of individuals with disabilities

» Explain to what degree a test's administration procedures can be modified and still be valid for use with individuals with disabilities

Understand measurement terminology such as reliability, validity, administrative feasibility, and objectivity when selecting measurement instruments for testing individuals with disabilities 4.08.03.02

» Explain how tests that are not administratively feasible can adversely affect performance for individuals with disabilities

» Explain the relationship between a test's validity and the decision-making process relative to eligibility, program planning, IEPs, and placement decisions; reporting progress; and measuring achievement of individuals with disabilities

PRETEST PLANNING: Demonstrate knowledge of preparation that occurs before assessing individuals with disabilities

Understand the purposes for assessing in physical education

Understand screening, diagnostic assessment, and evaluation relative to individuals with disabilities 4.09.01.01

» Coordinate the assessment of motor performance from screening to program evaluation

» Establish criteria for screening that can be implemented consistently

Know the unique roles of instructional assessment, diagnostic assessment, and monitoring progress in programs for individuals with disabilities 4.09.01.02

» Understand and describe the purposes for assessment at each stage of the assessment process

» Explain the purpose of different types of instruments used at each stage of the assessment process

Plan prior to conducting an assessment

Understand the importance of planning for ongoing assessment of individuals with disabilities 4.09.02.01

» Establish a plan for assessing individuals with disabilities on a regular basis

» Select appropriate times, facilities, and instruments or procedures for assessing a variety of individuals with disabilities

» Identify and use appropriate communication techniques required by some individuals with disabilities

Understand what equipment is needed for administering the selected instruments to individuals with disabilities 4.09.02.02

» Obtain equipment necessary for conducting the assessment apart from the test itself

» Maintain consistency in assessment conditions such as using the same equipment, facility, and instructions

Understand and complete the training needed to accurately administer the selected instruments to individuals with disabilities 4.09.02.03

» Videotape and analyze your performance administering the selected instruments to a variety of individuals with disabilities until you can produce consistent/reliable results

» Compare your assessment results with those of other trained and experienced adapted physical educators

PERFORMANCE STANDARDS: Demonstrate knowledge of how to apply and interpret test standards

Compare and contrast norm-referenced, criterion-referenced, and **content-referenced standards**

Understand how norm-referenced, criterion-referenced, and content-referenced tests can be used to assess individuals with disabilities 4.10.01.01

» Explain how the Test of Gross Motor Development can be used as a norm-referenced test or as a criterion-referenced test

Understand the relative value of norm-referenced, criterion-referenced, and content-referenced standards needed for the decision-making process 4.10.01.02

» Understand how norm-referenced, criterion-referenced, and content-referenced standards can be used when making eligibility decisions

» Understand how norm-referenced, criterion-referenced, and content-referenced standards can be used when making program planning decisions

» Understand how norm-referenced, criterion-referenced, and content-referenced standards can be used when making IEP decisions

» Understand how norm-referenced, criterion-referenced, and content-referenced standards can be used when making placement decisions

Demonstrate an understanding of the process of developing norm-referenced and criterion-referenced standards

Understand the differences between norm-referenced and criterion-referenced standards 4.10.02.01

» Explain when norm-referenced standards can be used with individuals from a given population

» Explain when criterion-referenced standards can be used with individuals from a given population

Understand the similarities between norm-referenced and criterion-referenced standards for individuals with disabilities 4.10.02.02

» Describe how norm-referenced and criterion-referenced tests can both be standardized

» Describe how norm-referenced and criterion-referenced tests can both be used to determine individual performance

» Describe how norm-referenced and criterion-referenced tests should both demonstrate validity and reliability

DATA GATHERING: Demonstrate knowledge that the process of gathering information on individuals for the purpose of assessment may take the form of formal or informal; objective or subjective assessment and use norm-, criterion-, or content-referenced standards

Utilize informal measures such as checklists, task analysis, rubrics, **curriculum-embedded** measures, and behavioral observation (see Standard 10)

Understand the use of informal measures with individuals with disabilities 4.11.01.01

》 Observe an individual's motor behavior during unstructured and unplanned play and record on a rating scale

》 Maintain anecdotal records related to an individual's IEP

Understand the use of systematic observational techniques such as academic learning time (ALT) and opportunity to respond for individuals with disabilities 4.11.01.02

》 Use **event recording** techniques to observe behavior

》 Use **duration recording** techniques to observe behavior

》 Use interval recording techniques to observe behavior

Understand the use of individual reports in the process of gathering data on individuals with disabilities 4.11.01.03

》 Use individual self-report evaluations when appropriate

》 Use peer evaluations when appropriate

Understand various protocols used in the administration of tests such as performance assessment, direct measures, formal standardized procedures, informal unstructured activity, etc.

Understand various assessment protocols, forms of data gathering, environmental settings, and organizational structures used in physical education and the effects of these on the performance of individuals with disabilities 4.11.02.01

》 Describe various assessment protocols for measuring motor development, physical fitness, motor skill acquisition, and sensory-motor function

》 Describe various forms of data gathering for individuals with disabilities such as parent report, standardized testing, self-report, observation, task analysis, and direct measures

Understand the difference between coaching and encouraging an individual while administering a test to individuals with disabilities 4.11.02.02

》 Understand the test administration instructions and what prompts can be used to elicit performance from individuals with disabilities

》 Understand that prompts provided should not include instructional information or cues

Understand the effects of medication on attention, coordination, and responsiveness when administering tests to individuals with disabilities 4.11.02.03

》 Note the presence of psychotropic drugs in individuals with disabilities during assessment

》 Observe the motor behavior of an individual taking medication at various times during the day

Recognize the value of establishing rapport with individuals with disabilities prior to assessing 4.11.02.04

» Demonstrate the ability to establish rapport

» Validate the comfort level of individuals with the examiner by observing their interactions with other teachers

Understand the basic principles of subjective data gathering in contrast to objective assessment protocols

Understand the essential functional gross and fine motor performances marking significant motor milestones throughout the lifespan 4.11.03.01

» Modify test items to accommodate limited motor development

» Observe infants engaged in motor activity and report observations

Understand the biomechanical elements expected in fundamental motor patterns and skills for individuals without disabilities before assessing individuals with disabilities 4.11.03.02

» Describe when biomechanical elements of movement are absent, substituted, or changed by individuals with disabilities

» Explain the differences between observed biomechanical elements of movement and expected biomechanical elements

Understand data gathering through curriculum-based assessment of movement for individuals with disabilities 4.11.03.03

» Explain the individual's present level of performance within the curriculum

» Select curricular activities based on present level of performance

» Obtain measurements through video recording

» Obtain measurements using ecological inventories

Understand the value of conducting play-based assessment with individuals with disabilities 4.11.03.04

» Create a play-based environment for observing play behaviors and motor performances

» Use a variety of environments or settings in which to observe play behaviors and motor performance

» Gather data from the significant others regarding play behaviors and individual and/or family preferences and practices relative to physical activity

Understand the value of a task analysis of motor skills for gathering data on individuals with disabilities 4.11.03.05

» Use task analysis to develop criterion-referenced tests for measuring instructional content

» Use task analysis for defining instructional sequences

Understand how to gather data through review of written reports and medical records of individuals with disabilities 4.11.03.06

» Read written reports from other professionals and correlate with findings of motor performance assessment

» Read medical records and correlate with findings of motor performance assessment

Understand direct measures for gathering data other than through motor performance such as dynamometry, telemetry, and goniometry

Understand the need to use direct measures instead of performance measures of individuals with disabilities 4.11.04.01

» Use skinfold calipers for measuring body composition

» Use dynamometry for measuring strength

» Use goniometry for measuring range of motion

Understand the use of screening methods

Know the legislative restrictions on the use of screening methods with individuals with disabilities 4.11.05.01

» Use screening methods as an informal procedure to gather initial data

» Limit screening activities to those allowed under federal legislation and the guidelines for the local educational agency

Understand how screening methods can be used as an informal procedure to validate other data on individuals with disabilities or when other procedures are untenable 4.11.05.02

» Use an informal checklist or rubric of behaviors (e.g., attention, comprehension of instruction, effort) to validate formally obtained data

» Write a descriptive narrative of the motor performance (e.g., supports provided, behaviors that interfere with performance, adaptations to assessment, etc.) when individuals have demonstrated difficulties with the assessment process

Understand the advantages of individual versus mass organizational assessment such as reliability and validity of scores, consistency of motivation, and precision of performance

Know the types of assessment environments appropriate to the characteristics of individuals with disabilities 4.11.06.01

» Arrange the assessment environment appropriate to the characteristics of the individual with a disability

» Provide a distraction-free assessment environment for individuals with attention disorders

Understand the effects of mass versus individual assessment on individuals with specific disabilities 4.11.06.02

» Determine which type of assessment is appropriate based on the characteristics of an individual with disabilities

» Provide opportunities for practice trials in a mass assessment environment when appropriate

Understand the limitations of individual versus mass assessment of classes of individuals with disabilities 4.11.06.03

» Describe the prerequisite competencies needed in a mass assessment environment

» Verify the validity of test results obtained from an individual assessment versus results from a mass assessment environment

PERFORMANCE SAMPLING: The practice of measuring representative factors of motor performance as a means of obtaining an overview of an individual's true ability

Understand the concept of **performance sampling** using objective and subjective testing

Understand the use of performance sampling in determining an individual's eligibility for adapted physical education 4.12.01.01

» Identify motor parameters to be sampled when considering eligibility for adapted physical education services

» Determine an efficient and effective sampling procedure

» Explain the benefits of performance sampling across multiple days/sessions

Understand the use of baseline data collection for program development for individuals with disabilities 4.12.01.02

» Use multiple trials to establish baseline performance

» Re-establish baseline performance at each annual review

» Use baseline data to write **annual goals** and objectives

Understand the concept of performance generalization across contexts for individuals with disabilities 4.12.01.03

» Provide opportunities for motor performance of a given skill in a variety of contexts

» Evaluate the ability of individuals with disabilities to apply newly acquired skills in community-based settings and activities

HISTORY AND PHILOSOPHY

HISTORY AND PHILOSOPHY

STANDARD 5

EDUCATIONAL REFORM: Knowledge of educational reform regarding individuals with disabilities

Understand the evolution of educational reform in relation to individuals with disabilities

Understand the historical treatment of individuals with disabilities with regard to educational, emotional, social, and medical treatment 5.01.01.01

>> Explain persecution of individuals with disabilities in society before the 1800s

>> Explain neglect of individuals with disabilities with regard to education prior to the 1800s

Understand segregated educational placements for individuals with disabilities 5.01.01.02

>> Explain strengths of segregated educational placements

>> Explain weaknesses of segregated educational placements

Understand regular education initiative/total inclusion 5.01.01.03

>> Explain regular education initiative/total inclusion from a positive position

>> Explain regular education initiative/total inclusion from a negative position

Understand the evolution of physical education for individuals with disabilities

Understand the practice of physical education in separate schools and separate classes 5.01.02.01

>> Explain the advantages of separate physical education classes

>> Explain the disadvantages of separate physical education classes

Understand the concept of least restrictive environment for individuals with disabilities in the physical education setting 5.01.02.02

>> Explain least restrictive environment in physical education

>> Explain continuum of placement alternatives in relation to least restrictive environment in physical education

>> Explain how to determine the least restrictive environment in physical education for an individual with a disability

Understand evolution of multidisciplinary concepts in education

Understand multidisciplinary, interdisciplinary, and cross-disciplinary/transdisciplinary approaches with regard to adapted physical education 5.01.03.01

» Explain the adapted physical educator's role on the multidisciplinary team

» Explain the adapted physical educator's role on an interdisciplinary team

» Explain the adapted physical educator's role on a cross-disciplinary/trans-disciplinary team

» Explain the importance of the adapted physical educator when collaborating on multidisciplinary, interdisciplinary, and cross-disciplinary/transdisciplinary teams

Understand evolution of funding education for individuals with disabilities

Understand funding terminology in relation to individuals with disabilities legislation 5.01.04.01

» Explain authorization of funds in relation to legislation for individuals with disabilities

» Explain appropriation of funds in relation to legislation for individuals with disabilities

» Explain discretionary funds in relation to legislation for individuals with disabilities

LAW: Knowledge of public laws that affect physical education, non-academic, and **extracurricular services** (e.g., interscholastic athletics) for individuals with disabilities

Understand major components of the Individuals with Disabilities Education Act (IDEIA, 2004) in relation to physical education and physical activity

Understand free, appropriate public education for individuals with disabilities 5.02.01.01

» Explain the concept of a free, appropriate public education for an individual with a disability

» Explain what an individualized education program (IEP) is

Understand least restrictive and most restrictive environments in physical education for individuals with disabilities 5.02.01.02

» Explain the least restrictive environment for an individual with a disability

» Advocate for a variety of placements in physical education for individuals with disabilities

» Advocate for a variety of supports in the general physical education setting

Understand the meaning of direct and indirect services in the law 5.02.01.03

» Explain the difference between direct and indirect services in physical education

» Explain the legal definition of special education

» Explain the legal definition of physical education

Understand the meaning of related services for individuals with disabilities 5.02.01.04

» Explain the legal definition of related services

» Explain the scope and types of related services

» Suggest related services, such as physical and **occupational therapy**, when needed in order to succeed in physical education

Understand parental and guardian involvement in the education of all children and youth with disabilities 5.02.01.05

» Discuss the parent and/or guardian role in the IEP process

» Discuss the parent and/or guardian input in the planning and evaluation of the adapted physical education program

» Explain **due process** in relation to the parent and/or guardian involvement

Understand how age impacts the services provided to individuals with disabilities under IDEIA 5.02.01.06

» Know that **Individual Family Service Plans** (IFSPs) are to be developed for students ages 0 to 3

» Know that IEPs are to be developed for students ages 4 to 21

» Know that Individual Transition Plans (ITP) are to be developed for students ages 14 to 21

» Know that adapted physical education services can be provided to individuals with disabilities from age 0 to 21 years of age if prescribed on the IFSP, IEP or ITP

Understand the Individual Family Service Plan in relation to families and individuals with disabilities (see Standard 9) 5.02.01.07

» Explain components of the Individual Family Service Plan such as family needs and resources

» Explain how physical activities are a part of the Individual Family Service Plan

Understand the categories of disability that are included in IDEIA, Part C (2004) 5.02.01.08

» Define and explain "at risk for developmental delay"

» Define and explain "developmentally delayed"

Understand transition services 5.02.01.09

» Explain how physical activities are a part of the Individualized Transition Plan

» Describe the adapted physical educator's role in the transition from home to school

» Describe the adapted physical educator's role in transition from school to vocation and the community

Understand the change in age for services for individuals with disabilities 5.02.01.10

» Advocate for physical activities for individuals birth through 21

» Advocate for **community resources** for physical activities for individuals birth through 21 and their parents and guardians

Understand major components of the Individuals with Disabilities Education Act (IDEIA, 2004) and the Americans with Disabilities Act (ADA, 1990), in relation to non-academic and extracurricular services (e.g., interscholastic athletics)

Understand that the clause describing the inclusion of individuals with disabilities mandates an equal opportunity for participation in non-academic and extracurricular programming (e.g., interscholastic athletics) 5.03.01.01

» Advocate for individuals with disabilities in school-based **inclusive sport opportunities** as well as disability integrated and **segregated sport opportunities**

» Be aware of the innovative school-based programs for including individuals with disabilities in sport and recreational activities

Understand major components of the Rehabilitation Act of 1973 (Section 504), the Amateur Sports Act of 1978, the Americans with Disabilities Act of 1990 (ADA), and the Every Student Succeeds Act of 2016 in relation to physical education and physical activity

Understand the nondiscrimination clauses referenced in the Rehabilitation Act of 1973 (Section 504), the Amateur Sports Act of 1978, and the Americans with Disabilities Act of 1990 (ADA) 5.04.01.01

» Advocate for individuals with disabilities in integrated and segregated sports programs

» Be aware of the innovative programs for including individuals with disabilities in sport and recreational activities

» Advocate for qualified individuals with disabilities to participate in interscholastic athletics and extracurricular class activities

» Advocate for activities to be conducted in architecturally accessible structures

» Advocate for program accessibility

Understand the difference between Section 504 and the ADA as they relate to physical activity and physical education programming 5.04.01.02

» Know the difference between a **504 plan** and an IEP

» Know that adapted physical education (APE) services can be included on a 504 plan

» Describe program accommodations

» Know how program accessibility is impacted by the ADA

Understand the implications of the Every Student Succeeds Act of 2016 5.04.01.03

» Explain the Every Student Succeeds Act (ESSA) 2016 in relation to preparing, training, and recruiting qualified school personnel, including physical educators and adapted physical educators

» Explain the definition of a well-rounded education in relation to physical education for students with disabilities

» Explain ESSA 2016 in relation to supporting safe and healthy students, including those with disabilities

» Apply the requirements of ESSA 2016 to adapted physical education

HISTORY: Knowledge of the history of physical education for individuals with disabilities

Understand the medical model

Understand **medical gymnastics** and its early role in the adapted physical education movement 5.05.01.01

» Identify individuals associated with the medical gymnastics movement

» Explain components of medical gymnastics that have had an impact on current adapted physical activity practices such as individually prescribed exercises

Understand corrective/**remedial physical education**

Understand corrective/remedial physical education and its impact on early adapted physical education services 5.05.02.01

» Identify individuals associated with corrective/remedial physical education

» Explain components of corrective/remedial physical education such as orthopedic and **structural remediation** that have an impact on current practices in adapted physical education

Understand the shift in service delivery models from adapted physical education services being provided in primarily separate settings to being provided in more inclusive physical education settings

Understand that **specially-designed physical education** (i.e., adapted physical education services) is a direct instructional service that must be provided in the least restrictive environment 5.05.03.01

» Explain components of the ABC model of adapted physical education service delivery process: program planning, assessment, implementation, and evaluation

» Explain how placement decisions are made in the program planning processes in adapted physical education

Understand the concept of least restrictive environment as it applies to adapted physical education 5.05.04.01

» Explain the continuum of placements in adapted physical education

» Advocate for service delivery in the least restrictive environment

» Philosophy: Knowledge of physical education, sport, and recreation

Understand there are multiple definitions of physical education (e.g., IDEIA, SHAPE America National Standards, etc.)

Understand the definition of physical education included in IDEIA 5.06.01.01

» Explain the five components of physical education as set forth in IDEIA

» Explain the implications for programming planning for physical education for individuals with disabilities served under IDEIA

» Know the differences that may exist between the definition of physical education in IDEIA and definitions of physical education set forth by professional organizations and/or state content standards

Understand the role of physical education in the school curriculum

Understand how physical education contributes to the total development of individuals with disabilities 5.06.02.01

» Explain how physical education teaches the motor skills needed for an active lifestyle

» Explain how physical education teaches the health-enhancing behaviors needed to be active in adulthood

Understand the philosophy of physical education as education "of the physical"

Understand the importance of motor skills and physical fitness such as flexibility, agility, and strength as it relates to individuals with disabilities 5.06.03.01

» Explain the importance of motor skills in the life of an individual with disabilities

» Explain the importance of physical fitness in the life of an individual with disabilities

Understand the philosophy of physical education as education "through the physical"

Understand physical, cognitive, and affective outcomes in adapted physical education 5.06.04.01

» Explain physical outcomes of physical education for individuals who have a disability to other educators and parents and/or guardians

» Explain cognitive outcomes of physical education for individuals who have a disability to other educators and parents and/or guardians

» Explain affective outcomes of physical education for individuals who have a disability to other educators and parents and/or guardians

Understand the role of sport in the total physical education curriculum

Understand sport opportunities for individuals with disabilities 5.06.05.01

» Explain the benefits of disability sport opportunities

» Explain the benefits of inclusive sport opportunities

Understand the role of recreation across the lifespan of an individual with a disability

Understand physical education as the foundation for recreation opportunities for individuals with disabilities (see Standard I5) 5.06.06.01

» Advocate for recreation activities that are physically active and socially engaging

» Advocate for appropriate physically active recreation activities in **transition planning**

Understand the relationship between therapeutic recreation and adapted physical education 5.06.07.01

» Explain **leisure counseling** and its application to adapted physical education

» Explain therapeutic recreation as a related service

PHILOSOPHY: Special education

Understand the role of the multidisciplinary team

Understand the coordination of resources for individuals with disabilities 5.07.01.01

» Collaborate with other service providers

» Share resources to optimize educational goals

» Develop partnerships to maximize the use of resources for individuals with disabilities

Understand the educational philosophy behind the transition process

Understand transition services 5.07.02.01

» Explain the adapted physical educator's role in the transition process

» Advocate for the adapted physical educator's role in the transition process

» Explain the benefits of providing transition services in physical education

Understand the educational philosophy of least restrictive environment

Understand least restrictive and most restrictive environments in physical education for individuals with disabilities 5.07.03.01

» Explain the adapted physical educator's role in determining the least restrictive environment for an individual with a disability

» Explain the supports and services that can be provided in the general physical education setting to allow individuals with disabilities to participate successfully

» Explain the benefits of the least restrictive environment in physical education for individuals with disabilities

» Explain the benefits of the least restrictive environment in physical education for individuals without disabilities

Understand inclusion from a philosophical standpoint

Understand inclusion as it relates to physical education for individuals with disabilities 5.07.04.01

» Explain criteria for exclusion from general physical education

» Explain dual placement (i.e., partial placement in general physical education setting and partial placement in a more restrictive adapted physical education)

Understand rationale for educating children from birth to three years of age

Understand rationale for providing physical and motor activities to young children with disabilities 5.07.05.01

» Advocate for physical activity for young children with disabilities

» Advocate for an adapted physical educator to consult and assist in providing physical and motor activities for young children with disabilities

UNIQUE ATTRIBUTES OF LEARNERS

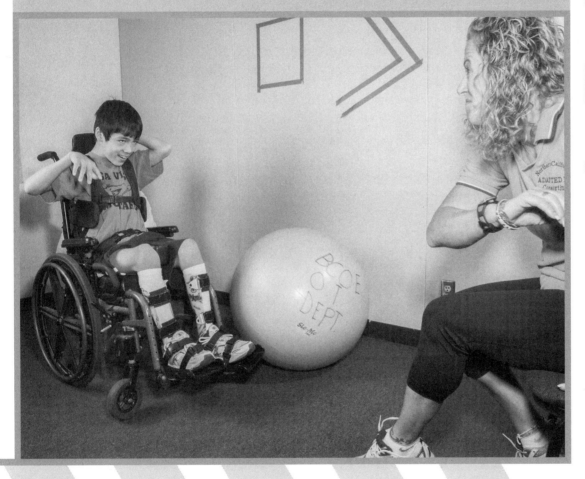

STANDARD 6

UNIQUE ATTRIBUTES OF LEARNERS: CONSIDERATIONS FOR PROFESSIONAL PRACTICE

AUTISM SPECTRUM DISORDER: Understand the unique attributes of individuals with autism spectrum disorder

As defined by IDEA, autism spectrum disorder (ASD) is "a developmental disability significantly affecting verbal and **nonverbal communication** and social interaction, generally evident before age three, that adversely affects a child's educational performance." 34 CFR §300.8

Understand the etiology of autism spectrum disorder and its impact on physical and motor attributes

Understand that ASD is a neurodevelopmental disorder that is caused by abnormalities in the structure or function of the brain (IV) 6.01.01.01

» Know that the exact cause of ASD is unknown though possible causes include heredity, genetics, and/or medical problems

» Know that males are five times more likely than females to be diagnosed with ASD

» Know that research specific to ASD is a rapidly evolving field of study that requires service providers to stay current with the literature

Understand the severity levels for autism spectrum disorder

Know there are three severity levels 6.01.02.01

» Know that level 1 is characterized as requiring support for social, communication, and restricted, repetitive behaviors

» Know that level 2 is characterized as requiring substantial support for social, communication, and restricted, repetitive behaviors

» Know that level 3 is characterized as requiring very substantial support for social, communication, and restricted, repetitive behaviors

Understand unique psychomotor considerations

Understand that individuals with ASD demonstrate delays in psychomotor development that impact motor performance 6.01.03.01

» Identify the challenges in evaluating motor performance needed to determine present level of performance

» Know that individuals with ASD may be motorically awkward

» Know that individuals with ASD may demonstrate stereotypic behaviors that interfere with motor performance

» Design instruction to provide structure and environmental prompts to elicit the appropriate motoric response

» Utilize appropriate instructional supports and strategies such as visual **demonstrations**, social stories, motivating equipment choices, and cue words and/or prompting to elicit the repeated trials necessary for motor learning to occur

Understand unique fitness considerations

Understand that individuals with ASD may demonstrate deficits in physical fitness 6.01.04.01

» Identify the challenges in evaluating physical fitness in individuals with ASD needed to determine present level of performance

» Know that individuals with ASD may lack the prerequisite motor skills needed to participate in physical activity sufficiently to develop and/or maintain physical fitness

» Know that individuals with ASD need sufficient supports to understand the feelings, sensations, and expectations of physical activity in order to persist in physical activity long enough to improve levels of physical fitness

» Design physical fitness instruction to provide structure and environmental prompts necessary to sustain physical activity participation needed to elicit changes or improve levels of physical fitness

» Utilize appropriate instructional supports and strategies such as visual demonstrations, social stories, motivating equipment choices, and cue words and/or prompting to elicit the appropriate frequency, intensity, and duration of physical activity necessary for maintaining or improving physical fitness

Understand unique cognitive considerations

Understand that most individuals with ASD demonstrate deficits in intellectual functioning which impacts learning in physical education 6.01.05.01

» Know that deficits in communication impact understanding of instruction and subsequent motor performance

» Know that individuals with ASD may demonstrate significant deficits in **executive functioning** that necessitate considerations in instructional and environmental design needed for learning to occur

» Design instruction in short, concise, sequential segments to maximize learning

» Know that it is important to only reinforce correct components of skill performance or personal social behaviors

» Know that individuals with ASD may perseverate which interferes with their learning and requires instructional supports such as social stories and global visual schedules

» Know that individuals with ASD may be attending to instruction and demonstrations though they may not be making eye contact

» Know and implement principles of **Universal Design for Learning** (UDL) in instruction and assessment

Understand unique affective and social skill considerations

Understand that individuals with ASD demonstrate marked deficits in affective and social skill development 6.01.06.01

» Know that individuals with ASD may demonstrate significant deficits in recognizing and responding to social cues necessary for appropriate social interactions

» Know that deficits in affective development and expressive language may lead to inappropriate responses in social interaction

» Recognize that deficits in **social imperception and social reciprocity** may lead to inappropriate and/or dangerous situations such as not recognizing a potentially dangerous situation

» Utilize appropriate instructional supports and strategies such as social stories, peer **modeling**, one-to-one instruction, video modeling, and/or prompting to elicit appropriate affective responses and social skills

» Know that individuals with ASD may require intensive instructional support in learning appropriate social skills such as social stories and peer modeling

» Recognize the physical educator's role in teaching and developing self-advocacy skills as well as providing opportunities to apply those skills

Understand health and medical issues

Understand that individuals with ASD may have a range of health and medical concerns such as diet, sleep, gastrointestinal, and/or sensory issues that impact learning and motor performance 6.01.07.01

» Know that individuals with ASD may demonstrate hypo- or hypersensitive responses to one or more sensory stimuli

» Know that individuals with ASD may engage in **self-stimulatory** or self-injurious behaviors that impact overall health status

» Know the effects of medications, commonly prescribed to individuals with ASD, on motor performance and behavior

» Collaborate with a multidisciplinary team to address health and medical issues

Understand unique communication considerations

Understand that individuals with ASD demonstrate marked deficits in speech and language development 6.01.08.01

» Know that significant deficits in speech production including issues with voice, articulation, and fluency will adversely affect communication

» Know that significant deficits in receptive and/or expressive language will impact communication of thoughts or feelings in social interactions

» Collaborate with a speech-language pathologist to maximize effective communication

» Use the current versions of aided (e.g., picture communication symbols and line drawings) and unaided (e.g., manual signs and gestures) **augmentative and alternative communication** methods along with appropriate transmission devices (e.g., iPads and **Dynavox** devices)

> **DEAF/BLIND:** Understand the unique attributes of individuals who are deaf/blind

As defined by IDEA, deafblindness means "concomitant hearing and visual impairments, the combination of which causes such severe communication and other developmental and educational needs that they cannot be accommodated in special education programs solely for children with deafness or children with blindness." 34 CFR §300.8

Understand the etiology of deafblindness and its impact on physical and motor attributes

Understand that deafblindness is caused by heredity, genetic, trauma, and/or medical conditions that lead to some level of vision and hearing loss 6.02.01.01

» Know that causes of deafblindness may include Usher syndrome, CHARGE (it stands for Coloboma of the eye, Heart defects, Atresia of the choanae, Retardation of growth and development, and Ear abnormalities and deafness) syndrome, as well as birth trauma, optic nerve atrophy, cataracts, glaucoma, macular degeneration, or diabetic retinopathy

» Know that individuals with deafblindness often present more than two concomitant disabilities

» Early detection and intervention is essential to development and the learning process

Understand the varying degrees of deafblindness and how each impacts physical education programming

Know that individuals with deafblindness can acquire hearing and vision loss at different times and exhibit varying degrees of hearing and vision loss that differentially impact learning 6.02.02.01

» Know that hearing and vision impairments can be stable or progressive

» Know that hearing and vision impairments can range from partial to complete

» Know that hearing loss can be bilateral or unilateral, symmetrical or asymmetrical, progressive or sudden, and fluctuating or stable

» Know that hearing and vision impairments can be congenital or acquired

» Know that the magnitude of learning difficulties will be greater for individuals with congenital hearing and vision loss versus individuals with acquired hearing and vision loss, particularly those who acquired hearing loss after language acquisition or vision loss after formative development

Understand unique psychomotor considerations

Understand that individuals with deafblindness may demonstrate delays in psychomotor development that impact motor performance 6.02.03.01

» Identify the challenges in evaluating motor performance needed to determine present level of performance

» Know that there will be significant delays in motor development

» Design instruction to provide extensive tactile and kinesthetic prompts to elicit the practice necessary for motor learning to occur

» Know that most individuals with deafblindness have the capacity to develop functional motor skills

Understand unique fitness considerations

Understand that individuals with deafblindness may demonstrate deficits in physical fitness 6.02.04.01

» Identify the challenges in evaluating physical fitness needed to determine present level of performance

» Know that the prerequisite motor skills needed to participate in physical activity sufficiently to develop and/or maintain physical fitness may be lacking

» Know that most individuals with deafblindness have the capacity to develop physical fitness levels

» Design instruction to provide extensive tactile and kinesthetic prompts to elicit the appropriate frequency, intensity, and duration of physical activity necessary for maintaining or improving physical fitness

» Utilize appropriate instructional supports and strategies such as motivating equipment, physical activity choice, communication methods, and prompting to elicit the appropriate frequency, intensity, and duration of physical activity necessary for maintaining or improving physical fitness

Understand unique cognitive considerations

Understand that individuals with deafblindness demonstrate academic delays that adversely affect learning in physical education 6.02.05.01

» Know that deficits in vision, hearing, and communication impact their understanding of instruction, the intended purpose for the movement, and their subsequent motor performance

» Design instruction in extremely small sequential segments employing all appropriate sensory stimuli to maximize learning

» Use multiple methods of presenting instructional information (see Standard 9) such as manual sign language, kinesthetic prompts, or tactile prompts to support instruction

» Know and implement principles of UDL in instruction and assessment

Understand unique affective and social skill considerations

Understand that individuals with deafblindness demonstrate deficits in affective and social skill development 6.02.06.01

» Know that significant deficits in affective development and language will limit social interaction

» Know that the demonstration of stereotypic behaviors interferes with social interactions

» Know that individuals with deafblindness with limited communication skills may become easily frustrated and/or feel socially isolated

» Know that intensive instructional support in learning appropriate social skills such as social stories and peer modeling may be required

» Recognize the physical educator's role in teaching and developing self-advocacy skills as well as providing opportunities to apply those skills

Understand health and medical issues

Understand that individuals with deafblindness may have a range of health and medical concerns such as heart conditions, cleft palate, and/or balance issues that impact learning and motor performance 6.02.07.01

» Collaborate with the multidisciplinary team to address health and medical issues

» Recognize safety and participation concerns associated with cochlear implants and hearing aids such as the impact of static electricity, blows to the head, and water exposure

» Collaborate with occupational therapists when working with individuals with sensorineural hearing loss to address issues associated with balance and vestibular impairments

Understand unique communication considerations

Understand that individuals with deafblindness demonstrate marked deficits in communication skills 6.02.08.01

» Understand communication challenges in the learning environment

» Encourage the use of cochlear implants and hearing aids and take measures to ensure safe handling in physical activity settings

» Collaborate with other professionals including audiologists, speech-language pathologists, deaf educators, and interpreters to maximize effective communication

» Recognize that individuals with deafblindness may attempt to communicate or interact socially through touch

» Know techniques to support communication (see Standard 9) such as manual sign language

» Recognize the physical educator's role in effectively receiving communication from individuals who are deaf-blind

DEAFNESS AND HEARING IMPAIRMENTS: Understand unique attributes of individuals who are deaf or have hearing impairments

As defined by IDEA, deafness means "a hearing impairment that is so severe that the child is impaired in processing linguistic information through hearing, with or without amplification that adversely affects a child's educational performance." 34 CFR §300.8

As defined by IDEA, hearing impairment means "an impairment in hearing, whether permanent or fluctuating, that adversely affects a child's educational performance but that is not included under the definition of deafness in this section." 34 CFR §300.8

Understand the etiology of deafness and hearing impairments and the impact on physical and motor attributes

Understand that deafness and hearing impairments are caused by abnormalities in the structure or function of the outer, middle and/or inner ear resulting in conductive or sensorineural hearing loss 6.03.01.01

>> Know that causes may include heredity, genetics, trauma and/or medical conditions

>> Know that individuals with sensorineural deafness or hearing impairment may have balance issues

>> Recognize that early detection and intervention is essential to language development and the learning process

Understand the types or classifications of deafness and hearing impairments and how each impacts physical education programming

Know that individuals with deafness and hearing impairments may have conductive, sensorineural, or mixed hearing loss 6.03.02.01

>> Know that conductive hearing loss is due to damage to the outer or middle ear and can be addressed by medical or surgical intervention (e.g., surgical placement of tubes) and/or the use of hearing aids that can magnify the sound

>> Know that sensorineural hearing loss is due to damage to the inner ear or the auditory nerve and may not be treated medically though individuals may benefit from cochlear implants

Know that individuals with deafness and hearing impairments can acquire hearing loss at different times and exhibit varying degrees of hearing loss that differentially impact learning 6.03.02.02

>> Know that hearing loss can be slight to profound depending on how well the individual can hear sound frequencies or intensities

>> Know that hearing loss can be bilateral or unilateral, symmetrical or asymmetrical, progressive or sudden, and fluctuating or stable

>> Know the magnitude of learning difficulties that will be greater for individuals with congenital hearing loss versus individuals with acquired hearing loss, particularly those who acquired hearing loss after language acquisition

Understand unique psychomotor considerations

Understand that individuals with deafness and hearing impairments may demonstrate delays in psychomotor development that impact motor performance 6.03.03.01

» Identify the challenges in evaluating motor performance needed to determine present level of performance

» Know that individuals with sensorineural deafness and hearing impairments may be motorically awkward

» Design instruction to provide structure and visual prompts to elicit the appropriate motoric response

» Utilize appropriate instructional supports and strategies such as visual demonstrations, visually engaging equipment choices, signs, and/or prompting to elicit the practice necessary for motor learning to occur

» Know that most individuals with deafness and hearing impairments have the capacity to develop motor skills comparable to their peers without disabilities

Understand unique fitness considerations

Understand that individuals with deafness and hearing impairments may demonstrate deficits in physical fitness 6.03.04.01

» Identify the challenges in evaluating physical fitness in individuals with deafness and hearing impairments needed to determine present level of performance

» Know that the prerequisite motor skills needed to participate in physical activity sufficiently to develop and/or maintain physical fitness may be lacking

» Know that most individuals with deafness and hearing impairments have the capacity to develop physical fitness levels comparable to their peers without disabilities

» Utilize appropriate instructional supports and strategies such as visual demonstrations, visually engaging equipment choices, appropriate communication methods, and environmental and visual prompting to elicit the appropriate frequency, intensity, and duration of physical activity necessary for maintaining or improving physical fitness

Understand unique cognitive considerations

Understand that individuals with deafness and hearing impairments may demonstrate academic delays that can adversely affect learning in physical education 6.03.05.01

» Know that deficits in communication impact understanding of instruction and subsequent motor performance

» Know that individuals with deafness demonstrate significant deficits in language development that impact their ability to learn until language proficiency is attained

» Design instruction in short, concise, sequential segments with visual supports to maximize learning

» Use multiple methods of presenting instructional information (see Standard 9) such as sign language, visual demonstrations, physical prompts, task cards, or other visual supports during instruction

» Know and implement principles of UDL in instruction and assessment

Understand unique affective and social skill considerations

Understand that individuals with deafness and hearing impairments demonstrate deficits in affective and social skill development 6.03.06.01

» Know that individuals with deafness and hearing impairments may demonstrate deficits in recognizing and responding to social cues necessary for appropriate social interactions

» Know that deficits in affective development and expressive language may lead to inappropriate responses in social interaction

» Recognize that age-appropriate motor skill functioning facilitates inclusion in physical activities with peers; however, deficits in social skill development may hinder successful interactions

» Know that individuals with deafness and hearing impairments may demonstrate stereotypic behaviors that interfere with social interactions

» Know that individuals with deafness and hearing impairments with limited communication skills may become easily frustrated

» Recognize the physical educator's role in teaching and developing self-advocacy skills as well as providing opportunities to apply those skills

Understand health and medical issues

Understand that individuals with deafness and hearing impairments may have a range of health and medical concerns such as ear/nose/throat, respiratory, mental health, and/or cochlear implant issues that impact learning and motor performance 6.03.07.01

» Collaborate with a multidisciplinary team, particularly with the speech-language pathologist, audiologist, and/or interpreter to address health and medical issues

» Recognize safety and participation concerns associated with cochlear implants and hearing aids such as the impact of static electricity, blows to the head, and water exposure

» Collaborate with physical therapists when working with individuals with sensorineural hearing loss to address issues associated with balance and vestibular impairments

Understand unique communication considerations

Understand that individuals with deafness and hearing impairments demonstrate marked deficits in speech and language development 6.03.08.01

» Know that there are communication challenges in the learning environment

» Encourage the use of interpreters, cochlear implants, and hearing aids and take measures to ensure safe handling in physical activity settings

» Use alerting devices to ensure learner is aware of safety issues such as fire or tornado warnings

» Know that there may be significant deficits in speech production including issues with voice, articulation, and fluency that adversely affect communication

» Know that there may be significant deficits in receptive and/or expressive language that impact communication of thoughts or feelings in social interactions

» Collaborate with audiologists, speech-language pathologists, and interpreters to maximize effective communication

» Use the current versions of aided (e.g., picture communication symbols and line drawings) and unaided (e.g., manual signs and gestures) augmentative and alternative communication methods along with appropriate transmission devices (e.g., iPads and Dynavox devices)

» Recognize that physical attempts to gain attention and communicate may be demonstrated

» Know techniques to support communication (see Standard 9) such as sign language, finger spelling, whiteboards, iPads, and placing individuals in good visual positioning to enhance lip reading

» Talk to the individual not to their interpreter

» Recognize the physical educator's role in effectively receiving communication

» Know and respect the individual's/family's preferred method for communication, such as signing, oral, or **total communication**

EMOTIONAL DISTURBANCES: Understand the unique attributes of individuals with emotional disturbances

As defined by IDEA, emotional disturbance means:
a condition exhibiting one or more of the following characteristics over a long period of time and to a marked degree that adversely affects a child's educational performance:

a. An inability to learn that cannot be explained by intellectual, sensory, or health factors

b. An inability to build or maintain satisfactory interpersonal relationships with peers and teachers

c. Inappropriate types of behavior or feelings under normal circumstances

d. A general pervasive mood of unhappiness or depression

e. A tendency to develop physical symptoms or fears associated with personal or school problems

Emotional disturbance includes schizophrenia. The term does not apply to children who are socially maladjusted, unless it is determined that they have an emotional disturbance. 34 CFR §300.8

Understand the etiology of emotional disturbances and the impact on physical and motor attributes

Understand that the cause of emotional disturbances remains idiopathic though heredity, brain disorder, diet, stress, trauma, and family functioning may be contributing factors 6.04.01.01

» Know that males are four times more likely to be diagnosed with an emotional disturbance than females

» Know that males are more likely to exhibit externalizing behaviors while females are more likely to exhibit internalizing behaviors

» Know that most individuals with emotional disturbances are not identified before school age with a majority of individuals receiving special education services for emotional disturbance during the middle and high school years

Understand emotional and behavioral disorders described in the *Diagnostic and Statistical Manual V (DSM-V)* and how each impacts physical education programming

Know that individuals may present with one or more disorders such as anxiety disorders, bipolar disorder, conduct disorders, or obsessive-compulsive disorder, and psychotic disorders may be present 6.04.02.01

» Know that varying degrees of impairment from mild to severe may be demonstrated

» Know that a variety of attributes such as hyperactivity, aggressive or self-injurious behaviors, and withdrawal that impact learning and performance in physical education may be demonstrated

Understand unique psychomotor considerations

Understand that delays in psychomotor development may be due to the nature of the emotional disturbance rather than motor abilities and may increase with age as the physical education curriculum becomes more complex and socially demanding 6.04.03.01

» Know that there may be delays in motor skill acquisition due to continual removal from the learning environment and learning opportunities because of behavioral issues

» Know that individuals may develop age appropriate motor skills but the application of these skills in a contextualized game setting may be hindered due to the competitive or social nature of the game

» Design instruction to provide structure and routine, consistency, and explicit behavioral expectations

» Utilize appropriate instructional supports and strategies such as start and stop signals, appropriate groupings, instruction latency, cooperative activities, and a balance of success and failure in learning trials

>> Incorporate the use of team building initiatives to prepare individuals for group or more demanding social activities (e.g., competitive games)

>> Employ a humanistic approach to **behavior management** to improve personal social responsibility, **self-management**, and character development in physical activity environments

Understand unique fitness considerations

Understand that individuals with emotional disturbance may demonstrate deficits in physical fitness 6.04.04.01

>> Know that the prerequisite motor skills needed to participate in physical activity sufficiently to develop and/or maintain physical fitness may be lacking

>> Know that the capacity to develop physical fitness levels comparable to their peers without disabilities is often present

>> Utilize appropriate instructional supports and strategies such as motivating equipment, physical activity choice, and cooperative activities to elicit the appropriate frequency, intensity, and duration of physical activity necessary for maintaining or improving physical fitness

>> Employ a humanistic approach to behavior management to improve personal social responsibility, self-management, and character development in physical activity and fitness environments

>> Utilize appropriate behavior management techniques such as goal setting, **behavior contracts**, and token economies to elicit the appropriate intensity and duration of physical activity necessary for maintaining or improving physical fitness

Understand unique cognitive considerations

Understand that individuals with emotional disturbance may demonstrate academic delays that can adversely affect learning in physical education 6.04.05.01

>> Design instruction in short, concise, sequential segments to maximize learning

>> Design instructional materials and content delivery to be appropriate for the academic achievement level of the individual with emotional disturbance such as increasing readability of instructional materials and cognitive assessments (e.g., end of unit quizzes)

>> Know and implement principles of UDL in instruction and assessment

Understand unique affective and social skill considerations

Understand that individuals with emotional disturbance demonstrate inappropriate social and affective behaviors as a manifestation of the emotional disturbance 6.04.06.01

>> Know that there may be deficits in adhering to social norms and behavioral expectations

» Know that individuals may demonstrate inappropriate responses in social interactions such as laughing when someone is injured, being overly sad, or unusually upset

» Know that individuals with conduct disorders may lack empathy

» Know that intensive instructional support in learning appropriate social skills such as social stories and peer modeling may be required

» Facilitate self-management and independent participation by designing the task and environment to meet the needs of individuals with emotional disturbance in order to develop motor skills

» Recognize that individuals may lack the ability to generalize newly acquired motor skills in novel contexts without appropriate structure and behavioral supports

» Recognize that age-appropriate motor skill functioning facilitates inclusion in physical activities with peers; however, inappropriate behaviors may hinder successful interactions

» Know that individuals with communication disorders may act out in response to frustration

» Understand that behavior problems such as **impulsivity** and noncompliance may lead to safety problems in physical activity settings

» Recognize the physical educators' role in teaching and developing self-advocacy skills as well as providing opportunities to apply those skills

Understand health and medical issues

Understand that individuals with emotional disturbance may have a range of health and medical concerns such as medication issues, appetite and nutrition issues, and addictive and risk-taking behaviors that impact learning and motor performance 6.04.07.01

» Collaborate with a multidisciplinary team, particularly with the school counselor, educational psychologist, social worker, and other mental health professionals, to provide comprehensive interventions

» Recognize safety and participation concerns that may arise in physical activity settings due to the inability to self-regulate behaviors

» Consult with school medical personnel on the side effects and contraindications of specific medications being used to manage behaviors

Understand unique communication considerations

Understand that individuals with emotional disturbance may have communication disorders that impact learning 6.04.08.01

» Know that receptive and/or expressive language disorders that create communication challenges in the learning environment may be present

» Know that difficulties with social reciprocity may be demonstrated when trying to communicate their needs, ideas, or feelings

HEARING IMPAIRMENTS: Understand unique attributes of individuals who have hearing impairments

As defined by IDEA, hearing impairment means "an impairment in hearing, whether permanent or fluctuating, that adversely affects a child's educational performance but that is not included under the definition of deafness in this section." 34 CFR §300.8

See relevant information under "Deafness and Hearing Impairments"

INTELLECTUAL DISABILITY: Understand unique attributes of individuals with intellectual disabilities

As defined by IDEA, intellectual disability means "significantly subaverage general intellectual functioning, existing concurrently with deficits in **adaptive behavior** and manifested during the developmental period, that adversely affects a child's educational performance." 34 CFR §300.8

Understand the etiology of intellectual disability and its impact on physical and motor attributes

Understand that intellectual disability is caused by idiopathic, chromosomal, metabolic, disease, toxic, trauma, and/or environmental conditions that lead to some level of impairment that adversely affects motor performance 6.06.01.01

» Know that intellectual disabilities may be congenital (e.g., chromosomal abnormalities) or acquired (e.g., toxic exposure to drugs and/or trauma)

» Know that individuals with intellectual disability may present with concomitant disabilities such as Down syndrome, cerebral palsy, hearing impairments, or blindness

» Early identification of needs and implementation of an intervention is essential to the development of **functional skills** including motor skills

Understand that intellectual disability includes limitations in intellectual functioning and adaptive functioning and that the severity of those limitations impact physical education programming (i.e., planning, assessment, implementation, teaching, and evaluation)

Understand that intellectual disabilities can range from mild to profound and result in varying degrees of impairment that differentially impact learning 6.06.02.01

» Know that programming will need to be designed to address the severity of the intellectual disability (i.e., mild, moderate, severe, or profound)

» Know that programming for individuals with more severe forms of intellectual disability will require extensive or pervasive educational supports

» Develop programming that establishes functional, meaningful, and generalizable goals

Understand unique psychomotor considerations

Understand that individuals with intellectual disability may demonstrate delays in psychomotor development that impact motor performance 6.06.03.01

» Identify the challenges in evaluating motor performance needed to determine present level of performance

» Know that there may be significant delays in motor development and/or significant challenges in motor planning

» Design instruction to involve multiple sensory modalities such as providing extensive visual, auditory, tactile, and kinesthetic prompts to elicit the practice necessary for motor learning to occur

» Know that there may be varying capacities to develop functional motor skills

» Know that it is beneficial to utilize task analysis and prioritization of learning focal points of motor skills

» Adapt activities to incorporate individuals who use various assistive devices such as wheelchairs or walkers

» Train paraeducators to be actively involved in the instructional process

Understand unique fitness considerations

Understand that individuals with intellectual disability may demonstrate deficits in physical fitness 6.06.04.01

» Identify the challenges in evaluating physical fitness needed to determine present level of performance

» Know that there may be a lack of the prerequisite motor skills needed to participate in physical activity sufficiently enough to develop and/or maintain physical fitness

» Know that there may be varying capacities to develop physical fitness levels

» Know that there may be a lack of intrinsic motivation to maintain appropriate intensity and duration of physical activity needed for physical fitness

» Know that the propensity for sedentary behaviors may contribute to obesity

» Design instruction to involve multiple sensory modalities such as providing extensive visual, auditory, tactile, and kinesthetic prompts to elicit the appropriate frequency, intensity, and duration of physical activity necessary for maintaining or improving physical fitness

» Adapt activities to incorporate individuals who use various assistive devices such as wheelchairs or walkers

» Train paraeducators to be actively involved in the instructional process

» Utilize appropriate instructional supports and strategies such as motivating equipment, physical activity choice, and prompting to elicit the appropriate frequency, intensity, and duration of physical activity necessary for maintaining or improving physical fitness

Understand unique cognitive considerations

Understand that individuals with intellectual disability demonstrate academic delays that adversely affect learning in physical education 6.06.05.01

» Know that deficits in cognitive functioning impact the understanding of instruction and the subsequent motor performance

» Know and implement principles of UDL in instruction and assessment

» Design instruction in short, concise, sequential segments employing all appropriate sensory modalities to maximize learning

» Know that additional time and prompts may be required in order to process input and effectively motor plan

» Design instruction for both developmental and age-appropriateness

Understand unique affective and social skill considerations

Understand that individuals with intellectual disability may demonstrate deficits in affective and social skill development 6.06.06.01

» Know that significant deficits in affective development and language will limit social interaction

» Know that intensive instructional support in learning appropriate social skills such as social stories and peer modeling may be required

» Know that social contexts (e.g., body language or tone of voice) may be misinterpreted

» Know that limited communication skills may cause individuals to become easily frustrated and/or feel socially isolated

» Collaborate with psychologist, behavior specialist, and/or other members of the functional behavioral assessment (FBA) team to improve social behavior

» Recognize the physical educator's role in teaching and developing self-advocacy skills as well as providing opportunities to apply those skills

Understand health and medical issues

Understand that individuals with intellectual disability may have a range of health and medical concerns such as heart conditions, respiratory issues, orthopedic impairments, gastrointestinal issues, mental health, and/or nutrition issues that impact learning and motor performance 6.06.07.01

» Collaborate with a multidisciplinary team to address health and medical issues

» Recognize the implications of susceptibility to respiratory infections in individuals with intellectual disability such those with Williams syndrome

» Recognize safety and participation concerns associated with individuals with intellectual disability such as individuals with tracheotomies and seizures

» Recognize safety and participation concerns associated with medications such as seizure medications, depressants, and stimulants

» Follow a pre-established universal precautions routine for handling body secretions in physical activity settings

Understand unique communication considerations

Understand that individuals with intellectual disability may demonstrate marked deficits in communication skills 6.06.08.01

» Understand communication challenges in the learning environment

» Utilize assistive technologies and communication devices to enhance participation in physical activity, and take measures to ensure safe handling of devices in physical activity settings

» Collaborate with other professionals such as speech-language pathologists, special educators, and paraeducators to maximize effective communication

» Recognize that in order to effectively communicate, physical educators may need to learn sign language and understand individual gestures or altered expressive language

Understand the considerations unique to individuals with specific conditions associated with intellectual disability

Understand the considerations unique to individuals with Angelman syndrome 6.06.09.01

» Know that individuals with Angelman syndrome may present with concomitant conditions such as epilepsy, sleep, gastrointestinal, and/or mental health disorders

» Know that individuals with Angelman syndrome may present with sensory issues (i.e., hyper- or hyposensitivity to environmental stimuli)

» Recognize the impact of communication issues and possible impulsive behaviors in the physical activity setting

Understand the considerations unique to individuals with Down syndrome 6.06.09.02

» Know the health and medical implications of atlantoaxial instability among individuals with Down syndrome

» Review medical records for results of cervical X-rays before starting programming

» Know the implications of hypotonicity and hyperflexibility

» Know the implications of medical conditions that are more common such as congenital heart defects, respiratory issues, hearing problems, childhood leukemia, and thyroid conditions

» Know the implications of unique physical features (e.g., small stature including small oral cavity and small hands and feet) in the physical activity environment

Understand the considerations unique to individuals with alcohol and drug-related birth defects 6.06.09.03

» Know the implications of **developmental delays** and abnormal movement patterns such as tremors and muscle spasms

» Know the implications of deficits in alertness and memory on the learning process

» Know the implications of congenital heart defects, kidney issues, or bone issues

MULTIPLE DISABILITIES: Understand unique attributes of individuals with multiple disabilities

As defined by IDEA, multiple disabilities means "concomitant impairments (such as [intellectual disability]-blindness or [intellectual disability]-orthopedic impairment), the combination of which causes such severe educational needs that they cannot be accommodated in special education programs solely for one of the impairments. Multiple disabilities does not include deaf-blindness." 34 CFR §300.8

Understand the etiology of multiple disabilities and their impact on physical and motor attributes

Understand that multiple disabilities are caused by heredity, genetics, trauma, and/or medical conditions that lead to some level of impairment across multiple areas of functioning that adversely affect motor performance 6.07.01.01

» Know that causes of multiple disabilities may include chromosomal abnormalities, premature birth, complications after birth, poor development of the brain or spinal cord, infections, genetic disorders, and injuries from accidents

» Early detection and intervention is essential to development and the learning process

Understand the types of multiple disabilities and how each impacts physical education programming (i.e., planning, assessment, implementation, teaching and evaluation)

Know that individuals with multiple disabilities can acquire multiple types of concomitant disabilities at different times and exhibit varying degrees of impairment that differentially impact learning 6.07.02.01

» Know that programming will need to be adjusted depending on how many disabilities are involved

» Know that programming will need to be adjusted depending on which disabilities are involved

» Know that programming will need to be designed to address the impact of the severity of the combined conditions

» Know that individuals with multiple disabilities often present with severe or profound disabilities and frequently require assistive technologies to access the physical education curriculum

Understand unique psychomotor considerations

Understand that individuals with multiple disabilities may demonstrate delays in psychomotor development that impact motor performance 6.07.03.01

» Identify the challenges in evaluating motor performance needed to determine present level of performance

» Know that individuals will present with significant delays in motor development

» Design instruction to involve multiple sensory modalities such as providing extensive visual, auditory, tactile, and kinesthetic prompts to elicit the practice necessary for motor learning to occur

» Know that most individuals have varying capacities to develop functional motor skills

» Adapt activities to incorporate individuals who use various assistive devices such as wheelchairs or walkers

» Train paraeducators to be actively involved in the instructional process

Understand unique fitness considerations

Understand that individuals with multiple disabilities may demonstrate deficits in physical fitness 6.07.04.01

» Identify the challenges in evaluating physical fitness needed to determine present level of performance

» Know that individuals may be lacking the prerequisite motor skills needed to participate in physical activity sufficiently to develop and/or maintain physical fitness

» Know that there are varying capacities to develop physical fitness levels

» Design instruction to involve multiple sensory modalities such as providing extensive visual, auditory, tactile, and kinesthetic prompts to elicit the appropriate frequency, intensity, and duration of physical activity necessary for maintaining or improving physical fitness

» Adapt activities to incorporate individuals who use various assistive and mobility devices to include wheelchairs, walkers, or parapodiums

» Train paraeducators to be actively involved in the instructional process

» Utilize appropriate instructional supports and strategies such as motivating equipment, physical activity choice, and cooperative activities to elicit the appropriate frequency, intensity, and duration of physical activity necessary for maintaining or improving physical fitness

Understand unique cognitive considerations

Understand that individuals with multiple disabilities demonstrate academic delays that adversely affect learning in physical education 6.07.05.01

» Know that deficits in cognitive functioning impact the understanding of instruction and the subsequent motor performance

» Design instruction in short, concise, and sequential segments employing all appropriate sensory modalities to maximize learning

» Know and implement principles of UDL in instruction and assessment

» Use multiple methods of presenting instructional information (see Standard 9) such as visual demonstrations, verbal cues, engaging equipment options, and kinesthetic prompts to support instruction

Understand unique affective and social skill considerations

Understand that individuals with multiple disabilities demonstrate deficits in affective and social skill development 6.07.06.01

» Know that significant deficits in affective development and language will limit social interaction

» Know that stereotypic behaviors that interfere with social interactions may be present

» Know that intensive instructional supports in learning appropriate social skills such as social stories and peer modeling may be required

» Know that those with limited communication skills may become easily frustrated and/or feel socially isolated

» Recognize the physical educator's role in teaching and developing self-advocacy skills as well as providing opportunities to apply those skills

Understand health and medical issues

Understand that individuals with multiple disabilities may have a range of health and medical concerns such as medication, heart conditions, respiratory issues, orthopedic impairments, gastrointestinal issues, mental health, and/or nutrition issues that impact learning and motor performance 6.07.07.01

» Collaborate with the multidisciplinary team to address health and medical issues

» Recognize safety and participation concerns such as tracheotomies, oxygen tanks, colostomies, **shunts** (i.e., with **hydrocephalus**), and catheters

» Recognize safety and participation concerns associated with medications such as seizure medications, depressants, and stimulants

» Collaborate with occupational therapists when working with individuals with multiple sensory impairments

» Collaborate with physical therapists when working with individuals with orthopedic impairments and/or balance issues

Understand unique communication considerations

Understand that individuals with multiple disabilities may demonstrate marked deficits in communication skills 6.07.08.01

» Understand communication challenges in the learning environment

» Utilize assistive technologies and devices to enhance participation in physical activity, and take measures to ensure safe handling of devices in physical activity settings

» Collaborate with other professionals such as audiologists, speech-language pathologists, special educators, paraeducators, and interpreters to maximize effective communication

» Recognize the physical educator's role in effectively communicating such as learning sign language and understanding an individual's gestures or altered expressive language

» Follow a pre-established universal precautions routine for handling body secretions in physical activity settings

ORTHOPEDIC IMPAIRMENT: Understand unique attributes of individuals with orthopedic impairment

As defined by IDEA, orthopedic impairment means "a severe orthopedic impairment that adversely affects a child's educational performance. The term includes impairments caused by a congenital anomaly, impairments caused by disease (e.g., poliomyelitis, bone tuberculosis), and impairments from other causes (e.g., cerebral palsy, amputations, and fractures or burns that cause contractures)." 34 CFR §300.8

Understand the etiology of orthopedic impairments and their impact on physical and motor attributes

Understand that orthopedic impairments are caused by heredity, genetic, trauma, and/or medical conditions that adversely affect motor performance 6.08.01.01

» Know that causes of orthopedic impairments may include birth defects, poor development of the brain or spinal cord, disease, genetic disorders, and injuries from accidents

» Identification of needs and implementation of intervention is essential to development of functional skills including motor skills

Understand the types or classifications of orthopedic impairments and how each impacts physical education programming

Know that orthopedic impairments can be congenital or acquired and result in varying degrees of impairment that differentially impact learning and mobility 6.08.02.01

» Know that programming will need to be adjusted depending on the severity (e.g., mild to severe) and degree (e.g., number of limbs involved) of orthopedic impairment

» Know that programming will need to be adjusted depending on whether the condition is progressive or stable

Understand unique psychomotor considerations

Understand that individuals with orthopedic impairment demonstrate delays in psychomotor development that impact motor performance 6.08.03.01

» Identify the challenges in evaluating motor performance needed to determine present level of performance

» Know that there will be significant delays in motor development

» Design instruction to involve multiple sensory modalities such as providing extensive visual, auditory, tactile, and kinesthetic prompts to elicit the practice necessary for motor learning to occur

» Know that there will be varying capacities to develop functional motor skills

» Know that prosthetics, assistive devices, orthopedic devices, such as wheelchairs, canes or walkers, may be used to enhance mobility

» Design motor skill activities to incorporate the use of various assistive devices (e.g., wrist splints and adapted grips) and mobility devices (e.g., wheelchairs and walkers)

» Know that joint and muscular injuries to the upper extremities are common overuse injuries

» Train paraeducators to be actively involved in the instructional process

Understand unique fitness considerations

Understand that individuals with orthopedic impairments may demonstrate deficits in physical fitness 6.08.04.01

» Identify the challenges in evaluating physical fitness needed to determine present level of performance

» Know that there may be a lack of prerequisite motor skills needed to participate in physical activity sufficiently to develop and/or maintain physical fitness

» Know that there will be varying capacities to develop physical fitness levels

» Provide accessible physical activity settings and adapted equipment (e.g., hand cycles and arm ergometers) needed to elicit the appropriate frequency, intensity and duration of physical activity necessary for maintaining or improving physical fitness

» Design fitness activities to incorporate the use of various assistive devices (e.g., wrist splints and adapted grips) and mobility devices (e.g., wheelchairs and walkers)

» Design fitness programs to prevent overuse injuries including joint and muscular injuries to the upper extremities

» Train paraeducators to be actively involved in the instructional process

» Utilize appropriate instructional supports and strategies such as physical activity choice, adaptive equipment, and prompting to elicit the appropriate frequency, intensity, and duration of physical activity necessary for maintaining or improving physical fitness

Understand unique cognitive considerations

Understand that individuals with orthopedic impairments may demonstrate academic delays that adversely affect learning in physical education 6.08.05.01

» Know that deficits in academic functioning are often the result of repeated periods of limited access to learning opportunities and environments (e.g., recovery periods from surgeries, broken bones, dependence on others for access to learning opportunities, etc.), which may impact the understanding of instruction and the subsequent motor performance

» Apply principles of UDL to assessment and instruction to maximize learning (see Standards 8, 9, and 10)

Understand unique affective and social skill considerations

Understand that individuals with orthopedic impairments may demonstrate deficits in affective and social skill development 6.08.06.01

» Know that repeated periods of limited access to social opportunities (e.g., recovery periods from surgeries, dependence on others for access to social opportunities, etc.) may impact their affective and social skill development

» Know that they may feel socially isolated in physical activity settings for reasons such as differences in mobility and/or appearance and limited opportunities to engage in social interactions

» Know that instructional support in learning appropriate social skills such as peer modeling may be required

» Recognize that it is the physical educator's role to teach and develop self-advocacy skills and provide opportunities for them to apply those skills

Understand health and medical issues

Understand that individuals with orthopedic impairments may have a range of health and medical concerns such as contractures, medication, skin conditions, and musculoskeletal, circulatory, respiratory, gastrointestinal, mental health, and/or nutrition issues that impact learning and motor performance 6.08.07.01

» Collaborate with members of the medical and multidisciplinary team to address health and medical issues

» Recognize safety and participation concerns regarding colostomies, shunts (i.e., with hydrocephalus), and catheters

» Recognize safety and participation concerns associated with sensory impairments including individuals with spinal cord injuries or spina bifida who require special attention to skin care and protection during transfers and participation

» Recognize safety and participation concerns associated with commonly taken medications such as anti-depressants, bowel or bladder control medications, and pain medications

» Collaborate with key related service personnel (e.g., physical and occupational therapists) to enhance functional performance in physical activity settings

» Collaborate with a school nurse and other school personnel to follow schedules for essential care including feeding, voiding, medications, etc.

Understand unique communication considerations

Understand that individuals with orthopedic impairments may demonstrate deficits in communication skills 6.08.08.01

» Know that repeated periods of limited access to communication opportunities (e.g., recovery periods from surgeries, dependence on others to carry or lift them in order to access opportunities for social and communication engagement, etc.) may impact their development of communication skills

» Recognize communication challenges in the learning environment such as those with cerebral palsy

» Utilize assistive technologies and devices to enhance participation in physical activity, and take measures to ensure safe handling of devices in physical activity settings

» Collaborate with other professionals such as speech-language pathologists, special educators, and paraeducators to maximize effective communication

» Recognize the physical educator's role in effectively receiving communication such as waiting for verbal responses from an individual with cerebral palsy and/or understanding the individual's gestures or altered expressive language of an individual who had a stroke

Understand the considerations unique to individuals with specific conditions associated with orthopedic impairments

Understand considerations unique to individuals with amputations 6.08.09.01

» Know the implications of decreased perspiration due to reduced cooling surfaces

» Know stump care considerations such as closely monitoring of the stump before and after physical activity and encouraging individuals to care for their stump

» Know the implications of skin irritations and skin breakdown on the stump

Understand considerations unique to individuals with cerebral palsy 6.08.09.02

» Know the types of cerebral palsy and how they impact movement including oral motor functioning

» Know the implications of variation in muscle tone on motor performance

» Know the implications of common procedures used to treat cerebral palsy, such as Achilles tendon release, Botox injections, and baclofen pump implants, on motor performance and participation

» Know the impact of limited range of motion on functional movement

» Collaborate with physical therapists and physicians on addressing issues such as avoiding contractures, positioning, controlling muscle imbalances, developing strength training programs, and maximizing the development of functional skills

» Know the implications of primitive reflexes, postural reflexes and perceptual motor deficits on motor performance

» Know the implications of secondary disabilities such as intellectual disabilities

Understand considerations unique to individuals with dwarfism 6.08.09.03

» Know that dwarfism is most commonly caused by a genetic disorder

» Know dwarfism can also be attributed to other causes including malnutrition, endocrine disturbances, kidney disease, or chronic diseases

» Know the multiple types of dwarfism

» Know that they may have proportionate or disproportionate short stature

» Know the implications of spinal anomalies such as atlantoaxial instability (C1-C2 instability) and scoliosis

» Know the implications of upper and lower body limitations such as bowed legs, frequent hip and knee dislocations, decreased limb length, and limited range of motion

» Know the implications of small chest size and narrow nasal passages

Understand considerations unique to individuals with Duchennes muscular dystrophy 6.08.09.04

» Know that Duchennes muscular dystrophy is a genetic disorder that primarily affects males, with symptoms often appearing between three and five years of age

» Know the implications of Duchennes muscular dystrophy on motor performance

» Know the disease progression, including presentation of Gower's sign, and the implications for participation in physical activity

» Consider factors related to muscle fatigue, such as time of day, when scheduling physical education

» Know the implications of muscle atrophy, muscle imbalance, and potential dislocations on performance of specific physical and motor skills

» Know the value of maintaining function including independent mobility and muscular strength and endurance

» Know the implications of respiratory fatigue on performing motor skills and physical fitness activities

» Know the emotional effect of a progressive disability on the individual and his or her family

» Know how to plan for and promote individual enjoyment within physical education activities

Understand considerations unique to individuals with osteogenesis imperfecta 6.08.09.05

» Know the types of osteogenesis imperfecta and implications of bone fragility

» Know the implications of spinal anomalies and chest deformities such as funnel chest

» Obtain medical clearance to determine contraindicated activities

» Know the impact of repeated hospitalizations or homebound periods particularly during adolescence

Understand considerations unique to individuals with posture disorders 6.08.09.06

» Understand various types of posture disorders such as scoliosis, lordosis, and kyphosis

» Know the role of braces, orthotics, and surgeries in treatment and the implications for participation in physical activity

Understand considerations unique to individuals with spina bifida 6.08.09.07

» Know the types of spina bifida and the implications for motor performance

» Know the implications of mobility impairment and limitations

» Know the implications of common overuse injuries such as wrist and shoulder injuries

» Know the implications of hydrocephalus including the use of shunts

» Know the implications of a latex allergy

» Know the potential for learning disabilities or intellectual disabilities secondary to spina bifida

Understand considerations unique to individuals with spinal cord injury 6.08.09.08

» Know the types of and classification systems for spinal cord injuries

» Know the level of spinal cord injury and the implications for functioning and sensation

» Know the signs, causes, and treatment of autonomic dysreflexia for individuals with injuries at or above T6

» Know the role of pads, braces, straps, and orthotics and the implications for participation in physical activity

» Know the implications of skin irritations and skin breakdown

» Know the implications of common overuse injuries such as finger, wrist, and shoulder injuries

---

OTHER HEALTH IMPAIRMENT: Understand unique attributes of individuals with other health impairment

---

As defined by IDEA, other health impairment means:
having limited strength, vitality, or alertness, including a heightened alertness to environmental stimuli, that results in limited alertness with respect to the educational environment, that—

i. Is due to chronic or acute health problems such as asthma, attention deficit disorder or attention deficit hyperactivity disorder, diabetes, epilepsy, a heart condition, hemophilia, lead poisoning, leukemia, nephritis, rheumatic fever, sickle cell anemia, and Tourette syndrome; and

ii. Adversely affects a child's educational performance. 34 CFR §300.8

Understand the etiology of other health impairments and their impact on physical and motor attributes

Understand that other health impairments may be caused by idiopathic, disease, environmental, heredity, genetic, trauma, and/or medical conditions 6.09.01.01

» Know that other health impairments may be congenital or acquired

» Know that the age of the individual at onset of the other health impairment may impact motor performance

» Know that other health impairments may be secondary to primary disabilities like autism spectrum disorder or intellectual disability

Understand the types or classifications of other health impairments and how each impacts physical education programming

Know that other health impairments are comprised of an array of disabling conditions that can result in varying degrees of impairment that differentially impact learning and performance 6.09.02.01

» Know that other health impairments include asthma, attention deficit disorder or attention deficit hyperactivity disorder, diabetes, epilepsy, a heart condition, hemophilia, lead poisoning, leukemia, nephritis, rheumatic fever, sickle cell anemia, and Tourette syndrome

» Know that other health impairments may be chronic or acute

» Know that programming will need to be adjusted depending on the severity (e.g., mild to severe) and status (e.g., progressive or stable) of the other health impairment

Understand unique psychomotor considerations

Understand that individuals with other health impairment demonstrate delays in psychomotor development that impact motor performance 6.09.03.01

» Identify the challenges in evaluating motor performance needed to determine present level of performance

» Know that they may range from mild (e.g., asthma) to severe (e.g., heart conditions) delays in motor development

» Know how to design instruction to address deficits in strength, vitality, and alertness such as providing extensive visual, auditory, and kinesthetic prompts to elicit the practice necessary for motor learning to occur

» Know that most individuals with other health impairments have varying capacities to develop functional motor skills

» Know how to train paraeducators to be actively involved in the instructional process

Understand unique fitness considerations

Understand that individuals with other health impairments may demonstrate deficits in physical fitness 6.09.04.01

» Identify the challenges in evaluating physical fitness needed to determine present level of performance

» Know that they may lack the prerequisite motor skills needed to participate in physical activity sufficiently to develop and/or maintain physical fitness

» Know that they have varying capacities to develop physical fitness levels

» Provide accessible physical activity settings and adapted equipment needed to elicit the appropriate frequency, intensity, and duration of physical activity necessary for maintaining or improving physical fitness

» Know how to incorporate the use of various assistive devices into fitness activities to maximize participation

» Utilize appropriate instructional supports and strategies such as physical activity choice, motivating equipment choices, and cooperative activities to elicit the appropriate frequency, intensity, and duration of physical activity necessary for maintaining or improving physical fitness

Understand unique cognitive considerations

Understand that individuals with other health impairments may demonstrate academic delays that adversely affect learning in physical education 6.09.05.01

» Know that deficits in academic functioning are often the result of repeated periods of limited access to learning opportunities and environments (e.g., recovery periods from acute attacks, recurrence of illness, dependence on others for access to learning opportunities, etc.), which may impact the understanding of instruction and the subsequent motor performance

» Apply principles of UDL to assessment and instruction to maximize learning (see Standards 8, 9, and 10)

Understand unique affective and social skill considerations

Understand that individuals with other health impairments may demonstrate deficits in affective and social skill development 6.09.06.01

» Know that repeated periods of limited access to social opportunities (e.g., recovery periods from surgeries and illness, dependence on others for access to social opportunities, etc.) may impact their affective and social skill development

» Know that they may feel socially isolated in physical activity settings for reasons such as differences in appearance and/or ability, and limited opportunities to engage in social interactions

» Know how to provide emotional support. Know that instructional support in learning appropriate social skills such as peer modeling may be required

» Recognize the physical educator's role in teaching and developing self-advocacy skills for individuals with other health impairments, and providing opportunities to apply those skills

Understand health and medical issues

Understand that individuals with other health impairments may have a range of health and medical concerns such as medication, and musculoskeletal, circulatory, respiratory, mental health, and/or nutrition issues that impact learning and motor performance 6.09.07.01

» Collaborate with members of the medical and multidisciplinary team to address health and medical issues

» Know the treatment and emergency action plan prescribed for the individual

» Recognize safety and participation concerns such as individuals with tracheotomies, colostomies, or catheters, or on oxygen

» Recognize safety and participation concerns associated with respiratory conditions including individuals with asthma or cystic fibrosis who require special attention to respiratory functioning during participation

» Recognize safety and participation concerns associated with commonly taken medications such as anti-depressants, stimulants, anticonvulsants, vasodilators, and pain medications

» Collaborate with key related service personnel (e.g., physical and occupational therapists) to enhance functional performance in physical activity settings

» Collaborate with a school nurse and other school personnel to follow schedules for essential care including feeding, breathing treatments, medications, etc.

Understand unique communication considerations

Understand that individuals with other health impairments may demonstrate deficits in communication skills 6.09.08.01

>> Know that repeated periods of limited access to communication opportunities (e.g., recovery periods from surgeries, acute attacks or illness recurrences) may impact their development of communication skills

>> Utilize assistive technologies and devices to enhance participation in physical activity, and take measures to ensure safe handling of devices in physical activity settings

>> Collaborate with other professionals such as speech-language pathologists, special educators, and paraeducators to maximize effective communication

Understand the considerations unique to individuals with specific conditions associated with other health impairments

Understand considerations unique to individuals with asthma 6.09.09.01

>> Know the implications of allergenic and non-allergenic asthma

>> Know the signs, precautionary measures, and treatment of asthma

>> Know how the individual's medical history impacts provision of physical activity outdoors or in aquatic environments

Understand considerations unique to individuals with attention-deficit/hyperactivity disorder (ADHD) 6.09.09.02

>> Know the difference between the types of attention-deficit/hyperactivity disorder

>> Know the implications of ADHD medications on motor performance and wellness

>> Know that there is a high comorbidity of ADHD with learning disabilities

>> Know that males are two to three more likely than females to be diagnosed with ADHD

Understand considerations unique to individuals with blood-related disorders 6.09.09.03

>> Know the blood-related disorders common in childhood and adolescence such as anemia, sickle cell anemia, and hemophilia

>> Know the implications of limited oxygen supply available to cells

>> Know the impact of increased heart rate and breathing rate on motor performance and participation in physical activities

>> Know the common signs and implications of heat intolerance

>> Know the common signs and implications of elevated blood pressure

>> Know common internal bleeding conditions associated with blood-related disorders such hemarthrosis and hematomas

>> Identify the early signs of internal bleeding such as swelling and heat in a joint

» In all situations, follow universal precautions for external bleeding

» Know the pre-established emergency procedures

Understand considerations unique to individuals with cardiac conditions 6.09.09.04

» Know the types and severity of cardiac conditions common in childhood and adolescence such as Marfans syndrome, heart arrhythmias, congenital heart disorders, and hypertrophic cardiomyopathy

» Know the signs and implications of cardiac conditions

» Collaborate with school and medical personnel to establish a protocol for selecting appropriate physical activities

» Recognize the potential for an emergency situation to occur in physical activity settings including the need to have an Automated External Defibrillator (AED) readily available

Understand considerations unique to individuals with childhood cancer 6.09.09.05

» Know the type and severity of childhood cancers including leukemia, brain or central nervous system tumors, neuroblastomas, lymphomas, bone cancers, and retinoblastomas

» Know the individual's present level of strength, vitality, and alertness during and immediately after active treatment

» Know the implications of chemotherapy, radiation therapy, and surgical treatments on learning, motor performance, and participation in physical activities

» Know the psychological and psychosocial needs of individuals adjusting to their physical appearance following surgical treatments

» Know the psychological and psychosocial needs of individuals adjusting to terminal diagnoses

Understand considerations unique to individuals with **developmental coordination disorder** (DCD) 6.09.09.06

» Know the types and severity of DCD including motor planning disorders, perceptual motor disorders, and dyspraxia

» Know the prevalence and comorbidity of DCD in school-aged children

» Know that males are two to five times more likely to be diagnosed with DCD than females

» Know the value of providing numerous opportunities to explore movement potential, use a variety of movement experiences, and use a gradual balance progression from static to dynamic

Understand considerations unique to individuals with diabetes 6.09.09.07

» Know the types, severity, and age of onset for diabetes

» Know the implications of varying blood sugar and insulin levels on motor performance and participation in physical activity

» Know the importance of testing blood sugar levels prior to participation in physical activity

» Know the implications of uncontrolled management of blood sugar and insulin level leading to secondary health complications later in life

» Know the signs and treatment of hypoglycemia and hyperglycemia

» Know the implications of skin care for diabetics

Understand considerations unique to individuals with human immuno-deficiency virus (HIV) 6.09.09.08

» Know the causes for HIV in childhood and adolescence

» Know the implications of fatigue on motor performance and participation in physical activity

» Know the susceptibility to infections and avoid close contact with an individual who has a cold or communicable disease

» Know how HIV is transmitted and use universal precautions

» Know to address the psychological needs including coping with prejudice and stigmatization

Understand considerations unique to individuals with Juvenile Rheumatoid Arthritis (JRA) (also known as Juvenile Idiopathic Arthritis) 6.09.09.09

» Know that JRA is an idiopathic autoimmune disease

» Know the types of JRA such as polyarticular, systemic, and pauciarticular JRA

» Know the implications of limited range of motion (ROM) or joint instability resulting from JRA

» Know the implications of chronic pain associated with JRA and the need to provide emotional support the individual who is afraid to perform physical activities

» Know the implications of changing symptoms such as stiffness on physical activity participation

Understand considerations unique to individuals with seizure disorders 6.09.09.10

» Know that a seizure refers to a single surge of electrical activity in the brain whereas a seizure disorder is a condition in which an individual has multiple seizures over time

» Know the types and classification systems for seizures such as absence seizures (formerly known as petit mal), tonic-clonic or convulsive seizures (formerly known as grand mal), atonic seizures (also known as drop attacks), clonic seizures, tonic seizures, and myoclonic seizures

» Know the signs of and professional responses (e.g., protecting the head, timing length of seizure, describing the severity) to various types of seizures

» Know the triggers for seizures such as stress, fatigue, and bright lights, and take precautionary measures to avoid seizures

» Know the implications of identified high-risk and contraindicated activities

» Know the importance of referring individuals to appropriate school personnel for medical care when under dosing, overdosing, or a missed dose of medication is suspected

SPECIFIC LEARNING DISABILITIES: Understand the unique attributes of individuals with specific learning disabilities

As defined by IDEA, a specific learning disability means "a disorder in one or more of the basic psychological processes involved in understanding or in using language, spoken or written, that may manifest itself in the imperfect ability to listen, think, speak, read, write, spell, or to do mathematical calculations, including conditions such as perceptual disabilities, brain injury, minimal brain dysfunction, dyslexia, and developmental aphasia." 34 CFR §300.8

Understand the etiology of specific learning disabilities and the impact on physical and motor attributes

Understand that specific learning disabilities may be caused by hereditary, teratogenic factors, medical factors, and/or environmental factors 6.10.01.01

» Know that specific learning disabilities may be congenital or acquired

» Know that males are four times more likely than females to be diagnosed

» Know that they account for over 47 percent of the school-aged population of individuals receiving special education services

Understand the types or classifications of specific learning disabilities and how each impacts physical education programming

Know that specific learning disabilities can result in varying degrees of impairment that differentially impact learning and performance 6.10.02.01

» Know that specific learning disabilities include conditions such as perceptual disabilities, brain injury, minimal brain dysfunction, dyslexia, and developmental aphasia

» Know that programming will need to be adjusted depending on the type of condition and the severity (e.g., mild to severe) of the condition

Understand unique psychomotor considerations

Understand that individuals with specific learning disabilities may demonstrate delays in psychomotor development that impact motor performance 6.10.03.01

>> Identify the challenges in evaluating motor performance needed to determine present level of performance

>> Know the sensory modulation continuum (hyper to hypo-responsivity) and the implications on learning

>> Know how to design instruction to address deficits in inner, expressive, or receptive language by providing instruction in the sensory modality that is most likely to elicit the practice necessary for motor learning to occur

>> Know that they have varying capacities to develop functional motor skills

Understand unique fitness considerations

Understand that individuals with specific learning disabilities may demonstrate deficits in physical fitness 6.10.04.01

>> Identify the challenges in evaluating physical fitness needed to determine present level of performance

>> Know that they may lack the prerequisite motor skills needed to participate in physical activity sufficiently to develop and/or maintain physical fitness, though for some individuals, physical fitness development is a strength

>> Know how to provide appropriate and motivating activities needed to elicit the frequency, intensity, and duration of physical activity necessary for maintaining or improving physical fitness

>> Utilize appropriate instructional supports and strategies such as motivating equipment, physical activity choice, and cooperative activities to elicit the appropriate frequency, intensity, and duration of physical activity necessary for maintaining or improving physical fitness

Understand unique cognitive considerations

Understand that individuals with specific learning disabilities demonstrate academic delays that may adversely affect learning in physical education 6.10.05.01

>> Know that deficits in academic functioning may impact the understanding of instruction and the subsequent motor performance

>> Know the impact of limited attention span in the learning environment

>> Apply principles of UDL to assessment and instruction to maximize learning (see Standards 8, 9, and 10)

Understand unique affective and social skill considerations

Understand that individuals with specific learning disabilities may demonstrate deficits in affective and social skill development 6.10.06.01

>> Know that deficits in processing language may frequently impact their affective and social skill development

>> Know that they may demonstrate inappropriate social behaviors in physical activity settings for reasons such as perceived differences in ability, experiences with bullying, limited positive social experiences, and issues with social imperception, **perseveration**, and impulsivity

» Know how to provide emotional support

» Know how to provide instructional support in learning appropriate social skills such as peer modeling

» Recognize the physical educator's role in teaching and developing self-advocacy skills, and providing opportunities to apply those skills

Understand unique communication considerations

Understand that individuals with specific learning disabilities may demonstrate deficits in communication skills 6.10.07.01

» Know that deficits in processing language may impact their development of communication skills

» Collaborate with other professionals such as special educators, school counselors, and paraeducators to practice effective communication in physical activity settings

SPEECH AND LANGUAGE DISORDERS: Understand unique attributes of individuals with speech and language disorders

As defined by IDEA, speech or language impairment means "a communication disorder, such as stuttering, impaired articulation, a language impairment, or a voice impairment, that adversely affects a child's educational performance." 34 CFR §300.8

Understand the etiology of speech and language disorders and the impact on physical and motor attributes

Understand that speech and language disorders may be caused by hearing loss, neurological disorders, brain injury, intellectual disability, drug abuse, physical impairments (e.g., cleft palate), vocal abuse or misuse, or idiopathic causes 6.11.01.01

» Know that speech and language disorders may be congenital or acquired

» Know that they may also present with other conditions such as ADHD, dyspraxia, apraxia, or identified developmental delays

» Know that individuals may have a speech and/or a language disorder (i.e., expressive or receptive language) that impacts the learning process

Understand the types or classifications of speech and language disorders and how each impacts physical education programming

Know that speech and language disorders can result in varying degrees of impairment that differentially impact learning and performance 6.11.02.01

» Know that speech disorders impact the ability to produce sounds correctly or fluently or create difficulties with voice such as stuttering

» Know that language disorders impact an individual's ability to understand others (i.e., receptive language) and/or share their thoughts, feelings and ideas (i.e., expressive language)

» Know that programming will need to be adjusted depending on the type of the condition and the severity (e.g., mild to severe) of the condition and the type of augmentative and alternative communication that is being used

» Know that individuals with receptive language disorders, such as receptive aphasia, may require multiple means of accessing and/or receiving instruction such as the use of sign language, gestures, pictures, or symbols

» Understand individuals with expressive language disorders, such as mechanical disorders and expressive aphasia, may need communication devices, additional time for responses, or assistance from an interpreter in the physical education setting

Understand unique psychomotor considerations

Understand that individuals with speech and language disorders may or may not demonstrate delays in psychomotor development that impact motor performance 6.11.03.01

» Identify the challenges in evaluating motor performance needed to determine present level of performance

» Know how to design instruction to address deficits in expressive or receptive language

» Know that they may have varying capacities to develop age-appropriate motor skills

Understand unique fitness considerations

Understand that individuals with speech and language disorders may or may not demonstrate deficits in physical fitness 6.11.04.01

» Identify the challenges in evaluating physical fitness needed to determine present level of performance

» Know that those who demonstrate developmental delays may lack the prerequisite motor skills needed to participate in physical activity sufficiently to develop and/or maintain physical fitness

» Utilize appropriate instructional supports and strategies such as motivating equipment, physical activity choices, and cooperative activities to elicit the appropriate frequency, intensity, and duration of physical activity necessary for maintaining or improving physical fitness

Understand unique cognitive considerations

Understand that individuals with speech and language disorders may demonstrate academic delays that adversely affect learning in physical education 6.11.05.01

» Identify the challenges in evaluating physical education content knowledge (e.g., knowledge of physical fitness, sports rules, game play strategies, etc.)

» Know that deficits in academic functioning as a result of expressive and receptive language delays may impact the understanding of instruction and the subsequent motor performance

» Apply principles of UDL to assessment and instruction to maximize learning (see Standards 8, 9, and 10)

Understand unique affective and social skill considerations

Understand that individuals with speech and language disorders may demonstrate deficits in affective and social skill development 6.11.06.01

» Know that deficits in processing language may frequently impact affective and social skill development

» Recognize the physical educator's role in teaching and developing self-advocacy skills as well as providing opportunities to apply those skills

» Know that they may demonstrate inappropriate social behaviors in physical activity settings for reasons such as difficulties handling communication frustrations, issues with impulsivity control, experiences with bullying, and/or self-limiting social experiences

Understand unique communication considerations

Understand that individuals with speech and language disorders may demonstrate deficits in communication skills 6.11.07.01

» Know that deficits in processing language may impact the development of communication skills

» Collaborate with other professionals such as speech and language pathologists, special educators, school counselors, and paraeducators to practice effective communication in physical activity settings

» Know that those who demonstrate deficits in communication skills may experience difficulties in physical activity settings that can result in withdrawal, experiences with bullying, and/or self-limiting social experiences

TRAUMATIC BRAIN INJURY: Understand unique attributes of individuals with traumatic brain injury

As defined by IDEA, traumatic brain injury (TBI) means:

an acquired injury to the brain caused by an external physical force, resulting in total or partial functional disability or psychosocial impairment, or both, that adversely affects a child's educational performance. Traumatic brain injury applies to open or closed head injuries resulting in impairments in one or more areas, such as cognition; language; memory; attention; reasoning; abstract thinking; judgment; problem solving; sensory, perceptual, and motor abilities; psychosocial behavior; physical functions; information processing; and speech. Traumatic brain injury does not apply to brain injuries that are congenital or degenerative, or to brain injuries induced by birth trauma. 34 CFR §300.8

Understand the etiology of traumatic brain injury and the impact on physical and motor attributes

Understand that traumatic brain injury is caused by an injury or trauma that leads to some degree of impairment and/or permanent loss across multiple areas of functioning adversely affecting motor performance 6.12.01.01

» Know that traumatic brain injury may be caused by injuries from accidents, falls, external physical force, or other traumas

» Know that traumatic brain injuries can be open or closed head injuries that result in impaired functioning in one or more areas (e.g., cognitive, memory, reasoning, motor planning, behavior, judgment, and speech)

Understand traumatic brain injury and how it impacts physical education programming (i.e., planning, assessment, implementation, teaching, and evaluation)

Know that individuals with traumatic brain injury can present with multiple types of concomitant disabilities and exhibit varying degrees of impairment that differentially impact learning 6.12.02.01

» Know that they may demonstrate multiple disabilities related to the degree and/or severity of the trauma and/or impairment

» Know that programming will need to be adjusted depending on the degree of severity of conditions associated with the individual trauma

» Know that programming must be adapted to accommodate the physical, cognitive, and affective constraints post TBI as the individual adjusts to the loss of function while adjusting to new ways of performing daily living skills

Understand unique psychomotor considerations

Understand that individuals with traumatic brain injury may demonstrate significant limitations in motor control that may limit or even prevent the acquisition of psychomotor skills 6.12.03.01

» Identify the challenges in evaluating motor performance needed to determine present level of performance

» Know that they may have significant limitations and/or varying degrees of motor control ability

» Design instruction to involve multiple sensory modalities such as providing extensive visual, auditory, tactile, and kinesthetic prompts to elicit the practice necessary for motor learning to occur

» Know that they have varying capacities to perform functional motor skills

» Adapt activities to incorporate individuals who use various assistive devices such as wheelchairs, walkers, or canes

» Train paraeducators to be actively involved in the instructional process

Understand unique fitness considerations

Understand that individuals with traumatic brain injury may demonstrate significant limitations which may limit or prevent their ability to develop appropriate levels of physical fitness 6.12.04.01

» Identify the challenges when evaluating physical fitness needed to determine present level of performance

» Know that they may no longer have the prerequisite motor skills needed to participate in physical activity sufficiently to develop and/or maintain physical fitness

» Know that they have varying capacities to develop physical fitness levels

» Know that instruction may need to be adapted to include multiple sensory modalities such as the use of visual, auditory, tactile, and kinesthetic prompts to elicit the appropriate frequency, intensity, and duration of physical activity necessary for maintaining or improving physical fitness

» Adapt fitness activities to incorporate individuals who use various assistive devices such as wheelchairs, walkers, or canes

» Train paraeducators to be actively involved in the training and instructional processes

» Utilize appropriate instructional supports and strategies such as motivating equipment, adaptive equipment, physical activity choices, and cooperative activities to elicit the appropriate frequency, intensity, and duration of physical activity necessary for maintaining or improving physical fitness

Understand unique cognitive considerations

Understand that individuals with traumatic brain injury may demonstrate a variety of learning challenges such as memory loss, attention deficit, anxiety etc. that adversely affect learning in physical education 6.12.05.01

» Apply principles of UDL to assessment and instruction to maximize learning (see Standards 8, 9, and 10)

» Know that deficits in cognitive functioning impact the understanding of instruction and the subsequent motor performance

» Design instruction in short, concise, sequential segments employing all appropriate sensory modalities to maximize learning

» Use principles of UDL such as visual demonstrations, verbal cues, engaging equipment options, and kinesthetic prompts to support instruction

Understand unique affective and social skill considerations

Understand that individuals with traumatic brain injury may be impacted by both the loss of prior abilities and the limitations imposed by existing functional capabilities that impact affective and social skill development 6.12.06.01

» Know that significant deficits in affective development and language will limit social interaction

» Know that they may demonstrate stereotypic behaviors that interfere with social interactions

» Know that they may require intensive instructional support in learning appropriate social skills such as social stories and peer modeling

» Know that those with limited or altered communication ability may become easily frustrated and/or feel socially isolated

» Know that they may demonstrate varying degrees of anxiety and depression as a result of acquiring a TBI which may cause the loss of prior abilities

» Know how to facilitate the development and acceptance of new self-identity and functional abilities

» Recognize the physical educator's role in teaching and developing self-advocacy skills as well as providing opportunities to apply those skills

Understand health and medical issues

Understand that individuals with traumatic brain injury may have a range of health and medical concerns such as heart conditions, epilepsy, respiratory issues, orthopedic impairments, mental health, and/or nutrition issues that impact learning and motor performance 6.12.07.01

» Collaborate with a multidisciplinary team to address health and medical issues

» Recognize safety and participation concerns such as tracheotomies, oxygen tanks, walkers, or other medical related devices

» Recognize safety and participation concerns associated with medications such as seizure medications, depressants, and stimulants

» Collaborate with rehabilitation specialists, physical therapists, and occupational therapists when working with individuals who present with multiple conditions associated with TBI

» Collaborate with physical therapists when working with individuals who require therapy to develop and/or regain fine and gross motor control

Understand unique communication considerations

Understand that individuals with traumatic brain injury may demonstrate marked deficits in communication skills 6.12.08.01

» Understand communication challenges in the learning environment such as perseveration, loss of speech, memory, motor planning, and echolalia

» Utilize assistive technologies and devices to enhance participation in physical activity and take measures to ensure safe handling of devices in physical activity settings

» Collaborate with other professionals such as audiologists, speech-language pathologists, special educators, paraeducators, and interpreters to maximize effective communication

>> Recognize the physical educator's role in effectively communicating such as learning sign language and understanding individual's gestures or altered expressive language

> **VISUAL IMPAIRMENTS INCLUDING BLINDNESS:** Understand the unique attributes of individuals who are blind or visually impaired

As defined by IDEA, visual impairment including blindness means "an impairment in vision that, even with correction, adversely affects a child's educational performance. The term includes both partial sight and blindness." 34 CFR §300.8

Understand the etiology of visual impairments, including blindness, and the impact on physical and motor attributes

Understand that visual impairment, including blindness, is caused by abnormalities in the structure or function of the eye or the brain as it relates to vision 6.13.01.01

>> Know that causes of visual impairments may include heredity, genetics, disease, age, trauma, and/or medical conditions

>> Know that the causes of visual impairments may be congenital or **adventitious**

>> Early detection and intervention is essential to orientation and mobility development

Understand the types or classifications of visual impairments, including blindness, and how each impacts physical education programming

Know that individuals with visual impairments, including blindness, can acquire vision loss at different times and exhibit varying degrees of visual impairment that differentially impact learning 6.13.02.01

>> Know that, even with correction, individuals with visual impairments have a visual acuity of less than 20/40

>> Know that visual impairments range from mild to total blindness including: mild (20/40-20/60), moderate (20/70-20/160), severe low vision (20/200-20/400), profound low vision (20/500-20/1000), near total blindness (less than 20/1000), and total blindness (no light perception)

>> Know that visual impairments may be due to issues with refractive vision and/or orthoptic vision

>> Know that visual impairments may develop progressively or come on suddenly and be fluctuating or stable in nature

>> Know the magnitude of learning difficulties that will be greater for individuals with congenital vision loss versus individuals with adventitious vision loss, particularly those who experienced vision loss later in life

Understand unique psychomotor considerations

Understand that individuals with visual impairments, including blindness, may demonstrate delays in psychomotor development that impact motor performance 6.13.03.01

» Recognize the impact of vision on movement exploration and motor development

» Identify the challenges in evaluating motor performance needed to determine present level of performance

» Design instruction to provide physical and auditory prompts to elicit the appropriate motoric response

» Utilize appropriate instructional supports and strategies such as tactile modeling, visually and auditorily engaging equipment choices, and/or prompting to elicit the practice necessary for motor learning to occur

» Know that most have the capacity to develop motor skills comparable to their peers without disabilities

» Know that body image and body awareness may be impaired

» Know the open and close nature of motor skills and use that knowledge to design or modify learning tasks

» Know that low levels of fitness and delays in fundamental motor skill development may negatively impact specialized motor skill performance and learning, as well as orientation and mobility

Understand unique fitness considerations

Understand that individuals with visual impairments, including blindness, may demonstrate deficits in physical fitness 6.13.04.01

» Identify the challenges in evaluating physical fitness needed to determine present level of performance

» Know that they may lack the prerequisite motor skills needed to participate in physical activity sufficiently to develop and/or maintain physical fitness

» Know that most have the capacity to develop physical fitness levels comparable to their peers without disabilities

» Recognize that many fitness activities are closed skills (e.g., bench press, push-up, riding a stationary bike, etc.) which lend themselves to successful participation and significant attainments in physical fitness

» Utilize appropriate instructional supports and strategies such as tactile modeling; safe and appropriate equipment choices; as well as environmental, auditory, and visual prompts in order to elicit the appropriate frequency, intensity, and duration of physical activity necessary for maintaining or improving physical fitness

» Utilize appropriate instructional supports and strategies such as auditory equipment, physical activity choices, and orientation and mobility supports to elicit the appropriate frequency, intensity, and duration of physical activity necessary for maintaining or improving physical fitness

Understand unique cognitive considerations

Understand that individuals with visual impairments, including blindness may demonstrate academic delays that can adversely affect learning in physical education 6.13.05.01

» Design instruction in short, concise, sequential segments to maximize learning

» Design instructional materials and content delivery to be appropriate for the academic achievement level

» Provide multiple methods of accessing instructional materials including using assistive technologies and/or using large print or Braille materials

» Apply principles of UDL to assessment and instruction to maximize learning (see Standards 8, 9, and 10)

» Recognize that instruction in physical education is often reliant on visual concepts (e.g., line up on the line, move in a clockwise direction, etc.)

Understand unique affective and social skill considerations

Understand that individuals with visual impairments, including blindness, may demonstrate deficits in affective and social skill development 6.13.06.01

» Know that they may demonstrate deficits in recognizing and responding to social cues necessary for appropriate social interactions

» Know that deficits in affective development may lead to inappropriate responses in social interactions

» Recognize that age-appropriate motor skill functioning facilitates inclusion in physical activities with peers; however, deficits in social skill development may hinder successful interactions

» Know that they may demonstrate stereotypic behaviors that interfere with social interactions such as rocking, head shaking, or eye pressing

» Know that they may engage in frequent, ongoing verbal exchanges with others as a way to better understand their placement/location in the learning environment, which may be perceived as distracting by their peers who do not understand why they are doing so

» Recognize that discrepancy in social and play interests may develop between them and their peers, which might increase with age

» Recognize the physical educator's role in teaching and developing self-advocacy skills as well as providing opportunities to apply those skills

Understand health and medical issues

Understand that individuals' visual impairments, including blindness, may have a range of health and medical concerns such as blood pressure issues, mental health issues, and specific concerns related to macular degeneration, glaucoma, and retinal detachment that impact learning and motor performance 6.13.07.01

» Collaborate with a multidisciplinary team, particularly with the school nurse, to address health and medical issues

» Collaborate with the orientation and mobility specialist to address safety, falling, and participation concerns associated with low vision and blindness

» Know that retinal detachment has implications for contact activities and jarring

» Know that glaucoma has implications on physical activity choices that increase pressure in the eye

Understand unique communication considerations

Understand that individuals with visual impairments, including blindness, demonstrate marked deficits in speech and language development 6.13.08.01

» Understand communication challenges in the learning environment

» Use alerting devices to ensure awareness of safety issues such as fire or tornado warnings

» Know that significant deficits in communication and language development may be due to the inability to see others and/or their environment

» Know that there may be significant deficits in receptive and/or expressive language that impact communication of thoughts or feelings in social interactions

» Talk directly to the individual, not to their guide

CURRICULUM THEORY AND DEVELOPMENT

CURRICULUM THEORY AND DEVELOPMENT

CURRICULUM DESIGN: Understand how to plan a sequence of learning experiences that lead to the achievement of specified goals or learning outcomes

Understand how philosophical, psychological, and sociological factors influence selection of curriculum goals

Understand the role of philosophical, psychological, and social views and values play in the selection of program goals for individuals with disabilities 7.01.01.01

>> Plan for program goals that are specifically designed to meet the long-term fitness, motor skills, physical activity, and recreational needs of individuals with disabilities and reflect the family and community values

>> Plan for program goals that facilitate inclusion of all students in school and community physical activities

>> Prepare all individuals without disabilities for inclusion of individuals with disabilities in physical education and physical activity

Recognize the existence of curricular models in physical education such as movement education, fitness, developmental, sports education, activity-based, humanistic/social development, and personal meaning

Understand the pros and cons of various curricular models used in general physical education and how they apply to individuals with disabilities 7.01.02.01

>> Explain when it is appropriate to use curriculum models specially designed for individuals with disabilities

>> Explain when and how to include or exclude individuals with disabilities in general physical education depending upon the curriculum model being employed

Understand the influence of educational trends such as **culturally responsive pedagogy**, inclusive education, evidence-based approaches, Universal Design for Learning, and outcome-based education on the physical education curriculum

Understand the adapted physical educator's role in facilitating and implementing educational trends in physical education that benefit individuals with disabilities 7.01.03.01

>> Collaborate with the general physical education teacher about the progress and participation of the individuals with disabilities placed in inclusive general physical education

>> Develop and assist in implementing plans and evidenced-based practices to enable individuals with disabilities to successfully and maximally participate in general physical education

STANDARD 7

» Develop curricula that are accessible and operationalize the concept of the least restrictive environment (LRE) in physical education

Understand the need for relevant assessment information for defining appropriate program goals for individuals with disabilities 7.01.03.02

» Anticipate and evaluate the long-term physical activity needs of individuals with disabilities

» Understand and evaluate community physical activity and recreational facilities and programs

» Understand how to solicit input from families on their physical activity behaviors and interests

Understand the steps in designing a functional physical education curriculum to meet the unique needs of students with disabilities 7.01.03.03

» Explain the curriculum committee composition and their various contributions to the planning process

» Explain how the philosophy statement is developed and why it is an essential element of the planning process

» Explain how **top-down** goals are identified and then task analyzed into appropriate learning objectives based on the needs and attributes of the learner

» Explain the relationship between available instructional time and student learning rates in delimiting the content included in adapted physical education curricula

» Explain how a developmentally sequenced plan of learning objectives for a series of long-term physical education goals is created and integrated into adapted physical education program curriculum scope and sequence

EVALUATE CURRICULUM APPROPRIATENESS: Understand how to evaluate and determine when the general physical education curriculum is appropriate for individuals with disabilities

Understand how the underlying curriculum assumptions of the general physical education curriculum (e.g., number and type of goals, number of objectives per goal, time allocated for achievement, etc.) and the available resources (e.g., instructional time allocated for physical education, class size, equipment, facilities, etc.) impact the nature and number of goals and objectives to be included in the general physical education curriculum

Understand how to evaluate the underlying assumptions of the general physical education curriculum to determine if these are applicable to individuals with disabilities 7.02.01.01

» Explain how a student's present level of performance can be used to evaluate the appropriateness of the general physical education curriculum

» Explain how a student's long-term physical activity needs may require different goals than those addressed in the general physical education curriculum

» Explain how the amount of content and the time allocated to achieve content in general physical education may not be appropriate for individuals with disabilities

Understand how to evaluate and determine the impact that the amount of resources allocated for physical education instruction has on the number of goals and objectives that can be included in physical education curricula for students with disabilities 7.02.01.02.

» Explain how class size and disparate ability ranges can adversely impact the learning of students with disabilities

» Explain how teacher competency in assessing and teaching students with disabilities is correlated with student achievement

» Explain how access to adequate instructional facilities and student to equipment ratios impacts student achievement

NEEDS ASSESSMENT: Understand how to conduct a learner needs assessment

Understand how a learner needs assessment can be used to evaluate the appropriateness of the general physical education curriculum for students with disabilities

Understand how to create a learner needs assessment derived from the scope and sequence of the goals and objectives in the general physical education curriculum 7.03.01.01

» Explain how to select and sequence the objectives into a developmental needs assessment instrument

» Explain how to construct the administration procedures to produce valid and reliable results

Understand how to administer, score, and interpret the results of a learner needs assessment 7.03.01.02

» Explain how to score, record the needs assessment results, and calculate a summative score

» Explain how to interpret and communicate the results of the needs assessment to students, parents, teachers, and administrators

» Explain how to determine the most appropriate placement for a student based on the results of the needs assessment

Understand that many students with disabilities may require specially designed physical education curricula to meet their physical education needs

Understand the process of designing top-down functional curricula for individuals with disabilities 7.03.02.01

>> Explain how developmental delays and individual learning rates impact the number of goals and objectives that can be included in adapted physical education curricula

>> Explain the relationship among student learning rate, the amount of instructional time available, and the scope of content that can be included in the curriculum

Understand how the scope and sequence of the adapted physical education curriculum and the general physical education curriculum are used in making LRE placement decisions 7.03.03.02

>> Explain how to define a continuum of placement options that facilitates inclusion of students with disabilities when their adapted physical education curriculum content aligns with the general physical education curriculum

>> Explain how students with disabilities can work on parallel skills from their adapted physical education curriculum so that they can be included in general physical education

>> Explain how alternative placements on the continuum of placement options may be necessary when the focus of the general physical education curriculum is unsafe or inappropriate for students with disabilities (e.g., regulation soccer unit for a student with osteogenesis imperfecta)

CURRICULUM OBJECTIVES AND CONTENT: Understand the relationship between the learning objectives stipulated in the curriculum and what content is assessed and taught

Understand how to specify learning objectives that are congruent with the stated goals of the curriculum

Understand that the learning objectives included in the individualized education program (IEP) are directly aligned with the learning objectives identified in the curriculum to be worked on that year in the adapted physical education top-down curriculum 7.04.01.01

>> Prior to each year's annual IEP meeting, evaluate the student's progress on the learning objectives targeted for achievement the previous year

>> Explain how to use student ongoing assessment data to ensure achievement of the learning objectives in both their IEP and their specially designed adapted physical education curriculum

Understand how to develop precise, measurable learning objectives

Understand the criteria required for writing measurable objectives as specified for the IEP 7.04.02.01

>> Write objectives that are aligned with the curriculum and relate directly to the individual's needs as determined by the physical fitness and motor assessments

>> Write objectives that are observable and measurable (see Standard 9)

LEARNING EXPERIENCES: Understand how to design and evaluate appropriate student learning experiences

Understand how to substantiate the selection of learning experiences

Understand the relationship between the student's curriculum scope and sequence of learning objectives and the annual goals and objectives included on the IEP 7.05.01.01

» Write short-term instructional objectives designed to meet **long-term goals** (see Standard 9)

» Use the appropriate developmental sequence of motor skills

» Evaluate, at least on an annual basis, adapted physical education curriculum goals and objectives commensurate with the individual's achievement and progress

Understand how to utilize individualization (such as learning style options, pacing, and level of difficulty) as a basis for implementing learning experiences

Understand how to design instruction in a manner that capitalizes on the learning styles of individuals with disabilities (see Standard 10) 7.05.02.01

» Use instructional cues that are consistent with the student's preferred learning modality

» Control and time the sequence of the lesson activities to maximize student attention, engagement, and learning

» Plan activities with varying levels of difficulty allowing students to progress at their own pace

» Use **paraprofessionals** and **peer tutors** to enable maximum participation of individuals with disabilities

» Prepare and use paraprofessionals and peer tutors to effectively instruct, give feedback, and assess individuals with disabilities

ASSESSMENT

STANDARD 8

ASSESSMENT

> **LEGISLATIVE ISSUES:** Legislation in regard to assessment of individuals with disabilities throughout the lifespan (see Standard 5)

Know federal and state legislation for assessment of individuals with disabilities

Understand personnel requirements for assessment under federal and state law 8.01.01.01

» Conduct adequate training for valid test administration

» Explain the personnel qualifications necessary for valid assessment of the motor domain as defined in both federal and state education laws

» Explain the differences in personnel requirements between federal and state level mandates

Understand the criteria that the instrument(s) used must be considered acceptable under the law in terms of validity and reliability 8.01.01.02

» Identify the measurement characteristics of instruments needed to comply with federal law

» Explain validity and reliability relative to test instruments

» Use instruments that meet criteria for validity and reliability under the law

Understand the process of assessment under the law 8.01.01.03

» Use multiple measures or assessments when determining eligibility or developing an individualized education program by including standardized assessment data as well as **informal assessment** information and input from teachers, parents, and the student, when appropriate

» Conduct assessment in a nondiscriminatory manner

» Complete the assessment process in all areas related to the suspected disability, including, if appropriate, health, vision, hearing, social and emotional status, academic performance, assistive technologies, communicative status, and motor abilities

» Assess according to the frequency required by law

Understand the difference between instructional services and related services for individuals with disabilities 8.01.01.04

» Explain the differences between instructional services and related services for individuals with disabilities to parents and guardians

» Recommend related services to parents and guardians as appropriate

Know state and school district regulations and guidelines for assessment of individuals with disabilities

Know Local Education Agency (LEA) eligibility criteria for adapted physical education 8.01.02.01

» Communicate the rationale and use of eligibility criteria for adapted physical education

» Implement eligibility criteria for placing students into adapted physical education

Know the referral process

Understand the processes involved in referring and assessing individuals with disabilities for special education services 8.01.03.01

» Comply with the timelines for responsiveness to a referral

» Complete the assessment process within the specified time required under the law

Understand the physical educator's responsibilities in the referral process relative to physical and motor performance 8.01.03.02

» Explain the responsibilities in the referral process related to physical education for individuals with disabilities

» Initiate the referral process by submitting a referral form or communicating the referral to appropriate personnel within the school district

Understand appropriate procedures for data gathering based on referral information and suspected areas of motor disability 8.01.03.03

» Conduct appropriate screening for individuals with suspected motor disabilities

» Relate areas of screening with parameters measured in the assessment process

Understand the roles of other professionals 8.01.03.04

» Refer individuals with disabilities to related services personnel, such as physical, occupational, and speech therapists

» Explain to parents and guardians the role and purpose(s) of various related services professionals

Understand the ethical issues of assessment such as unbiased assessment and the use of individual's native language or commonly used form of communication (see Standard 5)

Understand what is meant by informed consent of parents and guardians 8.01.04.01

» Ensure that informed consent for the assessment process has been obtained prior to assessing a student

» Explain a student's need for adapted physical education assessment to parents and guardians who are hesitant to give consent for assessment

Understand due process and its ethical implications 8.01.04.02

» Comply with the due process procedures for all physical education services

» Explain due process to parents and guardians as needed

Understand how sociocultural aspects can affect the assessment process 8.01.04.03

» Apply necessary modifications in the assessment process for any influences due to culture and/or language

» Use an interpreter in instances in which individuals do not speak English as their primary language

Understand the need for confidentiality of records 8.01.04.04

» Read appropriate records for an individual prior to gathering assessment data

» Obtain information discretely from the classroom teacher and other professionals prior to gathering data

Acknowledge the rights of parents or guardians to obtain an appropriate and objective evaluation of performance by personnel outside the educational agency

Understand the relationship between the results of an outside evaluation and the results of motor assessment conducted by appropriately trained professionals under the law 8.01.05.01

» Communicate, when appropriate, with outside personnel who conducted the evaluations

» Resolve or validate the results of motor assessment with the results of assessment by outside personnel

TERMINOLOGY: The nomenclature used in the specialized field of motor assessment of individuals with disabilities

Awareness of the differences among screening, assessment, measurement, and evaluation

Understand the purpose of screening 8.02.01.01

» Conduct appropriate screening

» Articulate the findings of the screening process to other professionals, parents, and guardians

Understand the purpose of assessment 8.02.01.02

» Explain the various purposes for which assessment data are collected

» Describe the primary purposes for which assessment data are used in adapted physical education

Understand the purpose of measurement 8.02.01.03

» Distinguish between the purposes of measurement of individuals with disabilities and measurement of individuals without disabilities

» Describe how measurements are used in adapted physical education

Understand the purpose of program evaluation 8.02.01.04

» Compare and contrast the purposes of program evaluation for individuals with disabilities and individuals without disabilities

» Explain how program evaluation can be used for comparing adapted physical education to general physical education programs

Understand the purpose of individual evaluation 8.02.01.05

» Compare the individual's present level of performance with initial assessment and learning expectations targeted by the teacher

» Compare the individual's present level of performance with expected achievement outcomes stipulated in the IEP and APE curriculum

» Explain how to effectively communicate individual evaluation results to students and parents or guardians

Know formal and informal methods for gathering qualitative as well as quantitative data on motor performance

Understand how to use the various forms of data collected related to individuals with disabilities 8.02.02.01

» Use diagnostic evaluations, instructional assessment, individual evaluation, and program evaluation for monitoring progress

» Integrate information obtained from parent and guardian reports and other informal measures with formally obtained performance measures

Know curriculum-embedded methods of gathering data

Understand the process of gathering data on motor behavior 8.02.03.01

» Administer one or more curriculum-based evaluation procedures such as Smart Start, Everyone CAN **Data-Based Gymnasium**, and ABC

» Use data gathered on motor behavior in reporting present levels of performance of individuals with disabilities

» Use data gathered on motor behavior in reporting individual student and class progress

Know terminology such as eligibility criteria, individualized education program, and present level of performance

Know the terminology related to motor assessment 8.02.04.01

» Communicate utilizing terminology unique to assessment of individuals with disabilities

» Explain how multiple baseline measures may be needed to obtain accurate performance measures for many students with disabilities

» Teach colleagues appropriate terminology for movement parameters

» Apply the eligibility criteria established within the school district to the assessment process in physical education

» Develop the individualized education program for physical education inclusive of the mandated components (e.g., duration and frequency of services, present level of performance, etc.)

» Determine the present level of performance

Understand reasons for discrepancies between performance on standardized tests and curriculum-embedded performance

Know how performance score discrepancies relate to individuals with disabilities 8.02.05.01

» Defend or refute scores on standardized tests against performance-based observations of an individual's present level of performance

» Use appropriate assessment procedures such as age-appropriate evaluation, functional skills assessment, life-skills measurement, developmentally appropriate assessment, and bottom-up and top-down approaches

ADMINISTRATION: Knowledge of various instruments measuring human performance related to physical education

Know instruments that measure the qualities necessary for physical and motor fitness: fundamental motor skills and patterns; skills in aquatics, dance, and individual and group games and sports; as well as functional living skills

Know how to administer curriculum-based assessment procedures such as Smart Start and Everyone CAN 8.03.01.01

» Use at least one curriculum-based assessment procedure

» Describe some of the administrative advantages of curriculum-based assessment procedures

Know the instruments most commonly used by adapted physical educators 8.03.01.02

» Use instruments measuring physical fitness such as the FitnessGram and Brockport Physical Fitness Test

» Use instruments measuring motor skill performance such as Test of Gross Motor Development

» Use tests measuring motor development such as Brigance Diagnostic Inventory of Early Development, Denver Developmental Screening Test, and Peabody Developmental Motor Scale

Know other measurement and evaluation procedures prescribed by the state (SEA) or local education agency (LEA) 8.03.01.03

» Use the measurement and evaluation procedures used by the SEA or LEA when appropriate

» Explain advantages of the SEA or LEA's prescribed measurement and evaluation procedures (e.g., local norms) to other professionals

Know when it is appropriate to administer informal assessments including **authentic assessments** 8.03.01.04

» Explain the advantages of using authentic assessment practices to identify needs and monitor progress

» Use a teacher-developed or curriculum-specific checklist as appropriate to monitor individual progress

Know other measurement and evaluation procedures used by related services personnel 8.03.01.05

» Explain to related services professionals how motor limitations may impact performance on instruments measuring language and cognitive function

» Explain procedures used by other professionals to evaluate movement including reflex, mobility, and flexibility testing; sensory motor, gross motor, and fine motor skills testing; positioning/handling techniques; and leisure skills education

» Distinguish interrelationship of motor skills with related services such as speech-language pathology services and occupational and **physical therapy**

» Recognize the variety of motor skills and abilities assessed by other professionals on the multidisciplinary team

ADMINISTRATION: Demonstrate knowledge of an assortment of instruments measuring all aspects of human performance

Recognize the need for staff training, additional administrative support, and reallocation of resources in utilizing a diversity of instruments

Understand how to determine the level of need for inservices on test administration for individuals with disabilities 8.03.02.01

» Provide an inservice to general physical educators related to test administration based on the data gathered through a needs assessment survey

» Provide inservice to general physical educators on screening procedures for making appropriate referrals for adapted physical education based on data gathered through a needs assessment survey

INTERPRETATION: Gaining clarification and meaning of measurement results

Understand the use of measurement results for the purpose of identifying educational needs

Understand how to interpret measurement results of screening and diagnosis 8.04.01.01

>> Use the measurement results of screening and diagnosis to refer individuals with disabilities for further assessment

>> Use the measurement results of screening and diagnosis to write annual instructional goals

Understand how to interpret norm-referenced, criterion-referenced, and content-referenced results for individuals with disabilities 8.04.01.02

>> Use the results of norm-referenced, criterion-referenced, and content-referenced instruments in determining annual instructional goals and **short-term objectives**

>> Use the results of norm-referenced, criterion-referenced, and content-referenced instruments in prescribing programs for individuals with disabilities

Understand how to establish norm-referenced and criterion-referenced standards for qualifying students for placement in adapted physical education 8.04.01.03

>> Use the established entrance standards to recommend adapted physical education services for individuals with disabilities

>> Explain the entrance standards to parents or care providers and other professionals during the IEP meeting

Understand the use of measurement results for instructional planning

Understand how to interpret measurement results and use them in the instructional planning 8.04.02.01

>> Show evidence of using measurement results in the development of the instructional plans

>> Modify expectations for student performance based on measurement results

Understand how to interpret measurement results for monitoring progress of individuals with disabilities 8.04.02.02

>> Incorporate the measurement results when monitoring the program evaluation progress of individuals with disabilities

>> Use measurement results to give individuals feedback in the learning process

>> Use measurement results to develop progress reports for the individual and the parents

>> Use measurement results in the **summative evaluation**

Understand the relationships among measures of physical and motor fitness; fundamental motor skills and patterns; and skills in aquatics, dance, and individual and group games and sports as well as functional living skills

Understand how to incorporate integrated activities into the instructional plan 8.04.03.01

» Incorporate activities addressing reflex behavior, sensorimotor function, leisure skills, and functional skills into the instructional plan (see Standard 9)

» Integrate activities that foster the development of prosocial behaviors in the instructional plan

» Include lifetime activities in the instructional plan based on the results of assessment

Understand the importance of providing feedback for social, behavioral, and language skills as they relate to, and are demonstrated in, a motor performance context 8.04.03.02

» Incorporate the necessary feedback concerning social, behavioral, and language skills into the individual's overall physical education plan

» Use both general and specific feedback when implementing the physical education plan

Understand the connection between motor performance measures and self-help and mobility skills 8.04.03.03

» Incorporate self-help and mobility skills into the individual's physical education program when appropriate

» Identify self-help and mobility skill programs

Understand the importance of parental or guardians' input in the assessment process 8.04.03.04

» Actively seek parental or guardian input

» Include parents or guardians in the delivery of services by encouraging family activities

Understand the importance of effectively communicating the results of assessment

Understand how to communicate motor performance scores to parents or guardians 8.04.04.01

» Interpret motor performance scores to parents or guardians

» Explain the relationship between motor performance scores and play behavior observed by parents or guardians

Understand how to communicate motor performance scores to classroom teachers and other professionals 8.04.04.02

》 Interpret motor performance scores to classroom teachers and other professionals

》 Work cooperatively with other professionals to determine the need to refer for further testing for additional instructional or related services

Understand how to communicate motor performance scores to individuals with disabilities as appropriate 8.04.04.03

》 Interpret motor performance scores to individuals with disabilities as appropriate

》 Question individuals with disabilities on how they might improve their performance over the next review period

Understand that measurement results must reach a criterion in order to be determined eligible for adapted physical education

Understand the local measurement criteria for determining eligibility for adapted physical education 8.04.05.01

》 Interpret local criteria for determining eligibility for adapted physical education

》 Explain the difference between qualifying and non-qualifying performances relative to eligibility for adapted physical education

Understand the choices of services available to students with disabilities in the school district or local educational agency

Understand service delivery options for physical education in cooperation with a multidisciplinary team 8.04.06.01

》 Suggest the optimal service delivery option for physical education in cooperation with the multidisciplinary team

》 Agree on the service delivery options for physical education in cooperation with the multidisciplinary team

Understand adaptations or modifications of activities based on the individual's identified needs 8.04.06.02

》 Provide suggestions for adaptation or modifications of activities based on the individual's identified needs

》 Modify facilities and equipment as needed to accommodate the individual's identified needs (see Standard 9)

Recognize the need for staff training, additional administrative support, and reallocation of resources for effective administration of physical fitness and motor performance instruments and the interpretation of assessment results

Understand how to provide inservice training for general physical educators on measurement and interpretation of motor performance assessment 8.04.07.01

» Provide inservice on assessment to general physical educators on an ongoing basis

» Attend inservices, conferences, and workshops to keep current with assessment issues (see Standard 13)

Understand the need for classroom teacher involvement in physical and motor performance assessment interpretation 8.04.07.02

» Offer inservice to classroom teachers about measurement and interpretation of physical and motor performance assessment results as needed

» Provide guidelines for referral to adapted physical education

DECISION MAKING: The process of making choices from alternatives

Acquire knowledge of a theoretical framework with which to make comprehensive assessment decisions

Understand the nature of decisions to be made such as eligibility, program planning, placement, and instruction for individuals with disabilities 8.05.01.01

» Use the appropriate assessment instruments when making eligibility decisions

» Use the appropriate assessment instruments when making program planning decisions

» Use the appropriate assessment instruments when making placement decisions

» Use the appropriate assessment instruments when making instructional decisions

Understand the value of assessment as an ongoing process

Understand how ongoing assessment relates to programming decisions for individuals with disabilities 8.05.02.01

» Use ongoing assessment in program evaluation

» Use ongoing assessment of annual goals and objectives as a means to evaluate program effectiveness

Understand instructional decisions based on assessment results

Understand how to plan teaching based on assessment results 8.05.03.01

» Provide evidence of the effects of assessment on instructional decisions by changing teaching plans

» Demonstrate that expectations for performance of individuals is based on the results of assessment

Understand the difference between a full range of physical education services and essential physical education service options for individuals with disabilities 8.05.03.02

» Explain the difference between the two service options to parents, guardians, and other professionals

» Provide essential physical education services for individuals with disabilities

Know motor assessment resources available in the field

Understand how to locate names of local, state, and regional resources for assistance with motor assessment issues 8.05.04.01

» Provide parents, guardians, and other professionals with names of local/ state/regional resources for assistance with motor assessment issues

» Explain to parents or guardians their rights to obtain assistance with motor assessment from sources outside the school environment

SKILLS REQUIRED OF THE ASSESSMENT TEAM: The ability to work together with other professionals in a multidisciplinary team (see Standard 15)

Report the assessment results to parents, guardians, and other professionals

Understand how to use the appropriate statements with regard to the individual with a disability when reporting assessment results 8.06.01.01

» Distinguish among statements of fact, inference, and probability

» Use previous experience for establishing a context of reporting assessment results

Record assessment results for use by members of the multidisciplinary team

Understand the essential components of a comprehensive assessment report for use in making recommendations for programming 8.06.02.01

» State the essential dimensions of a summary report including demographics, overall summary of assessment results, specific behavioral observations during testing, specific subtest performances, and general recommendations regarding eligibility for services

» Include behavioral observations in physical education or other school-based settings, such as recess, as appropriate within the assessment summary report

» Discriminate between objective data and opinion

Understand how to interface the report of physical fitness and motor performance assessment and programming recommendations with the reports and programming of other team members

Understand the potential for developing collaborative lesson plans using assessment results provided by team members for general physical education classes and other inclusionary experiences 8.06.03.01

» Write rubrics in **collaboration** with the general physical educator

» Team teach with the general physical educator using a collaborative lesson plan

» Demonstrate the use of a task analysis when teaching as it relates to assessment results

Collaborate with team members to understand how to develop instructional strategies based on the team report that facilitate self-directed and independent participation of individuals with disabilities within the movement environment 8.06.03.02

» Collaborate with related service providers to improve independent participation through alignment of services such as improving dressing out for physical education

» Coordinate physical education goals and objectives with community-based physical activity experiences

» Coordinate community-based physical activity experiences with other professionals such as a therapeutic recreator or personal trainer

» Develop transition goals in physical activity to integrate the individual in community-based activities

Understand how to collaborate with and support other team members 8.06.03.03

» Engage other team members in discussion of the progress of individuals with disabilities at times other than formalized, planned meetings

» Use multidisciplinary strategies as appropriate

INSTRUCTIONAL DESIGN AND PLANNING

INSTRUCTIONAL DESIGN AND PLANNING

STANDARD 9

> **CURRICULUM PLAN:** Understand the factors needed to develop a systematic overall curriculum plan of instruction

Analyze individual strengths, needs, goals, and priorities

Understand individual strengths, needs, goals, and priorities specific to individuals with disabilities 9.01.01.01

» Determine long-term goals suitable for instruction given the individual's potential and time available to implement instructional programs, as well as, considering such factors as equipment, space, and number of individuals per class

» Determine the prerequisite behaviors and ancillary behaviors needed to complete the goals targeted for instruction

» Consider the individual's ability in the physical, cognitive, and social domains based on the assessment and evaluation of long-term annual goals and behavioral objectives

» Determine the individual's preferences for activities

» Consider sociocultural factors including family preferences in determining programming

» Consider the individual's various learning modalities such as visual, kinesthetic, or auditory

» Establish and promote behaviors with the most immediate value, such as those that allow individuals to function as independently as possible in the community and later in life

» Identify behaviors that offer long-term support and lifetime application

Analyze resources, constraints, and alternative delivery systems

Understand resources, constraints, and alternative delivery systems and strategies specific to meeting the needs of individuals with disabilities (see Standards 7 and 15) 9.01.02.01

» Collaborate with support personnel such as paraprofessionals and peer tutors to assist in planning for instruction (see Standard 15)

» Collaborate with community support services such as Special Olympics and YMCA for developing instructional programs

» Use existing resources in adapted physical education such as the ABC model for instructional planning

» Advocate for accessibility to facilities and teaching areas such as ramps for individuals who are wheelchair users as well as accessibility to pools and playground equipment

» Advocate for educational placement in the least restrictive environment

» Advocate for participation in intramural and interscholastic sport programs

Determine scope (goals and objectives) and sequence (when they will be taught) of the curriculum based on long-term goals, which will serve as the basis for the IEP and IFSP

Understand the concept of "planning down" to establish long-term goals 9.01.03.01

》 Select goals based on projected employment, living situation, cultural expectations, leisure preferences, and skill potential

》 Select goals based on access to facilities and equipment

》 Collaborate with other professionals to project long-term, community-based sport and adapted recreation goals

Understand the concept of instructional time and how it relates to planning functional curricula for individuals with disabilities 9.01.03.02

》 Calculate the total time available in the program

》 Adjust the amount of time based on access to facilities and equipment, student–teacher ratio, teacher competency, capability of individuals, and outside practice opportunities

Understand how to delimit the number of goals that can be achieved in the program by individuals with disabilities based on the amount of instructional time and the resources available 9.01.03.03

》 Determine goal emphasis

》 Establish time needed to achieve mastery of objectives

》 Plan time needed for retention and maintenance

Understand how to delineate and sequence the objectives across the years of the program so that the program goals can be achieved in the time available 9.01.03.04

》 Sequence objectives based on factors such as age-appropriateness, developmental level, and social skills

》 Determine when instruction should begin, when achievement is expected, and the relationship with the IEP such as when objectives should be included on the IEP

Understand how to use the scope and sequence of the objectives in the curriculum as the basis for program evaluation of individuals with a disability (see Standard 12) 9.01.03.05

》 Based on assessment data, determine if the program is being implemented as intended and when program revisions are needed

》 Communicate the program's purpose and the individual's progress

》 Monitor IEP progress using the curriculum scope and sequence

UNIT AND LESSON PLANS: Design units and lesson plans to maximize instruction

Plan lessons that acknowledge learner attributes and individual background

Understand that individuals with disabilities exhibit a unique array of characteristics such as limited attention span, distractibility, and hyperactivity (see Standard 6) 9.02.01.01

» Plan structured programs, class routines, and activities that include instructional learning cues to maintain attention (see Standard 10)

» Select equipment that maintains attention including varied colors, sizes, and shapes

» Plan a variety of presentations so that specific tasks can be altered, if needed, in order to maintain interest and attention

» Plan the use of a variety of teaching styles that will meet the needs of individuals with disabilities (see Standard 10)

Understand that the readiness level of individuals with disabilities may vary 9.02.01.02

» Plan programs to include appropriate modifications for individuals who learn at slower or different rates

» Plan programs to include appropriate skills and activities based on the individual's readiness level

Understand motivation levels of individuals with disabilities 9.02.01.03

» Plan programs with consideration of the teaching behaviors to promote and motivate the individual (see Standard 10)

» Plan programs with consideration to what the individual finds reinforcing to promote and motivate the learner

Understand there are multiple cultural variables that influence the perceptions and behaviors of individuals with disabilities 9.02.01.04

» Recognize the potential influence of age, gender, ethnicity, sexual orientation, socioeconomic status, and religious beliefs on physical activity behaviors

» Plan programs that appreciate the uniqueness of each individual

Understand the wide variety of individual differences among and within different types of individuals with disabilities 9.02.01.05

» Plan programs to account for individual differences among individuals, such as using various teaching styles

» Plan programs for appropriate use of environment, equipment, rules, materials, and activities (see Standard 10)

» Plan programs that include modified games and activities

Address the medical history of the individual within the instructional design

Understand the effect certain medical conditions may have when planning physical activity for an individual with a disability 9.02.02.01

» Check the individual's medical records (file) and be aware of his or her current medical condition including current medications

» Consult with a physician and other medical staff regarding recommended and contraindicated activities resulting from the individual's medical condition/medication

» Plan for recommended activities and exercises while avoiding contraindicated activities such as butterfly swim stroke and diving activities for individuals with atlantoaxial instability

» Organize the learning environment so that the impact of the disability is not magnified by factors such as strobe lights, flickering fluorescent lighting, or extraneous sounds that may trigger seizures

Understand the effect medication (type and dosage) may have on the behavior and performance of an individual with a disability when planning activities 9.02.02.02

» Plan programs that consider the effect medication has on the individual's physical fitness, motor skill abilities, and physical work capacity

» Plan programs that consider the effect medication has on the length of time an individual is able to remain on task or participate

» Be aware of medication schedule and consider charting the effect of the medications if they interfere with performance, such as fatigue, errors in movement, and distractibility

Plan for safety and risk management

Understand proper safety techniques and principles specific to individuals with disabilities 9.02.03.01

» Plan activities that account for the amount of risk involved by considering such factors as space available, floor surfaces, appropriate equipment, and types of activities offered

» Plan for safety procedures including handling wheelchair transfers, securing and strapping techniques, negotiating stairs and inclines, bracing, reinsertion of tracheotomy tube, and guiding techniques

» Identify and post safety procedures for specific emergency procedures

Plan for proper supervision following school policies

Understand potentially dangerous situations and activities specific to individuals with disabilities 9.02.04.01

» Share information and/or procedures with general physical educators and others regarding individuals with disabilities and their special needs

» Develop and post emergency plans specific to individuals with a disability such as emergency procedures to follow when an individual has a seizure

» Plan for directional, visual, auditory, and **tactile signals** alerting individuals with disabilities of potentially dangerous activities and emergencies

» Develop specific supervision and spotting procedures

Understand LEA policies with regard to safety of individuals and staff 9.02.04.02

» Implement safety policies specific to individuals with disabilities

» Maintain appropriate certifications such as first aid, Cardiopulmonary Resuscitation (CPR), and Crisis Prevention and Intervention that support safety of individuals and staff

» Complete appropriate incident forms as required by school policy

Consider student–teacher ratio

Understand that certain individuals with disabilities may need a small student–teacher ratio 9.02.05.01

» Utilize paraprofessionals and peer tutors for individuals who require greater attention to maintain appropriate behaviors, stay on task, or learn a skill

» Design activities that vary the assistance provided by the teacher such as the use of stations or reciprocal style teaching (see Standard 10)

» Train paraprofessionals and volunteers to assist individuals (see Standard 15)

Consider class size and composition

Understand the effect of class arrangement and formations when planning activities specific to individuals with disabilities 9.02.06.01

» Design for smaller group formations such as fewer individuals per station for individuals who are easily distracted and/or display difficulty staying on task

» Design a class formation for individuals who need preferential placement near the teacher such as individuals who are deaf or hard of hearing

» Utilize grouping strategies that create groups of individuals with and without disabilities

Plan for physical education classroom management, organization, and routines

Understand the importance of developing class management rules, routines, and transitions specific to individuals with disabilities (see Standard 10) 9.02.07.01

» Consider learner attributes when developing signals for getting the class's attention and starting and stopping the class

» Design consistent routines and **transitional procedures** that can be used by individuals as independently as possible

» Use peer tutors to assist in class management and activity transitions

Plan for appropriate use of environment, equipment, rules, materials, and activities

Understand how to adapt the environment, equipment, rules, materials, and activities specific to individuals with disabilities 9.02.08.01

» Use equipment that is developmentally appropriate and meets the needs of individuals with disabilities

» Modify the size and shape of the court/field to meet the needs of individuals with limited fitness levels

» Include adapted sport within the curriculum such as beep baseball or goal ball to address the needs individuals who are visually impaired or blind

Plan for modifications of environment

Understand the concepts and strategies necessary to modify the environment to meet the needs of individuals with disabilities such as adjustments to the play area 9.02.09.01

» Reduce the playing area for individuals who have limited mobility

» Use hard surfaces or play indoors for individuals using mobility devices and aids such as wheelchairs, gait trainers, walkers, or **Segways**

» Lower the basket or net to varying heights in games such as basketball or volleyball, for individuals with low stamina or deficient skill levels

» Use sound devices, bright equipment, and hand signals or flags for individuals with visual disabilities

» Mark goals and boundaries for individuals who need visual supports within game play

» Increase the size of the goal for individuals with an eye–hand coordination problems

» Provide visual cues on the wall to assist individuals with short-term memory or language barriers

Plan for modifications of equipment

Understand the concepts and strategies necessary to plan for the modifications of equipment specific to individuals with disabilities such as weight, size, color, and texture 9.02.10.01

» Use different size balls for individuals who have difficulty with motor coordination

» Use a contrasting background during physical activities such as when catching a ball outside (i.e., yellow ball against a blue sky)

» Use activities and equipment that are motivational such as activities that include music and activities using brightly colored balls

» Use equipment that will attract attention such as beep baseball or bell ball for individuals who are blind

» Decrease the speed of a moving object by using modified versions of the equipment, such as a sensory ball, adding or reducing the weight of the object, deflating the ball, or putting a tail on the object

» Shorten the length of the handle on a striking implement such as a racket, bat, or golf club

» Use large visual targets for individuals with visual impairments

» Use soft and/or lightweight equipment such as a sponge Frisbee or ball for individuals who have difficulty handling objects or are fearful of catching the moving object

» Make objects stationary such as using a batting tee for individuals who have difficulty striking a moving object

» Use Velcro mitts and balls for individuals who have difficulty catching

Plan for modifications of rules

Understand the concepts and strategies necessary to modify rules specific to individuals with disabilities 9.02.11.01

» Use rules from various adapted or disability sport associations and organizations such as Challenger Little League Baseball, National Wheelchair Basketball Association (e.g., use two pushes in wheelchair basketball)

» Play with a different number of players on the floor than the rules permit to make the game more achievable and equitable such as three players on a side for tennis or badminton

» Use modifications such as having individuals positioned closer to the net or serving from inside the court in games like volleyball or badminton

» Reduce the number of rules to simplify the game or activity

» Preserve the purpose of the game when modifying rules

Plan activities and games that meet the needs of individuals with disabilities

Understand the concepts and strategies necessary to design and implement activities and games specific to the needs of individuals with disabilities 9.02.12.01

» Avoid elimination games

» Consider a cooperative approach by using collective score among teams (i.e., combining points of the teams)

» Emphasize cooperation over winning among teammates as well as opponents

» Plan games and activities that stress participation for everyone

Plan for appropriate time spent in the lesson

Understand the importance of planning to maximize learning time for individuals with disabilities 9.02.13.01

» Maximize learning time by matching the difficulty of the task with the unique ability levels of individuals

» Plan lessons that address the need of individuals who require more time to complete tasks and need time for review

» Sequence lesson plan activities according to unique needs of individuals

» Modify the lesson plan format and progression of activities according to unique needs of individuals such as providing frequent rest periods for individuals with low physical vitality

Understand the importance of planning for optimal instruction time with individuals with disabilities 9.02.13.02

» Teach individuals using effective and multiple modes of communication to ensure comprehension

» Provide short and simple instructional sets for individuals with cognitive disabilities

» Use cue words or commands to elicit the desired response or behavior

Understand the importance of planning to reduce **transition time** for individuals with disabilities 9.02.13.03

» Arrange the environment to allow for smooth and short transitions when working with individuals who have limited attention spans or who have difficulty traveling from one location to another

» Allow adequate time for individuals to change in and out of physical education clothes and provide assistance with dressing out to individuals such as those with orthopedic disabilities and/or multiple disabilities

Determine individual progression through a **formative evaluation** plan

Understand the importance of evaluating the progress of individuals with disabilities (see Standards 4 and 8) 9.02.14.01

» Chart progress of the individual's curricular goals on the IEP and/or transition plan

» Chart progress of the family goals on the IFSP

» Evaluate individuals using individualized evaluation standards that determine the mastery of a skill or activity such as using a task analysis

» Evaluate individual program progression supported instruction toward independent completion of the activity

Understand the importance of selecting realistic lesson plan goals and objectives that can be successfully attained by individuals with disabilities 9.02.14.02

» Include individuals as part of the process of planning goals and objectives

» When appropriate, include individuals in recording and monitoring progress

» Select functional skills for instruction and evaluation that match the needs and interests of the individuals

Understand the importance of evaluating the functional aspects of performance for individuals with disabilities 9.02.14.03

» Evaluate performance authentically in the environments in which individuals will perform the skill

» Evaluate performance based on criteria determined as necessary for successful participation in the community such as being able to bowl at a bowling center

Plan for paraprofessionals, volunteers, and peer tutors

Understand the importance of planning for paraprofessionals, volunteers, or peer tutors to assist with teaching individuals with disabilities 9.02.15.01

» Establish a system for recruiting, training, and communicating with paraprofessionals and volunteers/peer tutors such as providing training on how to monitor behaviors with a checklist or a rubric

» Establish a system for providing feedback to paraprofessionals and volunteers/peer tutors such as feedback about how to modify a skill for an individual using a wheelchair

IEP AND IFSP: Understand federal mandates involved in planning programs of physical education for individuals with disabilities

Know the IEP process

Understand present level of performance as it relates to individuals, 3 to 21 years old, with disabilities relative to the development of physical fitness, fundamental motor skills, games, sport, aquatics, dance, and leisure skills 9.03.01.01

» Write present level of performance statement based on assessment information from norm-referenced test scores, criterion-referenced test scores, and/or informal test methods (see Standard 4)

» Write present level of performance statement based on how the individual is progressing in relation to the physical education curriculum

Understand how to develop annual goals based on assessment data and the specific needs of individuals with disabilities 9.03.01.02

» Write annual goals based on assessment and present level of performance information

» Write goals that are specific, observable, measurable, achievable, relevant, and time-bound

Understand that short-term instructional objectives in physical education lead toward performance mastery 9.03.01.03

» Write instructional objectives in behavioral terms based on present level of performance

» Match objectives to previously established annual goals, when appropriate

Understand that a continuum of least restrictive environments in physical education must be made available to individuals with disabilities requiring special education services 9.03.01.04

» Work with members of the IEP team to place the individual with disabilities in the least restrictive physical education environment for service provision

» Work with other physical education service delivery providers to meet the needs of individuals with disabilities in the least restrictive environment

Understand that related services, such as physical and occupational therapy, must be made available to an individual with a disability if they are needed to benefit from special education 9.03.01.05

» Collaborate with related service providers in meeting an individual's established goals and objectives

» Coordinate the scheduling of physical education instruction relative to related services to maximize the benefits to the individual, such as scheduling physical therapy prior to physical education

Understand how to project dates for the initiation and duration of physical education services 9.03.01.06

» Coordinate the initiation and duration of the individual's physical education program with all service providers

» Implement a physical education program for the appropriate duration to meet needs of the individual

» Monitor program progress for the duration of the established physical education program or until goals/objectives are met

Understand the physical education transition from school to community 9.03.01.07

» Implement a transition plan to teach the skills needed to access community-based services within the existing physical education structure

» Collaborate with the support services and other service providers in implementing the transition plan

» Write age- and ability-appropriate transition goals and objectives according to the individual's ability and interest

Know the IFSP process as it applies to infants and toddlers

Understand the individual's present level of performance by identifying the family's knowledge of their child's motor skills through various data collection methods including formal assessment, verbal communication, and observation 9.03.02.01

» Record the information collected from the family concerning their young child's motor skills and development

» Write present level of performance based on information gathered from assessment, verbal communication, and observations

Understand the motor outcomes expected to be achieved by the young child and family by developing a sequential instructional plan of motor skill activities that includes realistic goals and objectives for the family to implement with their child 9.03.02.02

» Write realistic annual goals for the young child that include the needs of the family

» Write objectives that reflect the present level of performance

» Write a motor program that the family can implement that matches the stated goals and objectives

Understand how to determine family timelines to meet motor outcome progress 9.03.02.03

» Write timelines related to the mastery of a young child's stated physical education goals and objectives

» Write timelines that are monitored by the family and the physical educator

Understand how to plan for services to meet the young child's motor needs 9.03.02.04

» Monitor various services for the family needed to meet the established goals and objectives including community-based services, educational supports, and other private and public services

» Collaborate with various early intervention service providers supporting the motor development needs of the young child so that cooperation occurs and services are not duplicated

» Solicit feedback from the family regarding the individual's progress in motor development and performance

Understand how to establish dates for the implementation and evaluation of an IFSP 9.03.02.05

» Write dates for the implementation of the program, including gathering or purchasing of equipment, amount of time involved in teaching, and time to locate and schedule adequate space

» Coordinate the young child's motor program with the family and early intervention service providers

» Monitor motor development skill sequence and acquisition timeline

» Monitor program progress and service providers' ability to implement the child's established motor program for the duration of the needed service

Understand how to plan for transition from early intervention to school 9.03.02.06

» Determine the similarities and differences between the early intervention environment and that of the educational setting

>> Determine the similarities and differences between the individual's motor needs in the home in contrast to those same needs in school

>> Collaborate with the support services and other service providers in implementing transition programming

TECHNOLOGY APPLICATIONS: Demonstrate knowledge of communication systems sanctioned by the American Speech-Language-Hearing Association

Understand that verbal communication is a medium of oral communication that involves the use of linguistic code (language)

Understand the importance of using oral communication in physical education class with individuals with language disabilities 9.04.01.01

>> Rephrase thoughts or ideas during communication

>> Use appropriate vocabulary

>> Recognize when an individual with disabilities is tacting and manding within the physical education setting

Understand that receptive and expressive language, which can be communicated through verbal speech, impacts learning and performance in the physical education environment

Understand the difference between receptive and expressive language and how to support individuals with language disorders in the physical education environment 9.04.01.02

>> Rephrase thoughts or ideas during communication for individuals with disabilities who have deficits in receptive language

>> Use appropriate vocabulary to meet the needs of individuals with language disorders

>> Support tacting and manding within the physical education environment for individuals with expressive language disorders

Understand that augmentative and alternative communication includes all forms of communication (other than oral speech) that supplement or replace speech or writing for individuals with impairments in the production or comprehension of language

Understand how unaided communication systems support individuals with speech and language disorders such as those who are deaf or hard of hearing 9.04.02.01

>> Collaborate with other professionals, especially the speech-language pathologist, to determine the most appropriate unaided communication system such as sign language to use in a physical education environment

>> Demonstrate proficiency in unaided communication using sign language or gestures in physical education environments

Understand how aided communication systems serve to communicate for individuals with speech and language impairments 9.04.02.02

» Collaborate with other professionals to determine the most appropriate aided communication system to augment communication in a physical education environment

» Demonstrate a proficiency in communicating in physical education using speech generating devices such as a **Touch Talker**, Go Talk, or **Canon Communicator**; and/or **communication boards**, books, or handheld or notebook computers

ASSISTIVE DEVICES: Knowledge of adaptation of assistive devices to enhance participation in physical education

Understand how physical positioning can facilitate movement in physical education

Identify types of equipment used to position individuals with disabilities 9.05.01.01

» Use bolsters, wedges, and/or lying wedges for positioning to facilitate movement

» Use strapping to maintain appropriate body alignment

» Use a standing frame for positioning to facilitate movement

Understand how modified seating can enhance movement for individuals with disabilities 9.05.01.02

» Use adaptations to the wheelchair such as removal of armrests to facilitate movement

» Use alternative seating such as on a bench, beanbag, or the floor to enhance movement

Understand how canes enhance mobility in physical education

Know types of canes used by individuals with orthopedic impairments 9.05.02.01

» Collaborate with other professionals to determine what type of cane would be the most appropriate to use in the physical education environment

» Incorporate use of a quad cane, tripod cane, and/or cane tips to enhance mobility

Understand how crutches enhance mobility in physical education

Identify types of crutches that are most often used by individuals with disabilities such as amputees, long leg brace users, and individuals with a temporary disability 9.05.03.01

» Collaborate with other professionals to determine which type of crutches would be the most appropriate to use in a physical education environment

» Incorporate the use of the Lofstrand crutch or forearm support crutch, platform crutch, and/or underarm crutch to enhance mobility

Understand how walkers and gait trainers can provide greater independence during physical education activities

Know different types of walkers and gait trainers that are often used by individuals with orthopedic impairments 9.05.04.01

» Collaborate with other professionals to determine which walker or gait trainer would be best to use in the physical education environment

» Incorporate use of a gait trainer, pick-up walker, rolling walker, forearm support walker, and/or the Kaye posture control walker during physical education activities

Understand that an **orthosis** is a positioning device for support or immobilization, and is used to prevent or correct a deformity, or to assist or restore function

Know the types of orthotic devices for individuals with lower extremity disabilities 9.05.05.01

» Collaborate with other professionals to determine which type of orthotic devices would be appropriate to use in the physical education environment for an individual with a lower extremity disability

» Incorporate the use of ankle-foot orthoses, hip-knee-ankle-foot orthoses, knee-ankle-foot orthoses, and reciprocating gait orthoses during physical education activities

Know the types of orthotic devices for individuals with upper extremity disabilities 9.05.05.02

» Explain the use of different types of orthotic devices for individuals with upper extremity disabilities

» Incorporate the use of wrist and hand orthoses or hand splints during physical education activities

Understand that a **prosthesis** is a substitute for a missing extremity

Know prosthetic devices for lower extremity amputees 9.05.06.01

» Be familiar with the strengths and limitations of a variety of prosthetic devices

» Know prosthetic devices that can be used by individuals with a lower extremity amputation and their strengths and limitations

» Incorporate the use of foot prostheses such as the Seattle Foot and lower limb prostheses during physical education activities

» Know the appropriate care of a prosthetic, such as how an individual's prosthetic device articulates with their stump

Know prosthetic devices for upper extremity amputees 9.05.06.02

» Be familiar with the strengths and limitations of a variety of prosthetic devices that can be used by individuals with an upper extremity amputation

» Incorporate the use of a **myoelectric arm** and/or upper extremity prosthesis during physical education activities

» Know the appropriate care of a prosthetic device, such as how an individual's prosthetic device articulates with their stump

Understand adaptations of equipment used for sport and recreational activities

Understand specific adaptations of equipment for individuals with visual impairments 9.05.07.01

» Collaborate with other professionals, including the orientation and mobility specialist, to determine which specific equipment adaptations would be appropriate in the physical education environment for an individual with a visual impairment

» Use beepers to help locate a target

» Use handrails to adjust body posture

» Use beeper or bell balls in throwing, rolling, or catching activities

Understand specific adaptations of equipment for individuals with orthopedic impairments 9.05.07.02

» Enlarge the handle of striking implements for improved grip

» Use strapping such as Velcro to attach striking implements to the arms of amputees or individuals who cannot grasp the implement

» Use Velcro gloves or mitts for individuals with upper extremity impairments to make catching easier

» Use modified skis, such as sit skis, to enable individuals with lower extremity involvement in skiing

» Modify a walker by adding skis to enable individuals with orthopedic impairments to stand while skiing

MOBILITY DEVICES: Knowledge of various mobility aids to enhance participation in physical education

Understand that wheelchairs either provide or enhance mobility for individuals with orthopedic impairments

Understand types of manual wheelchairs such as medical model, lightweight or sport, and racing or track wheelchairs used by individuals with disabilities 9.06.01.01

» Incorporate the use of lightweight stainless-steel manual wheelchairs

» Incorporate tilt-in-space wheelchairs designed for individuals with severe physical disabilities

» Incorporate lightweight or sport wheelchairs

» Incorporate track wheelchairs for racing activities

Understand components of manual wheelchairs 9.06.01.02

» Demonstrate ability to lock brakes and adjust armrests and footrests on a wheelchair to facilitate participation in physical activity

» Suggest modifications to casters, wheels, hand rims, chair backs, and seats to facilitate participation in physical activity

Understand components of power or motorized wheelchairs used by individuals with disabilities 9.06.01.03

» Accommodate the use of standard upright power wheelchairs to facilitate participation in physical education activities

» Demonstrate knowledge of control box mechanism needed to facilitate participation in physical education activities

» Explain procedure to engage and disengage motors

Understand that scooters are a means for increasing mobility and enhancing participation in physical education

Know a variety of scooter boards for use with individuals with disabilities 9.06.02.01

» Collaborate with other professionals to determine the appropriate scooter board to use in the physical education environment for an individual with orthopedic impairments

» Incorporate use of regular and long scooter boards and/or modified pediatric scooters, such as a Jettmobile or Scooot, to facilitate participation in physical education activities

Understand that bicycles and tricycles increase mobility in physical education

Know various bicycles and tricycles used by individuals with orthopedic impairments 9.06.03.01

» Collaborate with other professionals to determine the most appropriate bicycle or tricycle with possible modifications for an individual with an orthopedic impairment

» Attach a unicycle to the front of the wheelchair to convert the wheelchair into a tricycle

» Incorporate the use of hand crank cycle and/or standard adult tricycle to facilitate participation in physical education activities

Know adaptations made to cycles to accommodate individuals with orthopedic impairments 9.06.03.02

» Collaborate with other professionals to determine the appropriate adaptations for a cycle for an individual with an orthopedic impairment

» Incorporate the use of foot sandals, hip and chest straps, and/or back and neck supports to facilitate participation in physical education activities

Understand how the use of mobility aids enhances participation in physical education activities for individuals who are visually impaired

Know types of mobility aids for individuals with visual impairments 9.06.04.01

» Collaborate with other professionals to determine the appropriate mobility aids for an individual with a visual impairment participating in a physical education environment

» Incorporate cane walking, sighted guide techniques, partner assists, and/or guide wire or rope to enhance participation in physical education activities

TEACHING

STANDARD 10

TEACHING

> **TEACHING STYLES:** Demonstrate various teaching styles in order to promote learning in physical education

Understand the **command style of teaching**

Understand the effectiveness of using the command style of teaching with individuals with disabilities in order to promote learning in physical education 10.01.01.01

>> Provide clear, concise, and simple language when needed

>> Use specific, clear, concise verbal cues to highlight points

>> Use total communication as needed

>> Use visual cues to demonstrate skill such as using a colored sock to show kicking foot

Understand the effectiveness of demonstrating an activity using a command-style approach for individuals with disabilities 10.01.01.02

>> Secure individuals' attention through a command or other communication means before demonstrating

>> Perform demonstrations in an environment that minimizes distractions for individuals who have short attention spans or who are easily distracted

>> Perform demonstrations with verbal cues to maximize sensory information input

>> Perform demonstrations in a position that allows the individual to best receive information such as individuals who are deaf or hard of hearing

Understand the effectiveness of class organization and control using the command style of teaching 10.01.01.03

>> Organize the class so that individuals with disabilities such as autism spectrum disorder or intellectual disabilities perform skills under structured class rules and conditions

>> Structure the class to allow the completion of assigned skills on command

>> Establish a physical activity environment that remains the same in terms of format, procedures, and routines for individuals with disabilities, such as autism spectrum disorder, intellectual disabilities, and blindness

>> Teach class so that individuals practice the activity together under the direct supervision of the general physical educator

Understand the **reciprocal style of teaching**

Understand the effectiveness of using the reciprocal style of teaching with individuals with disabilities in order to promote learning in physical education 10.01.02.01

》 Guide peers to be peer tutors or partners to teach individuals with disabilities

》 Design activities that allow individuals to work together in pairs

》 Design activities so peer tutors can see progress

Understand the importance of training peer tutors to effectively participate in a reciprocal teaching environment with individuals with disabilities in order to promote learning 10.01.02.02

》 Train peer tutors to provide a continuum of prompts from minimum to maximum

》 Train peer tutors to communicate effectively

》 Train peer tutors to provide appropriate and specific feedback

》 Train peer tutors to use their initiative and provide alternative progressions and skill techniques when their partner is not experiencing success with the activity being attempted

Understand what qualities to look for when selecting and assigning peer tutors to work with individuals with disabilities 10.01.02.03

》 Identify peer tutors with a tolerant positive nature and mature disposition

》 Identify peer tutors with good communication skills, preferably in more than one mode of communication, such as ability to use communication boards or an additional language such as sign language, Spanish, etc.

》 Identify peer tutors with ability to model skills correctly

Understand the **task teaching style**

Understand the effectiveness of using the task teaching style with individuals with disabilities in order to promote learning in physical education 10.01.03.01

》 Design activities and instructions to the ability level of the individual such as using picture activity cards to depict the desired skill to be performed

》 Use a variety of equipment, modified if necessary, in each activity to ensure successful completion of each assigned task

》 Select tasks that can be safely performed individually or with a partner

》 Identify and develop goals and objectives for each skill or activity that will allow for the achievement of individual levels of success at the same task

Understand how to organize a class environment to promote a task teaching style method for individuals with disabilities 10.01.03.02

》 Design the class activities in a **circuit type or station arrangement**

》 Arrange the class so that individuals can move quickly and safely from one task to the next

》 Arrange the class so that individuals can perform tasks independently and safely

» Design tasks with multiple successful outcomes to allow individuals to develop coping and adapting strategies

Understand how to effectively analyze progress and provide feedback to individuals with disabilities using a task teaching style method 10.01.03.03

» Identify goals and objectives specific to the needs of the individual

» Use self-recording to allow individuals to monitor their own progress and assess their own gains

Understand the individualized style of teaching

Understand the effectiveness of using the individualized style of teaching with individuals with disabilities in order to promote learning in physical education 10.01.04.01

» Design physical activities based on the specific needs of the individual

» Create an individualized education program based on the specific needs of the individual

» Use individualized charts and reports to determine the progress of the individual

» Create activity opportunities with variable levels of success (e.g., using stations) to enable all individuals to achieve some measure of success in the same activity

» Provide instruction and feedback in the individual's primary mode of communication

Understand how to assess individuals with disabilities to determine their present level of performance and develop goals for the IEP 10.01.04.02

» Select appropriate assessment instruments specific to the individual (see Standards 4 and 8)

» Develop instruments based on the task analysis

» Determine the level of independence for each individual based on assessment information

» Develop goals for the IEP based on the individual's present level of performance

Understand how to provide effective feedback using an individualized style of teaching 10.01.04.03

» Provide personal recording methods such as self-recording progress cards and charts

» Design tasks and activities that provide individualized feedback of results and information on the successful completion of the task such as lights and buzzers that sound when the ball has gone through the hoop

Understand the **guided discovery style of teaching**

Understand the effectiveness of using the guided discovery style of teaching with individuals with disabilities in order to promote learning in physical education 10.01.05.01

» Develop problem-solving techniques involving challenging questions and tasks to promote adaptation and coping strategies

» Develop problem-solving techniques based on naturally occurring obstacles and challenges that occur in the everyday environment

» Guide the individual, when appropriate, to efficient task completion

» Develop a hierarchy of problem solving from single to multiple tasks

Understand the **divergent or exploratory style of teaching**

Understand the effectiveness of using the divergent or exploratory style of teaching with individuals with disabilities in order to promote learning in physical education 10.01.06.01

» Select tasks for instruction that have multiple methods of successful completion

» Use praise and specific feedback to foster alternative methods of completing the skill or task

» Use the concept of generalization to challenge individuals to complete a specific task under different environmental conditions and circumstances

» Encourage and praise effort and creativity in addition to task completion

Understand how to present tasks using a divergent or exploratory style of teaching that is appropriate for the individual with disabilities 10.01.06.02

» Identify tasks and skills that are developmentally as well as age appropriate

» Use group activities to promote **cooperative learning** and development

Understand how to effectively use feedback and praise when using a divergent or exploratory style of teaching for individuals with disabilities 10.01.06.03

» Use corrective feedback, which provides information that indicates the correct way to perform the task

» Use comments that promote alternative variations to complete the task to foster independent coping and adapting strategies

Understand the cooperative learning style of teaching

Understand the effectiveness of using the cooperative learning style of teaching with individuals with disabilities in order to promote learning in physical education 10.01.07.01

» Use group activities to foster learning of **social values** and **interaction skills**

>> Use noncompetitive tasks and environments to promote cooperation and interaction among individuals with disabilities and individuals without disabilities in a nonthreatening environment

>> Use group activities that include individuals with disabilities to challenge current concepts on how some tasks should be performed and to promote variations that allow everyone to successfully complete the task

>> Provide culminating activities that reinforce cooperation

TEACHING BEHAVIORS: Understand the various teaching behaviors needed to promote learning

---

Understand various instructional cues such as **verbal directions**, demonstrations, and **physical guidance**

Understand the importance of using various instructional cues to prompt certain individuals with disabilities to complete tasks 10.02.01.01

>> Implement instructional and environmental cues based on the needs of individuals from least to most intrusive

>> Implement instructional and environmental cues based on the unique needs of individuals such as having an individual with intellectual disability step on a poly spot shaped like a foot in order to cue him or her to step with opposition while throwing

>> Avoid unknowingly eliciting abnormal **reflexes** when providing physical guidance

>> Use other types of instructional cues if one is not effective in communicating to the individual's unique needs or disability such as Braille for an individual who is blind

>> Use peers to demonstrate instructional cues

>> Avoid over cueing or over demonstrating in the selected modality for an individual with a disability such as an individual with attention-deficit/hyperactivity disorder

>> Transition individual reliance on instructional cues to independent completion of the task

---

Understand the process of task analysis

Understand the use of task analysis procedures to promote skill learning in individuals with disabilities 10.02.02.01

>> Break skills down along a hierarchy in order to meet the unique needs of the individual

>> Provide the prerequisite and **ancillary skills** needed to complete the skill targeted for instruction

>> Develop an ecological task analysis that includes the unique needs of the learner and the environment such as teaching the skill in various settings (i.e., school and community)

» Assess skill development and progress using a skill- or individual-specific task analysis assessment instrument (qualitative) that also accounts for level of independence or dependence during evaluation and teaching (see Standard 8)

Understand the concept of **time on task**

Understand the importance of providing maximal time on task in each lesson to maximize learning for individuals with disabilities in physical education 10.02.03.01

» Plan lessons allowing the individual to receive as many opportunities to perform the task as possible

» Organize the teaching environment so that transition time between task responses and activities is kept to a minimum

» Use behavior management techniques such as positive reinforcement or incentives for task initiation or completion

» Use teaching environment strategies such as removing other items or activities that may distract the individual in order to sustain performance during time on task

» Keep instructional information concise by focusing on key words and phrases

Understand qualitative skill teaching

Understand the importance of teaching qualitative aspects of skills and activities to individuals with disabilities 10.02.04.01

» Teach the correct form necessary to perform the skill

» Promote qualitative aspects of skills that facilitate normalization and are socially inconspicuous such as pedaling an exercise bicycle

» Promote generalization such as how to correctly and safely use a stair climber exercise machine at the local gymnasium or health club

» Use modified equipment to enable individuals to complete the task in as close to a typical manner as possible or on a functional skill level

Understand **quantitative skill teaching**

Understand the importance of using quantitative aspects of skills to teach individuals with disabilities in physical education 10.02.05.01

» Emphasize the product outcome of a skill such as scoring a basket in basketball

» Use group cooperation activities in **integrated settings** to promote task completion

» Emphasize outcome aspects of skill instruction that allow the individual to successfully participate in a socially inclusive environment such as hitting a tennis ball back over the net and into the court in a game of tennis

» Use adapted equipment such as using a bowling ramp to bowl that allows the individual to participate successfully in a socially inclusive environment

Understand teacher pacing of lesson

Understand the importance of pacing activities to meet the unique needs of the individual with a disability 10.02.06.01

>> Time activities to maintain interest

>> Plan activities of short duration in a lesson for individuals with a short attention span

>> Plan frequent rest breaks in a lesson for individuals such as those with low fitness levels or obesity

>> Establish a lesson activity sequence that alternates high- and low-intensity activities to foster fitness improvement

Understand how to communicate learner expectations and content

Understand the importance of using various means of communication to provide teacher expectations to individuals with disabilities such as the latest communication technology (see Standard 9) 10.02.07.01

>> Communicate with individuals in their primary learning modality (e.g., total communication with individuals who are deaf)

>> Keep communication simple for those individuals who are limited in cognition (e.g., posting pictures of class rules for those who cannot read)

>> Allow individuals to record their own results so they can monitor their progress toward the established goals

>> Allow individuals with disabilities to be part of program planning and where applicable have them sign the program plan

Understand the type of social climate that promotes interaction

Understand how to use peer tutors to promote social interaction and social values with individuals with disabilities 10.02.08.01

>> Select peer tutors with appropriate communication skills, social skills, and maturity level

>> Select peer tutors from the community who demonstrate skills needed by individuals with disabilities

>> Train peer tutors to communicate and interact with individuals with disabilities

>> Provide partner and group activities that foster appropriate interactions for individuals with and without disabilities

>> Play **cooperative games** that foster social interaction and trust for individuals with and without disabilities (see Standard 9)

Understand knowledge of feedback, knowledge of performance, and knowledge of results

Understand the importance of providing positive, specific, and immediate feedback to individuals with disabilities 10.02.09.01

» Provide feedback that is easily understood such as using short action word statements for individuals with intellectual disabilities

» Design activities that provide knowledge of performance through auditory and visual feedback

» Provide immediate feedback to establish a response–consequence relationship between the feedback and the performed behavior

» Provide the majority of feedback in a positive way

Understand how to determine progress and make changes to fit individual needs

Understand the importance of monitoring progress specific to individuals with disabilities 10.02.10.01

» Use appropriate assessment that is relevant to the specific individual and his or her disability (see Standard 8)

» Conduct informal and formal assessment of the progress of the individual on a regular basis

» Use multiple instruments and assessment methods and criteria to determine progress

Understand how to make changes in teaching to meet the needs of individuals with disabilities based on assessment data 10.02.10.02

» Reevaluate goals and objectives (program, student, teacher) on a regular basis

» Develop task analysis checklists with sequential steps that are appropriate to the needs and developmental level of individuals

» Use task analysis breakdowns to determine intermediate steps for skills that have not been attained at the end of the teaching period

» Use adapted equipment and/or alternative teaching techniques to make immediate changes during the lesson when an individual continually fails to complete a task or activity with existing teaching methods

Universal Design for Learning: Understand the principles of Universal Design for Learning

Understand that learners differ in the ways that they perceive and comprehend information that is presented to them 10.03.01.01

» Provide information through a number of different modalities such as vision, hearing, touch, or **kinesthesis**

» Provide information in a format that allows the individual to adjust to meet his or her needs such as large print, volume or rate of speech or sound, contrast between background and text, color used for information, or speed or timing of video

» Anchor instruction by linking to and activating relevant prior knowledge

» Use multiple examples and nonexamples to emphasize critical features

» Use cues and prompts to draw attention to critical features

» Highlight previously learned skills that can be used to solve unfamiliar problems

Understand that learners differ in the ways that they can navigate a learning environment and express what they know 10.03.01.02

» Provide alternatives in the requirements for rate, timing, speed, and range of motor action required to interact with instructional materials, physical **manipulatives**, and technologies

» Use social media and interactive web tools such as discussion boards, chats, web design, or animation presentations

» Provide text to speech software, human dictation, or recording

» Provide differential feedback

» Show representation of progress such as charts showing progress over time, portfolios, before and after photos

Understand that learners differ in the ways in which they can be engaged in the learning process and motivated to learn 10.03.01.03

» Provide individuals with as much discretion and autonomy as possible by providing choices in such areas as level of perceived challenge, type of reward available, or technique used to assess skills

» Involve individuals in setting their own personal performance goals

» Provide tasks that allow for active participation, exploration, and experimentation

» Develop an accepting and supportive classroom climate

» Involve all participants

» Emphasize process, effort, and improvement in meeting standards as alternatives to external evaluation and competition

» Develop cooperative learning groups with clear goals, roles, and responsibilities

» Use rubrics to develop expectations for projects

APPLIED BEHAVIOR ANALYSIS PRINCIPLES: Understand the principles of applied behavior analysis to promote learning

Understand how to select and define specific behaviors to be changed or maintained

Understand that individuals with disabilities may exhibit more severe and unique behaviors (see Standard 6) 10.04.01.01

» Identify self-injurious behaviors that may be exhibited by individuals with autism, depression, serious emotional behaviors, and other disabilities

» Identify aggressive behaviors that may be harmful to others

Understand how to observe, record, chart, and analyze the behavior to be changed

Understand how to systematically observe, record, chart, and analyze the unique behaviors exhibited by individuals with disabilities 10.04.02.01

》 Use members of the multidisciplinary team to assist with observing, recording, charting, and analyzing the behaviors

》 Analyze individual information from a variety of formal and informal settings

》 Use frequency, duration, and intensity recording procedures when needed (see Standard 4)

》 Use continuous interval recording or time sampling procedures when needed (see Standard 4)

Understand a variety of strategies for changing behaviors

Understand that individuals with disabilities may require the application of a number of unique behavior change strategies and programs 10.04.03.01

》 Implement a continuum of behavior change strategies depending on the needs of the individual from prevention to **punishment**

》 Implement consistent behavior change strategies with other team members and when possible across various settings such as the classroom, physical education setting, and home

》 Implement a variety of behavior change strategies as appropriate

Understand how to evaluate the behavior change plan

Understand the importance of evaluating the behavior intervention plan in individuals with disabilities in order to meet the unique needs necessary to change behavior 10.04.04.01

》 Include behavior intervention plan information with the individual's IEP, teaching units, lesson plans, and other progress reports

》 Communicate behavior change plan results with other team members who work with the individual

PREVENTATIVE STRATEGIES: Understand preventative management strategies in order to promote learning

Understand how to use signals for getting the class's attention and for starting and stopping the class

Understand the use of specific signals to get the attention of individuals with disabilities 10.05.01.01

》 Use sound signals (i.e., tambourine, whistle) for individuals with disabilities such as those who are blind

» Use visual and tactile signals for individuals with disabilities such as those who are deaf

Understand how to use routines and transitional procedures from one activity to the next

Understand the routines and transitional procedures that can be used with individuals with disabilities 10.05.02.01

» Communicate class routines in a meaningful way such as posting schedules or using flip charts

» Communicate clear, concise transitional procedures such as rotating clockwise from one activity to the next

Understand how to organize the class into groups and formations based on the nature of the activity

Understand that certain individuals with disabilities may need a smaller student–teacher ratio (e.g., distribution of students) 10.05.03.01

» Use paraprofessionals and peer tutors for individuals who require more attention

» Use stations or a reciprocal teaching style

» Use small group formations (e.g., only one or two individuals at a station)

Understand how to deal with interruptions while teaching

Understand that certain individuals with disabilities such as those with attention span deficits may seek constant attention and interrupt the class 10.05.04.01

» Identify cause(s) of interruption(s) that may be specific to an individual

» Implement specific plans and strategies such as **proximity control**, **extinction**, or **time-out** procedures

Understand how to teach individual goal-setting strategies

Understand the importance of setting realistic goals based on the limitations, needs, and strengths of individuals with disabilities 10.05.05.01

» Use goal setting to motivate individuals to participate in various adapted physical education environments

» Implement realistic, sequential steps to achieve goals

Understand how to teach self-management

Understand the importance of self-management at a developmentally appropriate level for individuals with disabilities 10.05.06.01

» Identify the most appropriate self-management techniques for the developmental level of the individual

» Teach individuals to use self-management techniques

INCREASING BEHAVIORS: Knowledge of positive teaching methods for maintaining and increasing individual behavior in order to promote learning

Understand modeling as a teaching method

Understand the importance of the teacher and individuals without disabilities modeling appropriate behavior to individuals with disabilities 10.06.01.01

>> Model appropriate behavior

>> Use peer tutor models to demonstrate appropriate behavior

Understand prompting as a teaching method

Understand the use of prompts such as verbal, demonstration, and physical guidance and the hierarchy of prompts from less intrusive to more intrusive based on the individual's disability 10.06.02.01

>> Select prompts based on individual needs (e.g., physical prompts for individuals who are blind)

>> Use more intrusive prompts as needed

>> Avoid physical guidance for individuals with tactile sensitivity

>> Fade prompts while maintaining performance

Understand **shaping** as a teaching method

Understand how to use shaping strategies such as task analysis and successive approximation with individuals with disabilities 10.06.03.01

>> Teach and reinforce only those parts of the skill that are necessary

>> Use qualitative and quantitative aspects in developing a shaping plan

Understand chaining as a teaching method

Understand when to use forward chaining, backward chaining, and total task presentation depending on the individual's disability 10.06.04.01

>> Use total task presentation prior to forward or backward chaining

>> Implement different forms of progressive forward and backward chaining of skills depending on the needs of the individual

>> Use backward chaining when needed

Understand social reinforcement as a teaching method

Understand how to use various nonverbal and verbal social reinforcement strategies based on the individual's disability 10.06.05.01

>> Identify a variety of **social reinforcers** that may appeal to individuals, such as age-appropriate social reinforcers (e.g., smile, high five, shaking hands)

» Use verbal reinforcement at a level the individual can comprehend such as using action words or simple two-word statements

» Use **mercury switches** to activate reinforcers

Understand **tangible reinforcement** as a teaching method

Understand the use of tangible reinforcers with individuals with disabilities 10.06.06.01

» Select reinforcers that are highly reinforcing for each individual

» Provide age-appropriate tangible reinforcers

» Monitor progress when using tangible reinforcers

» Continue social reinforcement and fade tangible reinforcers as appropriate

Understand **physical activity reinforcement** as a teaching method

Understand the use of physical activity reinforcers with individuals with disabilities 10.06.07.01

» Use physical activity reinforcers to assist individuals to make progress toward IEP goals and objectives

» Use physical activity reinforcers to develop leisure and recreational choices for community involvement

Understand reinforcement menus, **token economies**, and point systems as teaching methods

Understand the use of reinforcement menus, token economies, and **contingency** point systems with individuals with disabilities 10.06.08.01

» Match system (e.g., token economy) to the individual's comprehension level

» Use age-appropriate items on reinforcement menus

» Identify individual reinforcers that are highly reinforcing

» Monitor progress when using these techniques

» Fade reinforcement techniques while maintaining progress

Understand written contracts as a teaching method

Understand the value of written contracts when developing accountability in individuals with disabilities 10.06.09.01

» Use written contracts modified to the comprehension level of the individual

» Include essential components of a written contract such as the target behavior and consequences

Understand group and individual contingencies as teaching methods

Understand value of group and individual contingencies in changing behaviors in individuals with disabilities 10.06.10.01

» Use group contingencies when peer pressure is effective in changing behavior such as with individuals with a behavior disorder

» Provide contingencies that are achievable for the lowest functioning individual within a group

» Develop different individual contingencies for those individuals who cannot conform to the **group contingency**

Understand **reinforcement schedules** as a teaching method

Understand reinforcement schedules and their progression to use with individuals with disabilities 10.06.11.01

» Provide **continuous reinforcement** to those individuals learning a skill for the first time

» Provide reinforcement schedules such as ratio and **interval reinforcement** to assist individuals who are learning to maintain or generalize a behavior over time

» Implement a ratio schedule of reinforcement by reinforcing the specified frequency of responses

» Implement an interval schedule of reinforcement by reinforcing the specified duration of the performance of behavior

Understand **differential reinforcements** (DR) as a teaching method

Understand that DR is a method of manipulating the reinforcement schedule and may be used to increase or decrease the rate at which an individual with a disability exhibits a behavior 10.06.12.01

» Identify DR as a viable strategy to increase appropriate behavior and decrease inappropriate behavior

» Use DR for omission of an inappropriate behavior for a specified period of time (zero times in 10 minutes)

» Use DR for maintaining a low rate of behavior for a specified period of time (less than two times in 15 minutes)

» Use DR to reinforce incompatible behaviors

» Use DR to reinforce alternative behaviors

DECREASING BEHAVIORS: Use different methods, along a continuum from less to more intrusive, only after positive methods have been ineffective

Understand extinction as a teaching method

Understand the importance of using extinction for individuals with disabilities 10.07.01.01

» Ignore mild forms of inappropriate behavior with individuals who are constantly seeking attention while reinforcing alternative forms of appropriate behaviors

» Avoid using extinction with severe behaviors such as self-abuse

» Recognize that extinction is effective when attention is acting as the reinforcer

Understand **response cost** as a teaching method

Understand response cost is a technique that removes reinforcement to decrease a behavior and may be effectively used with individuals with disabilities 10.07.02.01

» Withdraw earned reinforcers contingent on the occurrence of the inappropriate behavior

» Use response cost as an alternative to physically or psychologically **aversive** strategies

» Use reinforcement of an appropriate behavior in conjunction with response cost to deter an inappropriate behavior

» Use response cost effectively with both individuals and groups

Understand **overcorrection** as a teaching method

Understand the value of overcorrection in teaching appropriate behavior while eliminating inappropriate behavior in individuals with disabilities 10.07.03.01

» Use **restitutional overcorrection** such as cleaning gymnasium walls by allowing the individual to experience the effort required by others to restore the damaged environment

» Use **positive practice overcorrection** by allowing the individual or group to practice the correct behavior numerous times

Understand time-out procedures as a teaching method

Understand that different time-out procedures are effective for individuals with disabilities such as observation, seclusion, and isolation 10.07.04.01

» Identify legal aspects involved with time-out procedures

» Administer the proper steps for using time-out procedures

» Use observational time-out by having the individual placed in time-out and allowed to continue to observe the activity

» Use seclusion time-out by allowing the individual to remain in the geographical area but not observe the activity

» Use isolation time-out by requiring the individual to leave the physical activity environment under supervision

Understand **associative learning** (pairing primary and **secondary reinforcers**) as a teaching method

Understand that associative learning may be used for both increasing and decreasing behaviors in individuals with disabilities 10.07.05.01

» Use associative learning to reinforce incompatible behaviors

» Combine reinforcement and punishment techniques to increase the effectiveness of a form of punishment that is not effective in reducing a behavior

» Use associative learning techniques with individuals with more severe disabilities

Understand strong punishers (**corporal punishment**) as a teaching method

Understand that the use of strong punishers with individuals with disabilities such as aversives, physical restraints, and corporal acts are very controversial and may not be allowed in many school districts or by an individual's parents 10.07.06.01

» Modify management techniques based on the knowledge that the administration of strong punishers is usually not a behavior builder

» Modify management techniques based on knowledge that administration of strong punishers is usually considered beyond the expertise of the adapted physical educator and should only be used with proper training, parental permission, and the approval of the multidisciplinary team and must be written into the individual's behavior intervention plan

» Explain the negative side effects of using corporal punishment

» Explain what the moral, ethical, and legal issues are for using corporal punishment

OTHER MANAGEMENT METHODS: Use other management methods/models for increasing, maintaining, and decreasing behavior in order to promote learning

Understand the personal and social responsibility model as a teaching method

Understand that most individuals with disabilities can benefit from programs that promote self-control of behaviors 10.08.01.01

» Develop social skills by using the personal and social responsibility model hierarchy of levels (e.g., irresponsibility, self-control, involvement, self-responsibility, and caring)

» Use appropriate strategies such as modeling, behavior contracts, goal setting, reflection time, student sharing, and journal writing to implement the different levels of the personal and social responsibility model

Understand teacher effectiveness training as a teaching method

Understand the value of effective communication between the teacher and individuals with disabilities 10.08.02.01

» Use effective communication methods with the individual such as active listening

» Use two-way communication to enhance learning and minimize behavioral problems in the physical education setting such as using a chalkboard to foster communication and questioning between an instructor and an individual who is deaf

CONSULTATION AND STAFF DEVELOPMENT

CONSULTATION AND STAFF DEVELOPMENT

STANDARD 11

MOTIVATION: Understand how motivation influences behavior

Understand **Maslow's theory** as the basis for planning consultation and staff development

Understand the motivation of general practitioners teaching individuals with disabilities 11.01.01.01

» Use a survey instrument to determine teachers' needs prior to inservice

» Use techniques to reduce intimidation and fear

» Provide successful experiences for teachers so they feel capable of teaching individuals with disabilities

ADMINISTRATIVE SKILLS: Knowledge of program organization and administrative hierarchy

Understand administrative organizational structure of education agencies/services

Understand how decisions are made in education agencies/services 11.02.01.01

» Identify the key personnel in the decision-making process

» Implement strategies to change organizational behavior

» Encourage administrators' interaction with teachers during inservice presentation

Understand program organization

Understand how curriculum decisions are made for teaching individuals with disabilities 11.02.02.01

» Explain the ABC model which includes program planning, assessment, implementation planning, teaching, evaluation, and modification strategy

» Monitor implementation of individualized education program in **general physical education** class

Understand effects of the living environment and the parent/guardian intervention

Understand strategies for communication with living environments 11.02.03.01

» Instruct parents and guardians on how to teach activities to enhance physical fitness and motor skills at home

» Encourage parents and guardians to be proactive in providing sport and leisure opportunities on a segregated and integrated basis

Know how to describe legal rights and responsibilities of parents and guardians of individuals with disabilities 11.02.03.02

» Identify advocates to assist parents and guardians in ensuring appropriate physical education programming

» Inform parents and guardians of their right to due process

Understand the role of community-based activity programs

Know how to identify community resources for individuals with disabilities 11.02.04.01

» Facilitate transportation possibilities for individuals to participate in community programming

» Develop physical fitness and motor skills that facilitate transition to community recreation facilities

Understand identification of funding sources

Know how to describe how funds can be obtained at various levels 11.02.05.01

» Seek funding from community service organizations

» Contact a grants officer for local education agency

» Contact a grants officer for state education agency

» Contact foundations that fund programs and equipment for individuals with disabilities

GROUP DYNAMICS: Demonstrate knowledge of team approaches for providing educational programs for all individuals

Understand the team approach for providing educational programs

Understand the multidisciplinary team process related to individuals with disabilities (see Standard 15) 11.03.01.01

» Establish a working relationship with members of a motor team such as physical therapists, occupational therapists, and speech therapists

» Use communication skills to enhance cooperation and mutual respect among team members

Understand the ecological approach related to individuals with disabilities 11.03.01.02

» Include families in the decision-making process (see Standard 15)

» Collaborate with the community professionals to provide physical education services to individuals with disabilities

» Use the available expertise when planning a physical education program for individuals with disabilities

Understand the nature of group cohesiveness

Understand the forces acting on members to remain in the group to improve physical education services provided to individuals with disabilities 11.03.02.01

» Create incentives for providing physical education services to individuals with disabilities

» Establish group goals so there is an expectancy of outcomes related to improving physical education services to individuals with disabilities

» Plan group activities that are valuable to the members and will improve physical education services to individuals with disabilities

» Evaluate success of the group related to the expected outcomes of improving physical education services for individuals with disabilities

Understand situational leadership

Understand the importance of developing professional relationships related to working with others to provide physical education services to individuals with disabilities 11.03.03.01

» Develop positive interactions with teachers who have effective teaching behaviors

» Use teachers with effective teaching behaviors to mentor other teachers who are less effective

Understand task orientation related to working with others to provide physical education services to individuals with disabilities 11.03.03.02

» Use explicit communication related to expectations in terms of performance in teaching physical education to individuals with disabilities

» Provide physical educators with the information they need to acquire the technical competence to teach physical education to individuals with disabilities

Understand cultural issues related to group dynamics

Understand differences in the behavior and lifestyle of other cultures 11.03.04.01

» Appreciate and accommodate differences in the behavior and lifestyle of other cultures

» Determine what language is spoken in the home environment

» Refrain from stereotyping individuals who look similar

» Establish rapport with ethnically diverse individuals by being sensitive to their cultural belief systems related to sport and exercise

INTERPERSONAL COMMUNICATION SKILLS: Knowledge of the ability to interact with, discuss, and write about individuals

Understand active listening as a communication skill

Know how to identify components of active listening useful in communication as an adapted physical education consultant 11.04.01.01

» Establish a physical education environment that will allow for good communication between the teacher and the consultant

» Use active listening when communicating with others

Understand the dynamics of advocacy groups

Know how to identify strategies used by advocacy groups for individuals with disabilities 11.04.02.01

» Teach individuals with disabilities about the laws that govern their right to access quality physical education, recreation, and sport programs and services

» Promote and defend the rights of individuals with disabilities to have access to public recreational facilities

PSYCHOLOGICAL DIMENSIONS: Knowledge of the cognitive processes that affect behavior

Understand attitude theories

Understand contact theory as related to individuals with disabilities 11.05.01.01

» Establish contact between individuals with and without disabilities that includes cooperative physical activities

» Establish contact between individuals with and without disabilities in a physical education setting that emphasizes the similarities between individuals with and without disabilities

Understand mediated generalization theory as related to individuals with disabilities 11.05.01.02

» Organize successful experiences in game and movement situations in which individuals with and without disabilities participate together

» Select game activities in which all individuals in an integrated physical activity program can perform and be successful

Understand assimilation-contrast theory as related to individuals with disabilities 11.05.01.03

» Use inservice training to promote positive attitudes toward individuals with disabilities

» Prepare the physical education class to receive a new student who has a disability

Understand stigma theory as related to individuals with disabilities 11.05.01.04

» Integrate individuals with disabilities into physical education activities with the support they need relative to type and degree of disability

» Integrate individuals with disabilities into activities that utilize abilities and strengths

Understand interpersonal relations theory as related to individuals with disabilities 11.05.01.05

» Design a peer tutoring program for physical education that is structured and long term (see Standard 10)

» Provide opportunities for individuals to observe highly competitive sporting events for individuals with disabilities, such as a track meet for individuals who are wheelchair users

Understand **group dynamics theory** as related to individuals with disabilities 11.05.01.06

» Provide input to teachers as to how their attitude toward individuals with disabilities affects others' attitudes

» Empower teachers to plan lessons that facilitate success and stress equity

Understand **cognitive dissonance** as related to individuals with disabilities 11.05.01.07

» Conduct activities that simulate disabling conditions during physical education

» Provide new experiences for students without disabilities, such as using a wheelchair for a day

Understand **reasoned action theory** as related to individuals with disabilities 11.05.01.08

» Provide a clear purpose and value for participation in adapted physical activities for all students before beginning the activity

» Motivate all students to participate together in an integrated physical activity setting

CONSULTING MODELS: Knowledge of how to utilize various consulting models

Understand prescription mode

Understand that adapted physical education consultants provide plans or aid in the selection of strategies for predetermined problems 11.06.01.01

» Conduct assessments and write the IEP for the direct service provider (see Standard 8)

» Provide one-to-one consulting sessions with the direct service provider

Understand provision mode

Understand that adapted physical education consultants provide direct services to individuals as needed 11.06.02.01

» Provide direct physical education services to individuals with disabilities when appropriate

» Model desired teaching behaviors

Understand collaboration mode

Understand that adapted physical education consultants respond to requests by engaging in mutual efforts to understand the problem, devise an action plan, and implement the plan 11.06.03.01

» Engage in a problem-solving relationship with the direct service provider

» Work with the direct service provider to select mutually agreeable strategies and ways to implement them

Understand mediation mode

Understand that adapted physical education consultants respond to requests from two or more consultees to help them accomplish an agreement or reconciliation by serving as a facilitator 11.06.04.01

» Facilitate solutions for quality physical education services for individuals with disabilities when teachers and administrators are in a disagreement

» Facilitate positive relationships between parents and guardians and direct service providers when disagreements occur, without dictating solutions

STUDENT AND PROGRAM EVALUATION

STANDARD 12

STUDENT AND PROGRAM EVALUATION

STUDENT OUTCOMES: Understand the value to program evaluation of measuring student achievement

Monitor the effectiveness of the **assessment plan** and make appropriate revisions

Understand different methods for evaluating program effectiveness 12.01.01.01

» Use individual progress on goals and objectives as an indicator of program effectiveness

» Use unanticipated outcomes as an indication of program effectiveness

Understand the advantages and limitations of formal assessment 12.01.01.02

» Select instruments that are valid for the age and suspected disability of the individual being tested

» Describe how the attributes of learners influence formal testing procedures

» Explain the effect of formal testing procedures on the preferred learning style(s) of individuals with disabilities

» Modify formal testing procedures to accommodate the preferred learning styles of individuals with disabilities

Understand the advantages and limitations of informal assessment 12.01.01.03

» Use informal assessment techniques to determine learner needs in authentic settings such as general physical education

» Use formative evaluation techniques with individuals with disabilities

» Use summative evaluation techniques with individuals with disabilities

» Modify evaluation instruments and explain the effect of these modifications on validity and reliability

» Write realistic and functional goals for individuals with disabilities utilizing appropriate standards of performance

» Explain the differences in validity and reliability between instruments that are used for making placement decisions and instruments used for determining individual progress

Understand how to use **student evaluation** data to communicate student progress 12.01.01.04

» Demonstrate how to create periodic progress reports to communicate students' progress on **short-term objectives** in their program plans and IEPs

» Demonstrate how to create cumulative progress reports that communicate students' progress on their long-term program goals

Understand how to use available resources to evaluate an individual's needs for modified equipment and/or learning materials 12.01.01.05

» Justify appropriate modification of equipment or materials

» Seek outside funding to supplement available resources as needed

Use existing criteria for quality physical education programs in terms of curriculum accessibility, appropriateness, as well as frequency and duration of program delivery

Understand how to compare curricula with existing criteria for quality physical education programs 12.01.02.01

» Use developmentally appropriate curricula for individuals with disabilities

» Use **functionally appropriate** curricula for individuals with disabilities

Understand how to justify program content based on evaluation standards 12.01.02.02

» Write goals and instructional objectives that are measurable and justifiable based on evaluation standards

» Discuss goals and instructional objectives with other professionals

» Use developmentally and functionally appropriate goals and instructional objectives for individuals with disabilities

Understand how to monitor the effectiveness of the program plan and make appropriate revisions in program content 12.01.02.03

» Select a timeline for implementing revised content for a smooth and easy transition for individuals with disabilities into general physical education classes

» Document intended program outcomes

Understand how to match program content with program components of activities addressing physical and motor fitness; fundamental motor skills and patterns; skills in aquatics, dance, and individual and group games and sports; as well as functional living skills 12.01.02.04

» Compare duration of time spent on program components with needs of individuals with disabilities

» Compare the developmental and functional appropriateness of program components with needs of individuals with disabilities

Understand how to measure the effectiveness of program implementation based on the plan and make appropriate revisions 12.01.02.05

» Distinguish between effective and ineffective service delivery for each individual with a disability

» Modify the service delivery model to meet the individualized needs of the student

Understand how to evaluate the effectiveness of various service delivery models such as collaboration, consultation, inclusion, and integration 12.01.02.06

» Discuss the strengths and weaknesses of various service delivery models as they relate to meeting the unique needs of individuals with disabilities

» Discuss the degree to which different service delivery models are being implemented in the LEA

PROGRAM OPERATIONS: Understand the importance of monitoring the quality of program operations

Understand the legal requirements for accessibility of physical education facilities for individuals with disabilities (see Standard 5)

Understand how to recognize and use instruments for evaluating accessibility of physical education facilities 12.02.01.01

» Evaluate accessibility of physical education facilities using architectural standards to accommodate individuals with disabilities

» Recommend modifications or retrofitting where needed to aid facility accessibility for individuals with disabilities

Recognize the importance of properly functioning wheelchairs and orthopedic devices

Understand how to evaluate the functional operations of wheelchairs and other orthopedic devices (see Standard 9) 12.02.02.01

» Describe adjustments for wheelchairs enabling sport participation by individuals with disabilities

» Describe adjustments for braces and other appliances enabling sport participation by individuals with disabilities

» Recommend available resources for the repair of wheelchairs and other orthopedic devices

Recognize the need for staff training, additional administrative support, and reallocation of resources for assessment

Understand how to contribute to staff training by submitting ideas for programs to meet the needs of personnel development 12.02.03.01

» Conduct sessions for staff training addressing needs of colleagues

» Participate in staff training to improve skills and competencies in adapted physical education (see Standard 13)

Understand how to contribute to training of parents and families by submitting ideas for presentations (see Standard 15) 12.02.03.02

» Develop videos for parent and family training on issues related to adapted physical education

» Conduct training sessions for parents and families on how to work with their children in physical activity

Understand various methods of describing and recording the results of measurement and evaluation

Understand systematic observational techniques for recording academic learning time (ALT) 12.02.04.01

» Use event recording techniques to observe behavior

» Use duration recording techniques to observe behavior

» Use interval recording techniques to observe behavior

» Use time sampling techniques to observe behavior

» Explain the uses and limitations of systematic observational techniques

» Use unobtrusive measures such as rating scales, case studies, and anecdotal records

» Graph baseline and intervention data that have been collected over a preset interval of time

Understand how to use student self-report and/or peer evaluation data 12.02.04.02

» Use student self-report data when appropriate in formulating individualized program plans and goals

» Use peer evaluation data when appropriate in formulating individualized program plans and goals

Use performance profiles in reporting student achievement

Understand how to create yearly student performance reports based on the objectives targeted for mastery in their APE program plans 12.02.05.01

» Identify and explain what content should be included in a yearly student performance report

» Explain how the content in the yearly student performance report should be interpreted and used

Understand how to create a cumulative student performance profile that shows progress on achieving the goals and objectives in their APE program plan 12.02.05.02

» Identify and explain what content should be included in a cumulative student performance profile

» Explain how the content in a cumulative student performance profile report should be interpreted and used

Understand how to interpret performance profiles in reporting student achievement 12.02.05.03

» Use age-appropriate award systems in rewarding and motivating achievers

» Use forms of recognition other than awards for student achievement

Use grades to report student progress

Understand how letter grades can be supplemented to report progress of individuals with disabilities 12.02.06.01

» Interpret letter grades with an accompanying narrative

» Use a performance profile to interpret letter grades

Recognize the need for staff training, additional administrative support, and reallocation of resources for recording and reporting student progress

Know resources available to support staff training 12.02.07.01

» Identify and recruit presenters for staff training

» Obtain additional resources for staff training

Demonstrate the ability to evaluate the degree to which a program meets professional standards of quality

Know how to conduct a self-study of program strengths and weaknesses 12.02.08.01

» Study the quality of the school–community environment in terms of mission, philosophy, climate, recognition of accomplishments, parent involvement, communication, and public relations

» Study the quality of the physical education program in terms of goals and objectives, curriculum organization, IEPs, equity, program evaluation process, program implementation, and dissemination of evaluation results

» Study the quality of the instruction in physical education in terms of individual characteristics, teacher characteristics, teacher–student interactions, classroom management, discipline, and individual evaluation

» Study the quality of facilities, equipment and safety practices, safety considerations, school medical records, and procedures (see Standard 9)

CONSUMER SATISFACTION: Monitor indications of consumer satisfaction

Demonstrate knowledge of the parents' or guardians' role in gathering information regarding students' attitudes toward physical education

Understand how to communicate with parents and guardians regarding students' attitudes toward physical education 12.03.01.01

> » Explain methods to parents and guardians for evaluating their children's attitudes towards physical education and physical activity

> » Establish ongoing communication with parents and guardians to obtain their input

Understand strategies to survey parents and guardians on their satisfaction with the physical education program 12.03.01.02

> » Conduct a satisfaction survey of parents and guardians

> » Explain how the results of a parent or guardian survey can be used

> » Recommend physical activity resources to parents or guardians

Recognize the value of individual feedback in program evaluation

Understand how to use different methods of soliciting feedback from individuals with disabilities regarding program merit and weaknesses 12.03.02.01

> » Survey individuals regarding their attitudes toward physical education

> » Survey individuals for suggestions on curriculum offerings in physical education

Understand how to survey individuals for suggestions on curriculum offerings in physical education 12.03.02.02

> » Explain how the results of an individual survey can be used

> » Use individual survey results to influence curricular offerings

Monitor individual's behavior relative to approaching or avoiding physical activity as an indication of their enjoyment or dissatisfaction with the movement medium

Understand how to use nonverbal indicators of an individual's satisfaction with curricular offerings 12.03.03.01

> » Record how frequently individuals initiate physical activity given a choice to select from a variety of activities

> » Provide recognition for individuals who engage in physical activity outside of school programs

Understand strategies for surveying individuals about the vigorousness of their leisure time activities 12.03.03.02

» Explain how survey results may be used

» Refer individuals to programs for leisure time participation

» Use survey results in program planning

CONTINUING EDUCATION

CONTINUING EDUCATION

STANDARD 13

> **PROFESSIONAL GROWTH:** Understand how to remain current on issues and trends that influence the field of physical education

Understand the impact of federal statutes and mandates on the provision of physical education service delivery

Understand how to access information in the *Federal Register* relative to the provision of physical education programs for individuals with disabilities 13.01.01.01

>> Apply information in the *Federal Register* to maintain compliance with current legislation related to individuals with disabilities such as in Individuals with Disabilities Education Improvement Act (IDEIA, 2004) and Americans with Disabilities Act (ADA, 2002)

>> Synthesize information with local practices pertaining to individuals with disabilities such as making **reasonable accommodations** within physical education programs

Understand information provided in the U.S. Department of Education Annual Report to Congress related to individuals with disabilities 13.01.01.02

>> Access a copy of the Annual Report to Congress related to individuals with disabilities

>> Interpret statistics relative to the implementation of IDEIA (2004) in state education agencies (SEAs) and local education agencies (LEAs)

>> Compare an LEA's implementation of IDEIA with that of other LEAs within a region of the state

>> Compare state statistics on implementation of IDEIA (2004) with other states

>> Assess an LEA's program to determine compliance with IDEIA

Understand the current federal nomenclature related to individuals with disabilities 13.01.01.03

>> Interpret federal abbreviations and acronyms such as Office of Special Education Programs (OSEP), free and appropriate public education (FAPE), least restrictive environment (LRE) and evidence-based practice (EBP)

>> Use federal abbreviations and acronyms in communications pertaining to compliance with federal regulations in physical education for individuals with disabilities

Understand how to access information through local offices of congressional leaders who are influential on matters related to individuals with disabilities

Know how to obtain the names of local legislators who are instrumental in the creation, review, and voting on legislation related to individuals with disabilities 13.01.02.01

>> Contact legislators who are instrumental in the passage of legislation related to individuals with disabilities

>> Participate in advocacy groups that attempt to lobby legislators who are instrumental in the passage of legislation related to individuals with disabilities

Understand how to identify how legislators vote on critical issues related to individuals with disabilities 13.01.02.02

>> Access information through newspapers or the *Congressional Record*

>> Use information from the voting records of decisions at the local, state, and federal levels regarding adapted physical education

Know current changes of public laws and how these changes affect adapted physical education 13.01.02.03

>> Use information about current changes in public laws to influence LEA policies and procedures related to the provision of adapted physical education

>> Use information about current changes in public laws to influence the best practices in adapted physical education

Access information through the State Department of Education

Know how to access an SEA's state plan for the implementation of IDEIA (2004) 13.01.03.01

>> Evaluate whether the state plan includes procedures for implementing physical education for individuals with disabilities

>> Evaluate procedures for implementing physical education mandates for students with disabilities

Know how to access an LEA's plan for the implementation of IDEIA (2004) 13.01.03.02

>> Evaluate whether local districts have developed procedures for implementing physical education for individuals with disabilities

>> Evaluate and compare procedures for implementing physical education mandates for individuals with disabilities

Understand current state and local nomenclature related to individuals with disabilities 13.01.03.03

» Interpret state and local terminology related to individuals with disabilities

» Use state and local terminology in communications pertaining to compliance with regulations that affect physical education for individuals with disabilities

Be aware of governance as it is conducted by an LEA

Understand how school boards or their equivalents operate on issues related to individuals with disabilities including the provision for adapted physical education 13.01.04.01

» Assist LEAs in monitoring compliance with legislation designed to ensure adapted physical education for individuals requiring such services

» Advocate for adapted physical education services when issues requiring a public hearing are necessary

Be aware of the positions of various professional organizations and groups on issues related to individuals with disabilities

Understand how to access information through professional organizations related to individuals with disabilities 13.01.05.01

» Attend local and state meetings to acquire legislative updates on issues related to individuals with disabilities

» Discuss current issues related to individuals with disabilities with other professionals in adapted physical education

Understand how to access information from individuals with disabilities 13.01.05.02

» Discuss current issues with parents/guardians or other advocacy groups for individuals with disabilities

» Discuss current issues with friends or colleagues with disabilities

Understand the nature of parent–professional communication to assist in the development of parent understanding of adapted physical education (see Standard 15) 13.01.05.03

» Involve parents/guardians in adapted physical education by making presentations or otherwise keeping them informed about their child's rights under IDEIA 2004

» Disseminate information to parents/guardians and community to assist them in determining if the provision for adapted physical education is appropriate

» Assist or organize parents/guardians to advocate for appropriate adapted physical education services in the community

CURRENT LITERATURE: Keep up to date with current literature in physical education

Subscribe to and read journals in physical education

Know how to review literature regarding physical education for individuals with disabilities 13.02.01.01

» Implement new evidence-based teaching strategies and methods for use in adapted physical education

» Support and use innovative ideas that are evidenced based

» Communicate with other professionals who work with individuals with disabilities relative to evidence-based practices related to adapted physical education

» Read journals from allied fields that address current issues related to the fields of adapted physical education and general physical education

Understand the implications for adapted physical education as they pertain to the literature from allied fields 13.02.02.01

» Apply multidisciplinary, evidence-based teaching methods to improve quality physical education programming

» Use most recent information on medically restricted conditions to enhance the quality of adapted physical education programming

PROFESSIONAL ORGANIZATIONS: Interact with professional organizations that address issues involving physical education

Support the activities of state, regional, and national organizations that promote physical education

Know the importance of professional commitment through attendance at regional, state, and national meetings sponsored by the NCPEID and/ or SHAPE America 13.03.01.01

» Make presentations related to adapted physical education

» Serve on committees that support the efforts of the organization as they relate to adapted physical education

Know the importance of professional commitment through service to local, state, and national organizations involving adapted physical education 13.03.01.02

» Chair or serve on committees involved in influencing policies and procedures concerning issues and concerns about individuals with disabilities

» Chair or serve on committees involved in the planning and conduct of **professional development** activities

» Provide consultation services to community members regarding adapted physical education

» Provide workshops to community leaders and professionals in adapted physical education

» Support activities of other organizations that may address issues directly or indirectly related to physical education such as the Council for Exceptional Children

Know how to contact the state department of education to obtain necessary information regarding professional development activities related to individuals with disabilities 13.03.02.01

» Attend workshops/courses that address issues indirectly related to adapted physical education

» Present at workshops/courses that address issues related to adapted physical education

Know how to join associations or organizations related to research and practice in adapted physical education 13.03.02.02

» Find associations and organizations related to research and practice in adapted physical education on the internet

» Join associations and organizations related to research and practice in adapted physical education by completing the registration on line

TECHNOLOGY: Understand how to use technology as a technique to disseminate information pertaining to physical education

Use Web pages, blogs, online updates (e.g., rich site summaries [RSS] feeds), specialized listservers, social media, and Internet search engines as a means of posting and retrieving information pertaining to physical education

Understand how to inform colleagues in LEAs, SEAs, and other professional and community organizations about current and new developments related to individuals with disabilities 13.04.01.01

» Stay informed of current and new developments in special education and adapted physical education and share that information with colleagues

» Share information with colleges and universities, special education centers, and schools

» Share information with local recreation centers, parks, and public facilities that provide community recreation programs for individuals with disabilities

» Access a variety of online resources such as **ERIC** and the OSEP Technical Assistance Centers (e.g., PBIS, Parent Resource Center) and share that information with colleagues

Know how to disperse information obtained from information retrieval systems to assist professionals and others to understand professional practice in adapted physical education 13.04.02.01

» Use information obtained from information retrieval systems to improve the quality of adapted physical education programming

» Use information obtained from information retrieval systems to assist professionals and others to remain updated with current theories, concepts, trends, and evidence-based practices in adapted physical education

Know how computers can assist IEP management 13.04.03.01

» Use computers to facilitate record keeping and data storage

» Use computers to manage and analyze IEP assessment data

» Use computers to generate adapted physical education IEP goals and objectives

» Use computers to generate IEP progress reports to be given to students and parents

» Use computers to disseminate information to others regarding the effectiveness of their physical education program

Know how to use word-processing software or applications to disseminate information related to adapted physical education 13.04.04.01

» Develop and disseminate adapted physical education newsletters

» Develop and disseminate personalized letters on issues related to adapted physical education

Know how to use spreadsheet software or applications to manage data relevant to adapted physical education service delivery 13.04.04.02

» Use spreadsheets to manage and calculate students' grades in adapted physical education

» Use spreadsheets to manage the adapted physical education budget

Know how to use database software or applications relevant to adapted physical education service delivery 13.04.04.03

» Use a database program to manage student performance data such as physical fitness and motor skill data in adapted physical education

» Use a database program to track student behaviors and progress in adapted physical education

» Use database programs to generate reports specific to student performance and program effectiveness

TEACHING CERTIFICATION: Understand the need to maintain current teaching certifications

Understand what mechanisms are available to maintain current teaching certifications

Know how to access professional development activities related to physical education for individuals with disabilities 13.05.01.01

» Enroll in adapted physical education coursework at local colleges/universities

» Maintain state or national adapted physical education certification (e.g., CAPE)

» Participate in adapted physical education workshops offered by non-degree granting agencies

» Use alternative means for acquiring or maintaining certifications such as online coursework

ETHICS

ETHICS

UNDERSTAND THE NEED FOR PROFESSIONAL STANDARDS

Understand and respect the roles and responsibilities of educators and other school-related professionals in upholding their professional standards (see Standard 15)

Understand the role of professional standards in guiding practice and preparation of all professionals who work closely with individuals with disabilities including adapted physical educators, special educators and related personnel such as occupational and physical therapists 14.01.01.01

» Apply the professional and ethical standards associated with preparation and certification as adapted physical educators

» Uphold the standards associated with certification as a teacher and an adapted physical educator

» Respect the need to monitor and enforce professional standards for adapted physical educators

UNDERSTAND AND VALUE APPROPRIATE PROFESSIONAL CONDUCT

Protect the privacy and security of the individual and the family information by complying with confidentiality policies including the Health Insurance Portability and Accountability Act (HIPAA) and Family Educational Rights and Privacy Act (FERPA), as well as state-level and local policies

Understand the need to protect the privacy and security of an individual's educational information by complying with confidentiality policies 14.02.01.01

» Protect individual confidentiality in electronic communications by eliminating identifying information such as using initials rather than names

» Put "confidential" in the subject line when using electronic communication

» Use secure or encrypted email servers rather than social media messaging when communicating individual information

» Know who has access to an individual's educational information

» Keep IEPs and other documents with parent and family information securely protected, not out on the desk

Accept the need for standards for a professional engaged in the education of children, youth, and adolescents

Understand the responsibility for developing and providing appropriate adapted physical education experiences 14.03.01.01

» Develop and implement programs for individuals with disabilities that are evidence based

>> Respect confidentiality and right to privacy in all matters related to the education of individuals with disabilities, including evaluation, assessment outcomes, and report writing

Understand the need to be respectful of all individuals with disabilities, parents, advocates, and other professionals 14.03.01.02

>> Interact with individuals with disabilities, parents, surrogates, advocates, and others in a professional and courteous manner

>> Be cognizant of how to respectfully use technology when communicating with parents (e.g., avoid colloquial speech, be protective of student data, be mindful of parent time)

>> Use appropriate terminology such as person-first language

>> Create an environment of respect and equality

Understand the need for continuous professional development

Understand the importance of participating in meetings, seminars, and conferences related to the education of individuals with disabilities (see Standard 13) 14.03.02.01

>> Attend courses, conferences, seminars, and other continuing education experiences on a regular basis

>> Provide and share professional information with others, including parents, guardians, and related personnel, that is accurate, current, and free of personal bias (see Standard 15)

Understand the responsibility to advocate for the educational needs of individuals with disabilities

Understand issues confronting individuals with disabilities and the relationship of these to programs designed to provide opportunities for physical activity 14.03.03.01

>> Articulate the challenges individuals with disabilities experience in accessing health-related facilities and programs

>> Support and promote individuals and organizations that provide physical activity and sport programs for individuals with disabilities

>> Cooperate with parent or guardian organizations and professional societies in promoting the health and fitness of individuals with disabilities (see Standard 15)

Understand the need to maintain credentials and professional standards

Understand the responsibility to earn credentials as an adapted physical educator as required by the state and/or a professional society 14.03.04.01

>> Advocate for the requirement of professional standards

>> Adhere to the requirements of professional standards and credentials in the practice of providing adapted physical education services

>> Earn and maintain state and/or national credentials as an adapted physical educator (e.g., CAPE)

» Advocate for professional preparation standards that are in alignment with the Adapted Physical Education National Standards

UNDERSTAND THE NEED TO ADVANCE THE PROFESSIONAL KNOWLEDGE BASE

Understand the need to conduct and support various forms of research (e.g., action, field, laboratory, qualitative) designed to expand the knowledge base

Understand the need to support research endeavors that advance programs and services for individuals with disabilities 14.04.01.01

» Engage and support research with special populations if it adheres to appropriate standards (i.e., approved by human subjects board)

» Use an informed consent process and respect the rights of individuals with and without disabilities who choose to participate in research studies

» Synthesize and report findings of studies that involve special populations to others

» Accept responsibility to conduct research that is relevant to the needs of individuals with disabilities (e.g., field based, socially valid)

» Acknowledge the contributions of others, including research participants, to the research endeavor

Understand the responsibility to incorporate research findings into practice

Know journals that provide current information about the latest research regarding programs and activities for individuals with disabilities 14.04.02.01

» Use research findings and incorporate evidence-based practices into adapted physical education programs and activities

» Evaluate new program ideas incorporated from research to assess their effectiveness on individual outcomes

ADVANCE THE PROFESSION

Serve on professional committees

Know adapted education professional organizations and their committee structures 14.05.01.01

» Volunteer to serve on committees and actively contribute

» Respond to requests for assistance from professional organizations such as completion of a survey

» Retain the rights to agree and disagree over professional matters, recognizing the need to do so in a courteous and professional manner

» Accept leadership opportunities consistent with talent, available time, and other responsibilities

COMMUNICATION

COMMUNICATION

STANDARD 15

PARENTS AND FAMILIES: Communication with parents and families

Understand the importance of parent and family intervention

Understand the importance of family support during the individualized education program (IEP), the individualized family service plan (IFSP), and other parent-teacher conferences/meetings 15.01.01.01

>> Explain physical education IFSP to family members

>> Explain the motor components of the IFSP to family members

>> Assist family members with the transition of the physical fitness and motor component from the IFSP to the IEP

Understand the skills families need to facilitate participation in play, sport, and physical activity with individuals with disabilities 15.01.01.02

>> Develop a management plan specific to a family's needs

>> Provide families with the specific management skills needed to implement a play, sport, or physical activity program

>> Provide families with strategies and teaching techniques to increase their effectiveness as instructors

Be a family advocate for physical activity

Understand the importance of family advocacy where parents can learn about physical activity programs for individuals with disabilities 15.01.02.01

>> Be an advocate for programs by working closely with the press and media such as writing newsletters

>> Volunteer to be a speaker at parent advocacy meetings

>> Provide information about local physical activity opportunities for individuals with disabilities to parent advocacy groups

>> Use social media to educate parents about the value and availability of physical activity programs for individuals with disabilities

Understand the value of home-based physical activity programs for families of children with disabilities 15.01.02.02

>> Design family home-based physical activity programs

>> Teach parents to implement a plan that includes long-range goals, behavioral objectives, lesson plans, teaching cues, and strategies for charting individual progress

>> Provide homework assignments for home-based activity programs

Disseminate knowledge of national agencies, organizations, and community programs that assist families in play, sport, and physical activity

such as Special Olympics and the United States Association of Blind Athletes 15.01.02.03

>> Assist families in contacting and getting involved in such national agencies, organizations, and community programs

>> Assist families in appropriate assessment procedures for placement in play, sport, and physical activity

>> Assist families in utilizing and adapting equipment in order to participate in physical activities

PUBLIC RELATIONS: Communicating the role of physical education (see Standard 5)

Acquire knowledge of physical education and be able to communicate the importance of physical activity

Understand and communicate the importance of physical activity for individuals with disabilities in the schools and community 15.02.01.01

>> Plan and implement programs that promote adapted physical education for parents and other groups

>> Take community-based educational trips and provide feedback to individuals with disabilities about how to be physically active within the community

>> Take integrated groups to community-based activities such as ice skating, bowling, and fitness centers

>> Advocate for adapted physical education programming as a part of transition services while serving on transition teams

>> Consult and/or collaborate with local physicians regarding the importance of adapted physical education programs

>> Advocate for inclusion of individuals with disabilities in intramural and athletic programs

>> Collaborate with local business and municipal recreation leaders in marketing recreational activities for all individuals, including those with disabilities

>> Speak to civic organizations about the right to recreate for individuals with disabilities by offering inclusive recreation/leisure opportunities

ROLES OF OTHER PROFESSIONALS: Understand other professionals who work with adapted physical educators and serve individuals with disabilities

Acquire knowledge of the roles and responsibilities of occupational therapists

Understand how occupational therapists can assist in programs of physical activity for individuals with disabilities 15.03.01.01

>> Confer with the occupational therapist on **activities of daily living** (ADL)

>> Meet regularly about the progress of individuals with disabilities relative to self-care, work skills, and daily activities to ensure that work toward goals is congruent

» Observe an occupational therapist working with individuals with disabilities and invite an occupational therapist to observe physical education/adapted physical education programming where an individual receiving occupational therapy is present

» Assist individuals with disabilities in identifying special interests in recreation/physical education that may require occupational therapist services

Acquire knowledge of the roles and responsibilities of physical therapists

Understand how the physical therapist can assist in programs of physical activity for individuals with disabilities 15.03.02.01

» Confer with the physical therapist on relevant issues such as the use and safety of wheelchairs and orthotics, transfers to and from wheelchairs, and positioning of individuals with reflexive movements

» Communicate with the physical therapist regarding assistive devices such as a sport wheelchair for active involvement of individuals with disabilities

» Collaborate with the physical therapist to develop appropriate stretching exercises for individuals with specific physical disabilities

Acquire knowledge of the roles and responsibilities of therapeutic recreators

Understand how the therapeutic recreation specialist can assist in community-based leisure activities for individuals with disabilities 15.03.03.01

» Confer with the therapeutic recreation specialist to identify leisure needs

» Confer with the therapeutic recreation specialist to identify what community recreation/leisure opportunities exist

» Confer with the therapeutic recreation specialist regarding ecological inventory and task analysis of community recreation/leisure activities

» Accompany individuals with disabilities on recreation/leisure trips to assess adapted physical education needs

» Contact agencies such as Easter Seals with the intent to cooperatively expand recreation activities such as horseback riding

» Confer with the therapeutic recreation specialist regarding camping, hiking, rock climbing, and canoe paddling activity options for individuals with disabilities

Acquire knowledge of the roles and responsibilities of **vocational specialists**

Understand the importance of physical fitness to enhance job skills and productivity 15.03.04.01

» Design physical fitness and physical activity programs to address needs of individuals with disabilities working in vocational work sites

» Accompany the vocation specialist to study work sites to assess physical abilities needed

» Collaborate with the vocational specialist to teach proper posture and body mechanics during manual labor

» Explore how physical fitness activities can be combined with work experiences such as walking or biking to work, stretching during work breaks, and performing low back exercises during breaks

Acquire knowledge of the roles and responsibilities of general physical educators

Understand how the general physical educator can assist in curricular and scheduling decisions for individuals with disabilities 15.03.05.01

» Consult with the general physical educator to understand how they are making appropriate modifications and/or accommodations within activities

» Consult with the general physical educator to discuss appropriate decisions about the least restrictive environment

» Collaborate with the general physical educator during the assessment process, in developing top-down curricula, and in the writing of goals and objectives

» Confer with the general physical educator to identify and access appropriate community recreation opportunities

» Work with the general physical educator to include individuals with disabilities in intramural programs

» Write grants cooperatively to improve programs such as acquiring sport wheelchairs to be used when appropriate in physical education classes by individuals who typically ambulate with crutches

Acquire knowledge of the roles and responsibilities of special education classroom teachers

Understand how the special education classroom teacher can assist in the appropriate placement of individuals with disabilities in such least restrictive environments as general or special education 15.03.06.01

» Collaborate with the special education classroom teacher regarding written work required for physical education

» Collaborate with the special education classroom teacher regarding behavior management in order to keep management techniques consistent across settings

» Inform the special education classroom teacher when routines or activities of individuals with disabilities will be changed in physical education settings

» Collaborate with the special education classroom teacher in establishing community recreation/leisure involvement for individuals with disabilities

» Collaborate with the special education teacher in developing the prerequisite physical skills needed by individuals with disabilities to transition to the community workforce

» Assist in developing activities for the special education classroom teacher and the general education classroom teacher providing opportunities for individuals with disabilities to practice skills in the classroom, during recess, at home, or in the community

Acquire knowledge of the roles and responsibilities of paraprofessionals and other volunteers

Understand how paraprofessionals and other volunteers can assist in the adapted physical education program 15.03.07.01

» Provide demonstrations on how to physically assist individuals with disabilities for paraprofessionals and volunteers assisting in the adapted physical education program

» Model how to sufficiently challenge individuals with disabilities during programming for paraprofessionals and volunteers

» Teach paraprofessionals and volunteers how to encourage peer partners

» Engage paraprofessionals and volunteers in the assessment process

» Train paraprofessionals and volunteers to take a lead role in teaching when the adapted physical educator is absent due to involvement in the assessment process or IEP meetings (depending on LEA policy)

» Teach paraprofessionals and volunteers how to use specialized equipment

» Evaluate the effectiveness of paraprofessionals and volunteers

Acquire knowledge of the roles and responsibilities of other school-based professionals who work with adapted physical educators and serve individuals with disabilities

Understand how to collaborate with these professionals to provide the appropriate educational services for individuals with disabilities 15.03.08.01

» Understand the roles and responsibilities of professionals such as principals, psychologists, physical educators, special educators, occupational therapists, physical therapists, and therapeutic recreation specialists

» Collaborate with other professionals regarding assessment and programming for individuals with disabilities

» Collaborate with other professionals regarding legal issues

» Collaborate with other professionals about issues related to school, state, and federal policies

TEAM APPROACH: Communicate effectively using a team approach

Acquire knowledge of differences among various team approaches

Understand which collaborative team approach should be used (see Standard 11) 15.04.01.01

» Collaborate and work effectively in a team by using such methods as consensus forming with the various members of the team

» Collaborate with other professionals regarding individual goals and objectives

» Explain how adapted physical education contributes to the overall growth of individuals with disabilities

Appendix A

National Consortium for Physical Education for Individuals with Disabilities

The purpose of the National Consortium for Physical Education for Individuals with Disabilities (NCPEID) is to promote research, professional preparation, service delivery, and advocacy of physical education for individuals with disabilities. The NCPEID provides public information and education, promotes the development of programs and services, and disseminates professional and technical information. The organization succeeded the National Committee on Physical Education and Recreation for Handicapped Children and Youth, formed in 1973, and was originally formed as the National Consortium for Physical Education and Recreation for Individuals with Disabilities.

NCPEID membership is open to all persons who are or have been involved in professional preparation, demonstration, or research activity related to physical education and physical activity for individuals with disabilities. University faculty in adapted physical education as well as public school and residential facility personnel from across the United States are encouraged to become members.

Related to the areas in the purpose of the organization, the membership works diligently to stimulate and conduct research efforts directed toward improving the lifestyle and well-being of individuals with disabilities through physical education and **life span** physical activity. In part, the membership works to monitor available research funding from governmental agencies by articulating current needs and collectively advocating for funding related to its mission. The membership also works to serve as a liaison to legislative organizations at the national, state, and local levels. An essential function of the NCPEID is to develop and foster the adoption of standards related to staff qualifications, services facilities, and recommended levels of support for recreational and physical education programs for persons with disabilities at national, state, and local levels. The NCPEID also serves its membership and the profession by holding an annual meeting wherein organizational activities as well as current issues and research are discussed. A goal of the NCPEID is to serve as a professional voice and collective force in support of physical education and life span physical activity for all people, including those with disabilities. This may be articulated through the development of national policy and position statements reflecting the contribution of physical education and life span physical activity on the lives of people with disabilities. Efforts are made to regularly and effectively communicate with the membership of the NCPEID and with other professional organizations that advocate for the rights of people with disabilities.

Appendix B

How the Adapted Physical Education Standards and National Certification Examination Were Developed

The purpose of the five-year special projects grant, funded in 1992 from U.S. Department of Education, Office of Special Education and Rehabilitation Services (OSERS) to the National Consortium for Physical Education and Recreation for Individuals with Disabilities (now the National Consortium for Physical Education for Individuals with Disabilities [NCPEID] and hereafter referred to as NCPEID) was to ensure that physical education instruction for students with disabilities was provided by qualified physical education teachers. The purpose of this project was to achieve the following two goals:

1. Develop national standards for the field of adapted physical education
2. Develop a national certification examination to measure knowledge of the standards

The Initial Project and Resulting Standards

The first two years of the Adapted Physical Education National Standards (APENS) project focused on developing the national standards. These standards would serve as the foundation for creating a national certification examination in years three and four, which would be administered nationally during the fifth year of the project. It is important to note that what was proposed and funded was a dynamic process for achieving these goals. This process served as the initial framework and was continuously shaped and refined with input from a variety of constituencies through an ongoing evaluation process.

Committees

The work force for the APENS project was composed of four committees and the project staff. Each of the major committees is briefly described in the following sections in terms of its membership and responsibilities.

Executive Committee (Six Members)

- Luke E. Kelly (chair), project director and past president of the NCPEID
- Jeff McCubbin, the president of the NCPEID at the time of the project
- Two members from the NCPEID board of directors appointed by the NCPEID board:
  - Patrick DiRocco, University of Wisconsin–La Crosse, who served as the official liaison between the project and the American Alliance for Health, Physical Education, Recreation and Dance (AAHPERD; now SHAPE America)
  - Hester L. Henderson, University of Utah, who served as the official liaison between the project and the Council for Exceptional Children
- Smokey Davis, who served as the National Association for State Directors of Special Education (NASDSE) representative
- Martha Bokee, who served as the OSERS Division of Personnel Preparation representative

This committee was responsible for (1) ensuring that the project was implemented as intended, (2) making all policy decisions, and (3) approving all materials and products produced by the various committees.

Steering Committee (Seven Members)

- Luke E. Kelly (chair), project director
- John M. Dunn, Oregon State University
- Willie Gayle, Wright State University
- Barry Lavay, California State University–Long Beach
- Monica Lepore, West Chester University
- Michael Loovis, Cleveland State University
- Janet A. Seaman, California State University–Los Angeles

The members of this committee applied for these positions and were reviewed and selected by the executive committee. The responsibilities of the steering committee were to (1) develop credentialing procedures and criteria for selecting the members of the standards committees and evaluation and review committee; (2) draft, implement, and monitor the development of the standards and the exam; (3) chair one of the standards committees; and (4) report progress on a regular schedule to the executive committee.

Standards Committees (72 Members)

There were six standards committees, each chaired by a member of the steering committee. The members on these committees applied for the positions and were selected by the steering committee and assigned to a standard committee based upon their area(s) of expertise and experience. The responsibilities of the standards committees were to (1) delineate the scope and sequence of the content in the standards they were assigned; (2) revise the content based upon the evaluation and review committee's feedback; (3) develop test items to measure the standards; and (4) revise the test items based upon the evaluation and review committee's feedback. The members of the standards committees are listed on page 214. Fifty-four percent of the committee members were female and 46 percent were male. The committee members were from 26 different states and from both K to 12 schools (45 percent) and colleges and universities (55 percent).

Evaluation and Review Committee (More Than 300 Members)

Members volunteered for the evaluation and review committee (ERC) and were appointed by the steering committee based on credentials. For evaluation tasks, multiple subevaluation groups composed of 30 members each were randomly formed from the pool of ERC members. The project director was responsible for instructing and monitoring the work of this committee. The ERC's responsibilities included validating the draft content of the standards and test items developed by the various standards committees. A total of 977 professionals expressed interest in working on the ERC. From this pool, 300 were selected to evaluate the draft standards based upon their willingness to perform this task and evidence that they were in fact practicing adapted physical educators with one or more years teaching experience. See appendix D for the names of these ERC members. Descriptive data on the ERC are shown in table B.1 on page 215. Review of the data in table B.1 reveals that 90 percent of the committee members were K to 12 adapted physical educators. They had a mean age of 40.36 years, an average of 11.28 years teaching experience, on average spent 80 percent of their time teaching adapted physical education, and represented 40 of the 50 states.

APE National Standards: Standards Committee Members

Judy Alexander	Constance Hayes	Gloria Palma
Bernadette Ascareggi	John Herring	Jan Patterson
James Ascareggi	Ric Hogerheide	Thomas Pennewell
Ted Baumgartner	Mike Horvat	Virginia Politino
Michael Berick	Cathy Houston-Wilson	Lynda Reeves
David Bermann	Joseph Huber	Jim Rimmer
Nick Breit	Charlotte Humphries	Catherine Schroeder
Sandy Brungardt	Daniel Joseph	Cindy Slagle
Stephen Butterfield	Monica Kleeman	Christine Stopka
Alana Campbell	Ellen Kowalski	Perky Stromer
Ellen Campbell	Karen Leightshoe	Christine Summerford
Judy Chandler	Lauren Lieberman	Paul Surburg
Charlie Daniel	Dwayne Liles	Ric Tennant
John Downing	Patrice Manning	Kathleen Tomlin
Gail Dummer	Nancy Markos	April Tripp
Charles Duncan	Deborah Maronic	Terri Troll
Peter Ellery	Elaine McHugh	Garth Tymeson
Steven Errante	Robert Merrifield	Dale Ulrich
M. Rhonda Folio	William Merriman	Vicki Vance
Sheri Folsom-Meek	Sue Ellen Miller	Paul Vogel
Georgia Frey	Duane Millslagle	Bill Vogler
Taralyn Garner	Thomas Murphy	Tim Wallstrom
Wanda Gilbert	Kathy Omoto	Robert Weber
Mike Haeuser	Michael Paciorek	Andrea Williams

Project Staff

The project staff was composed of the following: a project director, a research consultant, a project assistant, and a clerical assistant. The project staff were:

- Luke E. Kelly, project director, past president of the NCPERID, and director of the graduate adapted physical education program at the University of Virginia
- Dr. Bruce Gansneder, research consultant, from the Bureau of Educational Research, Curry School of Education, University of Virginia
- Four doctoral students at the University of Virginia serving as project assistants during the first two years of the project. These assistants were:
  - Jim Martindale
  - Morris Pickens
  - Katie Stanton
  - David Striegel
- A number of graduate students during the first two years of the project serving as clerical assistants, most notably:
  - Karen Etz
  - Alyssa Watkins
  - Jennifer Williams

Table B.1 Demographic Data on the ERC Members Used to Validate the Draft Standards

Variables	n	%		
GENDER				
Male	90	30		
Female	210	70		
TRAINING				
Bachelor's degree	279	93		
Master's degree	210	70		
Doctorate	45	15		
TEACHING LEVEL				
K-12 schools	269	90		
University	31	10		
STATES REPRESENTED	**40**	**80**		
Variables	n	Min	Max	Mean
Age	300	22.0	66.0	40.36
Years teaching	300	1.0	30.0	11.28
% time teaching APE	300	10.0	100.0	80.54

Standards Development Process

The first year of the project was devoted to achieving the following four objectives:

1. To review and compare our proposed procedures with those of other professional organizations that have already gone through the process of developing standards and national exams

2. To identify the roles and responsibilities adapted physical educators were being asked to perform in our nation's schools as well as the perceived needs of these educators

3. To interpret the job analysis data to determine the content that adapted physical educators need to know to perform their roles and responsibilities

4. To create a means of organizing this content

Since a number of other professional organizations have already developed national standards and certification exams, it seemed prudent to contact these organizations to see what could be learned from their experiences. To this end, the executive committee identified six professional organizations that were viewed as having elements of similarity to adapted physical education. Some of these elements were size, focus, need, and purposes for creating their standards and exams. These six organizations were the American College of Sports Medicine, the American Occupational Therapy Certification Board, the American Physical Therapy Association, the National Athletic Training Association, the National Council for Therapeutic Recreation Certification, and the National Organization on Competency Assurances. Extensive phone interviews were conducted with key members of these associations who had been involved in the standards or exam development processes of their respective organizations. The results of these interviews were compiled and reviewed by the members of the executive committee. Based on the review of the phone interviewers, the executive committee decided to invite three representatives to a two-day work session to discuss the proposed procedures for our project. These representatives were

- Patricia Tice, representing the American Physical Therapy Association;

- Maureen Plombon, representing the American College of Sports Medicine; and

- Mr. Paul Grace, representing the National Athletic Training Association and the National Organization on Competency Assurances.

Prior to the work session, each representative was sent a complete copy of the proposed project and the five-year project management plan. At the work session, the proposed procedures for developing the APENS and certification examination were confirmed by the representatives. They also provided a number of helpful suggestions, particularly related to developing and administering the exam, that have subsequently been added to the project management plan.

Determining the current roles, responsibilities, and perceived needs of practicing adapted physical educators required the creation of an appropriate tool to collect this information and the identification of a representative sample of practitioners to supply the needed information.

The first step in this process was to review previous needs assessment instruments that had been used in the profession and to solicit input from the executive and steering committees. With this information, the project staff developed a draft survey using the total design method (Dillman, 1978). The draft survey was reviewed by the executive and steering committees and revised accordingly by the project staff. The revised draft was field tested using small groups (total $n = 36$) of adapted physical educators identified by members of the steering committee. The field test results were compiled and reviewed by the steering committee, and final revisions were made to the instrument.

The second task related to the job analysis was to identify a representative sample of practitioners to receive the survey. The initial plan was to use the AAHPERD Adapted Physical Activity (APAC) membership list as the pool and to sample from this by region for the job analysis survey. However, a survey performed by the project director (Kelly, 1991b, 1991c) using this method revealed a number of limitations with this sampling plan. For example, the APAC membership list did not distinguish between K to 12 and college or university adapted physical educators, nor did it distinguish between members interested in adapted physical education versus those who were actually practitioners. Kelly (1991a) drew a random sample of 600 from the membership list of 1,500+ members. Based on a return rate of 81 percent ($n = 491$), only 22 percent of the respondents were full-time adapted physical educators at the K to 12 level. Since it was essential that the job analysis be completed by teachers who were actually practicing adapted physical educators, a more appropriate sampling plan was needed. Based on the recommendation of the steering committee, it was ultimately decided to identify K to 12 adapted physical educators in each state and then to use this group as the sample. A stratified sampling plan was developed. Each member of the steering committee was assigned several states. The steering committee members then contacted key leaders in adapted physical education in each of their assigned states. Depending upon the size of the state, the initial contact in a given state may have been asked to identify other leaders within the state to ensure the entire state would be represented. The contacts in each state were asked to collectively provide a specific number (based on state size) of names and addresses of adapted physical education practitioners in the state. The sample size obtained by state is illustrated in table B.2. This process resulted in a total sample of 585, with each state contributing a weighted number of subjects based on the population of the state. The committee was unable to secure the requested number of names and addresses of adapted physical educators in two states.

The final return rate was 55 percent (316/575). The results of the job analysis are contained in a separate report (Kelly & Gansneder, 1998). These results were reviewed by the steering committee and the content needed by practicing adapted physical educators divided into the 15 broad standard areas shown in table B.3. The members of the steering committee were then assigned two to three of these standard areas and were responsible for delineating the content with their standards committee.

One of the key decisions the steering committee had to make early on was the degree to which the content should be delineated. For example, should the standards be limited to just the unique content that adapted physical educators should know or should they include the prerequisite content that regular physical educators would be expected to know? In making this decision, the steering committee considered the following factors:

- The delineation of what general physical educators should know relative to the proposed 15 standards does not exist.
- The standards developed would be used by parents, state department officials, and others who probably would not have the training to deduce the prerequisite content.

Table B.2   Job Analysis Sample Distribution by State

Weighted number of teachers targeted by state to receive the national job analysis survey

State	Sample	State	Sample
Alabama	10	Montana	5
Alaska	5	Nebraska	5
Arizona	10	Nevada	5
Arkansas	10	New Hampshire	5
California	40	New Jersey	20
Colorado	10	New Mexico	5
Connecticut	10	New York	30
Delaware	5	North Carolina	15
Florida	25	North Dakota	5
Georgia	15	Ohio	25
Hawaii	5	Oklahoma	10
Idaho	5	Oregon	10
Illinois	25	Pennsylvania	25
Indiana	15	Rhode Island	5
Iowa	10	South Carolina	10
Kansas	10	South Dakota	5
Kentucky	10	Tennessee	10
Louisiana	10	Texas	20
Maine	5	Utah	5
Maryland	10	Vermont	5
Massachusetts	15	Virginia	15
Michigan	20	Washington	10
Minnesota	10	West Virginia	5
Mississippi	10	Wisconsin	10
Missouri	15	Wyoming	5

- What is defined as the minimum standards to be qualified may be interpreted by others as the absolute criteria.

Based upon these considerations it was decided that the delineation should include both the prerequisite content a general physical educator should know and the content an adapted physical education specialist should know. As a result, the content in each standard area was divided into the five levels shown in the sidebar with their corresponding descriptions.

Table B.3 Adapted Physical Education National Standards

The 15 standard areas and the steering committee member who was responsible for chairing the development of each standard

Standard	Title	Chair
1	Human Development	John M. Dunn
2	Motor Behavior	Michael Loovis
3	Exercise Science	Willie Gayle
4	Measurement and Evaluation	Janet A. Seaman
5	History and Philosophy	Monica Lepore
6	Unique Attributes of Learners	Monica Lepore
7	Curriculum Theory and Development	Michael Loovis
8	Assessment	Janet A. Seaman
9	Instructional Design and Planning	Barry Lavay Willie Gayle
10	Teaching	Barry Lavay
11	Consultation and Staff Development	Willie Gayle
12	Student and Program Evaluation	Janet A. Seaman
13	Continuing Education	Michael Loovis
14	Ethics	John M. Dunn
15	Communication	Barry Lavay

Illustration of the Five Levels

Level 1: Standard number and name (e.g., 2. Motor Behavior)

Level 2: Major components of the standard (e.g., theories of motor development, principles of motor learning, etc.)

Level 3: Subcomponents, dependent pieces of knowledge of fact or principle related to the major component that *all general physical educators* would be expected to know (e.g., stages of learning, knowledge of types of feedback, etc.)

Level 4: Adapted physical education content—additional knowledge regarding the subcomponents that teachers working with individuals with disabilities need to know (e.g., common delays in development experienced by individuals with severe visual impairments)

Level 5: Application of adapted physical education content knowledge from level 4 to teaching individuals with disabilities (e.g., can identify and interpret motor performance delays in children with disabilities)

The first three levels of each standard represent content that should be known by all physical educators. These levels were developed by the steering committee and reviewed and validated by the standards committees. The level 4 content represents the additional content adapted physical educators need to know to meet the roles and responsibilities of their positions. Level 5 contains example applications of the level 4 content that adapted physical educators would be expected to be able to demonstrate.

The majority of the work during year two of the project was devoted to delineating and validating the level 4 and level 5 content for each standard. The following process was used to create and validate the content:

- The steering committee members developed an example for each of their standards illustrating the five levels of content. Then they provided their standards committee members with the first three levels of the standard and an example of how to delineate the specific content they were being assigned to develop.

- The standards committee members delineated the content they were assigned and returned this information to their chair. Each chair then edited and compiled the results into a draft document, which was submitted to the project director.

- The project staff entered the draft standard content into a database and produced a series of ERC evaluation instruments for each standard. The typical ERC instrument was 8 to 10 pages in length and contained 50 to 60 content items to be evaluated. For some of the larger standards, the content was divided into two or more ERC instruments to keep the amount of content reviewed in any given evaluation reasonable.

- This project staff randomly drew a sample of 30 ERC members from the database of 300+ and sent them the ERC instrument. The ERC members were asked to complete and return the instruments as soon as possible. When the ERC instruments were returned, the project staff entered the ERC ratings into a Statistical Package for the Social Sciences (SPSS) data file. Summary statistics were computed and entered into the database for each content item. A summary statistics report was generated and sent to the appropriate member of the steering committee.

- The steering committee members reviewed the summary statistics for their standards and decided what revisions were warranted. This information was sent to the standards committee members with the request to revise or expand the content as indicated by the evaluation data.

The above process was repeated for the level 4 and 5 content of each standard until the steering committee, as a group, agreed it was acceptable. At this time, the steering committee identified and defined any terms they felt should be included in the glossary and added cross-references within the standards.

Dissemination

Given the goal of this project, to ensure that all students with disabilities received appropriate physical education services delivered by a qualified physical educator by developing national standards, a plan was included in the original proposal to disseminate the products of this project. Complimentary copies were sent to

- all state directors of special education;
- all state directors of physical education;
- all members of the National Consortium for Physical Education for Individuals with Disabilities;
- all identified directors of college or university adapted physical education programs;

- members of the executive, steering, and standards committees; and
- the executive directors of select professional and advocacy groups associated with physical education or serving the needs of individuals with disabilities.

2018 Standards and Exam Revisions

Approximately every 10 years, the NCPEID appoints a committee to review and revise the APENS and exam. In January of 2016, a committee was appointed to review and revise the 2006 version of the standards and the exam. This committee was composed of four members.

- Tim Davis, SUNY Cortland, Cortland, NY
- Suzanna Dillon, Texas Woman's University, Denton, TX
- Hester Henderson, University of Utah, Salt Lake, UT
- Luke Kelly (committee chair), University of Virginia, Charlottesville, VA

The committee was charged to review and revise the standards with regard to current standards of practice in the field of adapted physical education and in line with current federal mandates related to physical education for individuals with disabilities. In addition, the committee was charged to review the existing database of test items and to revise, delete, and add new items so that the test item database contained sufficient high quality items so that multiple comparable forms of the exam could be generated.

Standard Review and Revision Process

The standards were divided and distributed to the committee members according to their areas of content expertise. Each committee member reviewed the content in their assigned standards and identified any level 4 or 5 content they felt required either minor or major revisions. Minor revisions involved rewording statements to improve clarity, updating law references, or updating terminology such as changing mental retardation to intellectual disability. Major revisions involved reorganizing the content within a standard into more logical sequences. Two standards were reorganized during this revision: standards 6 and 7. Standard 6 was reorganized around the 13 Individuals with Disabilities Education Act (IDEA) special education disability definitions, and standard 7 was reorganized around the sequence of decisions made in curriculum development. For the major revisions, one committee member was charged with creating a draft of the revisions. The committee then met through video conferencing and two on-site meeting across 15 months to systematically review, discuss, and finalize all the content identified for both minor and major revisions.

Test Item Review and Revision Process

The test item review and revision process involved three steps.

1. All the items in the existing test item database were reviewed by the committee to verify the terminology was up to date. This involved updating things such as law references, test names, and disability terminology (e.g., changing *mental retardation* to *intellectual disability*).
2. All of the items were reviewed for overall clarity and relevance.

3. All the test items associated with level 4 content changes, where the level 4 content had been revised in the standard revision process, were reviewed. This involved removing test items from the database, if a level 4 statement had been deleted, or, in most cases, writing new items to reflect the revisions in the level 4 statements.

As a result of these procedures, a total of 600 new test items were created. The test item development process involved creating two new test items for each level 4 item requiring a new or revised item. Two test items were developed for each level 4 item with the goal of selecting the better of the two items to add to the test item database. Draft test items were created by the committee members according to their assigned standards. Draft test items were then reviewed by the entire committee via video conference calls. After full committee review, all new items were sent out for external review.

A modified version of the ERC structure used in the original APENS project was used to have the new test items reviewed by practicing adapted physical educators. All active certified adapted physical educators (CAPEs) were invited to participate in the evaluation of the new test items. CAPEs had to agree to evaluate five sets of 15 test items for a total of 75 items to participate on an ERC. Eight ERC committees were formed, each composed of 14 to 15 CAPEs. The CAPE members of the 2018 ERCs are shown in appendix D. Demographic information on the 70 females and 44 males that served on the ERC is provided in table B.4.

Each ERC was sent a series of five electronic surveys, each composed of 15 test items over a period of three months. On the survey, the ERC members were shown the relevant level 4 statement, the test item question, the four multiple choice

Table B.4 ERC Demographic Data

Demographic data on the ERC members used to validate the 2018 standards

Variables	%		
GENDER			
Male	32		
Female	68		
TRAINING			
Bachelor's degree	7		
Master's degree	71		
Doctorate	22		
TEACHING LEVEL			
K-12 schools	78		
University	22		
STATE REPRESENTED (N = 30)	**60**		
Variables	**Min**	**Max**	**Mean**
Age (years)	24	69	45.7
Years teaching	1	45	17.5
% time teaching APE	0	100	72.0

answers, and the correct answer. The ERC members were then asked to rate on a 100-point scale with 1 = low and 100 = high the following:

- The degree the test item measured the level 4 statement
- The quality of the test questions stem
- The quality of the four answer choices provided

After making each rating, they were prompted that if their rating was less than 80 percent, they were asked to explain why and to provide constructive recommendations for improvement. Finally, for each question they were asked, "What percentage of minimally competent adapted physical educators (who meets the APENS eligibility requirements and can pass the exam) do you feel would get this item correct?" This was a judgement of the ease or difficulty of each test item.

ERC evaluation data were summarized for each item and then sent to the APENS committee member who had created the item. The APENS committee members then reviewed the ERC data and revised their test items accordingly. All the revised test items were then reviewed and finalized by the full APENS committee via a series of video conference calls. Finally, since two draft test items were created for each level 4 statement, the APENS committee then selected the better of the two items to be added to the APENS new test item database.

Before items in the APENS new test item database can be added to the official APENS test item database, they have to be further validated. The NCPEID uses three methods to collect additional validation data. First, they include samples of 20 new test items on future APENS exams. The performance on these items is not included in the calculation of the APENS test score, but the performance of the new items is statistically analyzed and compared to the performance of the other items on the test. Second, they administer trial versions of the APENS exam at national and regional conferences. Third, they solicit CAPEs to complete trial versions of the APENS exam composed of new test items. After 100 responses are obtained on the new test items, the psychometric data are analyzed and then reviewed by the APENS committee and decisions made whether to add them to the official APENS test database. When items are added to the official database, the APENS committee assigns an Angoff score to each item. The APENS committee did not feel discussion of how Angoff scores are calculated and the related procedures in producing these scores were necessary in this brief overview.

Disclaimers

While significant progress has been made in defining the scope and sequence of the content that adapted physical educators should know, the current standards are viewed as only the initial steps of what will be an ongoing evolutionary process.

It was accepted as a limitation at the start of this project that measuring an individual's knowledge via a paper and pencil test was no guarantee that the knowledgeable individual would correctly apply this information when delivering services to individuals with disabilities. However, it was also clear that if teachers did not know what should be done or why, there was little likelihood that they would do it correctly. Therefore, it appeared reasonable, given the financial and time constraints of this project, to delimit this project to creating the initial version of the standards and a written test to measure knowledge of this content. It is anticipated that in the coming years, the standards will be expanded and the examination revised to include measures of knowledge, application, and demonstration.

The standards described in this document were developed in response to the roles, responsibilities, and perceived needs of practicing adapted physical educators. While many faculty from institutions of higher education (IHE) were involved, there was no attempt to limit the APENS to either what was currently being offered by IHEs or to what higher education faculty felt could be easily accommodated. As a result, it is possible that many IHEs may need to revise their training programs to adequately incorporate these standards. Any implications for change emerging from this project are intended to be positive and proactive and not as threats or criticisms of current training programs.

It may also be the case that the standards presented in this document vary from the standards in the 14 states that have established state certifications or endorsements for teachers of adapted physical education. The current APENS were not developed with the intent of challenging or interfering with state requirements. In fact, states that have credentials should be acknowledged for their initiative and proactive compliance with the mandates of IDEA. Hopefully, these states can take advantage of the up-to-date and national representation involved in the current APENS and use these standards as a basis for evaluating, and if needed, updating their state standards.

Finally, the APENS were developed and reviewed independently by many professionals using all available resources. Any specific mention in the APENS to any specific products, projects, programs, terms, resources, or references should not be interpreted as endorsements. Rather, these references should be viewed solely as illustrative examples.

Appendix C

Frequently Asked Questions

Over the past two decades, numerous professionals have had questions related to the Adapted Physical Education National Standards (APENS). The most commonly asked questions are related to the background, development, and history of the APENS and the APENS exam, eligibility to take the exam, and how to earn the certified adapted physical educator (CAPE) status and get recertified. Explanations to clarify some of these issues are presented in this appendix. If further information is required, please do not hesitate to contact the APENS National Office 607-753-4969, email APENS@ cortland.edu, or visit the APENS website at www.apens.org/index.html.

APENS

Why national standards for adapted physical education (APE)?

The Individuals with Disabilities Education Act (IDEIA, 2004), mandates that free and appropriate public education services for all children and youth with disabilities be provided by highly qualified professionals (the Every Student Succeeds Act uses the term *highly effective*). As defined in IDEIA (2004),

> Special education means specially designed instruction, at no cost to the parents, to meet the unique needs of a child with a disability, including— (i) instruction conducted in the classroom, in the home, in hospitals and institutions, and in other settings; and (ii) instruction in physical education. (Authority: 20 U.S.C. 1401[29])

Although physical education was clearly identified as the only specific curricular area to be provided to children and youth with disabilities in the federal legislation, the state educational agencies were given the responsibility to interpret the term *qualified professionals* within their respective states in order to develop or amend existing certification or licensing qualifications (Section 602[10][B-D] of IDEIA). Unlike other special education areas (teachers of individuals with intellectual disabilities, visual impairments, learning disabilities, etc.), most states did not have defined certifications for teachers of adapted physical education. While it is reported that 12 states have an endorsement or certification in adapted physical education at the time of this writing, there were 38 states and eight territories that had not yet defined the qualifications teachers need to provide adapted physical education services to their students with disabilities (Kelly & Gansneder, 1998). Some states also have add-on teaching licenses or certifications in adapted physical education. California, Louisiana, Maine, Michigan, Minnesota, Nebraska, Ohio, Oregon, Rhode Island, South Dakota, Wisconsin, and Wyoming have separate teaching licenses in adapted physical education. As a result of these findings, the National Consortium for Physical Education for Individuals with Disabilities (NCPEID) established a set of national standards that defined what an adapted physical educator should know in order to provide physical education services to children with disabilities.

When were the APENS first developed?

In the spring of 1991, the National Consortium for Physical Education and Recreation for Individuals with Disabilities (now known as the NCPEID), in conjunction with the National Association of State Directors of Special Education (NASDSE) and Special Olympics International conducted an action seminar on adapted physical education for state directors of special education and leaders of advocacy groups for individuals with disabilities. This conference had two goals:

1. Identify the barriers that were preventing full provision of appropriate physical education services to individuals with disabilities
2. Establish an action agenda for resolving these problems

Although numerous barriers were identified by the group, the most significant for state education leaders were that they did not know what adapted physical education was, how individuals with disabilities could benefit from appropriate physical education programming, or what competencies teachers needed to deliver appropriate physical education services to students with disabilities. In response to this need, it was recommended that the NCPEID develop professional standards and a means for evaluating these standards.

How was APENS developed?

As one of the many outcomes established during the 1991 action seminar, it was recommended that national standards be developed to guide the future of adapted physical education. Based on this recommendation, the NCPEID board voted unanimously to assume responsibility for developing national standards for adapted physical education. A grant proposal (number H029K20092) was submitted to the United States Department of Education, Office of Special Education and Rehabilitation Services, Division of Personnel Preparation, which was approved and used to fund a five-year project to develop national standards and a national certification examination for adapted physical education.

The first year, 1992, was devoted to conducting a national job analysis to determine what roles and responsibilities adapted physical educators were being asked to fulfill in their jobs. The second year focused on developing and validating content standards based upon these roles and responsibilities. The third year involved developing and evaluating a database of over 2,000 test questions from which to develop a set of certification exams. The fourth year was devoted to conducting a national validation study on the test items. Finally, the fifth year focused on creating and administering the first national certification exam, which was conducted at 46 sites across the country on May 10, 1997.

How do I know if the APENS are valid?

As part of a doctoral dissertation, (Davis, 2001) the APENS policies and procedures for development were reviewed, and sources of validity evidence established under the guidelines of the 1999 *Standards for Educational and Psychological Testing*. Specifically, five sources of validity evidence were used to investigate the validity of the APENS and national certification exam. The five sources included: (1) evidence based on test content, (2) response processes, (3) internal structure, (4) relationships to other variables, and (5) consequences of testing. Findings indicate the validity argument is supported by evidence contributed to four out of the five validity sources. Evidence based on test content indicated that the APENS exam measures what it purports to measure and that a test specification framework was used to guide the test item development. Expert judges were used throughout the entire APENS and national certification exam development process. Finally, issues surrounding the under- or overrepresentation of the construct, including bias, were controlled through a strong internal validity design.

Evidence based on response consequences supported the validity argument in that responses from a test validation study conducted during the test item development phase of the project were used to inform the item writing and selection process. Responses from exam candidates were analyzed using multiple regression. The findings support the eligibility criteria established to take the exam as well as the CAPE specialist profile. Predictors were in agreement with both the eligibility and CAPE criteria. Evidence based on internal structure suggested that the process and procedure used to develop the APENS and national certification exam were sound and controlled to construct irrelevant bias. An exploratory factor analysis was conducted on the results from the ($N = 219$) candidates who took the 1997 APENS national certification exam and confirmed the hypothesis that no factors would emerge due to the unique design and nature of the test items written for the exam. More recently, Davis and Dillon (2010) conducted a follow-up analysis on the change in eligibility criteria for taking the APENS exam using exam results posted from years 2010 to 2014 and reported similar findings.

What major organizations have endorsed the APENS?

In 1997, these organizations endorsed the APENS:

- American Alliance for Health, Physical Education, Recreation and Dance (AAHPERD) (now Society of Health and Physical Educators [SHAPE] America)
- American Association for Active Lifestyles and Fitness (AAALF)
- Adapted Physical Activity Council (APAC)
- National Association for Sport and Physical Education (NASPE)
- American Association of School Administrators (AASA)
- National Association of State Directors of Special Education (NASDSE)
- National Association of Secondary School Principals (NASSP)

APENS Exam

Where and when is the exam offered?

The APENS exam can be taken at most public schools on any date throughout the academic year. Please contact the APENS office at 607-753-4969 to learn more about this convenient process.

The exam can also be taken at the annual SHAPE America conference and at many state SHAPE America district and state conferences. Teachers who are interested in sitting for the APENS exam at one of the SHAPE America conferences should preregister two weeks prior to the conference by registering for the exam online at APENS.org or contacting the APENS office by email APENS@cortland.edu or by phone at 607-753-4969.

How much does it cost?

The APENS national certification fee is set by the NCPEID board. Check the APENS website (www.apens.org) for the most updated and current information.

Who is eligible to take the exam?

To be eligible to take the examination, teachers must meet the following criteria:

- Hold a bachelor's degree with a major in physical education or equivalent (e.g., sport science, kinesiology, etc.)
- Have 12 credits in adapted physical education and related areas. (nine hours in adapted physical education and three hours in a related area)
- Have a minimum of 200 hours of documented experience providing physical education instruction to individuals with disabilities
- Hold a current and valid teaching certificate in physical education

How is the exam formatted?

The exam is composed of 100 multiple choice questions designed to measure knowledge of adapted physical education. Teachers are given three hours to complete the exam. The questions are derived from the level 4 content from each of the 15 standard areas in the *Adapted Physical Education National Standards* manual.

What do you get for passing the examination?

Teachers who pass the exam are certified by the NCPEID for a period of seven years and listed in the NCPEID's national registry of certified adapted physical educators. The teachers are also provided with a one-year membership in NCPEID, which includes a free, one-year, subscription to *PALAESTRA: Forum of Sport, Physical Education, and Recreation*, the quarterly publication of NCPEID. Finally, teachers who pass the APENS exam receive a certificate documenting that they are certified adapted physical educators and are able to list the initials CAPE after their name (e.g., David Martinez, M.S., CAPE).

How was the APENS examination initially developed?

The initial APENS exam was the product of five years of development and evaluation work performed by over 500 members of the profession. Since 1997, the exam has been continuously reviewed and revised by the NCPEID APENS Committee. For more details, see appendix B. During year three of the project, a database of over 2,000 potential test questions was developed based upon the level 4 content in the APENS manual. Each of these test questions was sent to 30 adapted physical educators, chosen from the larger group, who were asked to evaluate the item according to eight criteria. Their responses were compiled and analyzed, and the questions were revised accordingly.

During the fourth year of the project, the test items were administered to a national sample of 3,000 preservice and in-service teachers, including adapted physical educators, special educators, general physical educators, and nonteaching physical education majors. The responses of these groups were used to calculate the psychometric measures for each item (item difficulty, discrimination index, etc.). All of the data on the test questions were then reviewed by the project executive and steering committees and used in selecting the final items that are used on the exam.

Finally, the validity of the exam was analyzed and tested. The validity analyzes whether the exam actually measures what it is intended to measure and whether the performance of an applicant on the exam is an indicator of performance on the job.

How does one become a CAPE?

All initial CAPE candidates must meet the aforementioned eligibility criteria and pass the APENS exam to earn the CAPE status. The CAPE certification lasts for seven years, and persons who wish to continue their certification do not have to retake the exam. Initial CAPE certification applicants can complete the online application or mail in a printed copy of the professional physical educator application (see www. APENS.org). Additional required items include a copy of the current teaching license, transcripts, and documentation of teaching students with disabilities in physical education. Please contact the APENS office with questions about application criteria and eligibility and testing sites, dates, and times.

Do CAPEs have to periodically renew their CAPE certification?

The field of adapted physical education is constantly evolving and expanding. In order for our certification to have meaning, it is essential that it be demonstrated that all CAPEs are current and actively engaged in the field. To do this, each CAPE must recertify every seven years. Recertification criteria can be found on the APENS.org website under recertification.

Website Information

Where can more information be obtained about APENS (e.g., applications, standards updates, newsletters, and resources)?

The APENS website can be viewed by visiting www.apens.org/index.html. Information can also be obtained by contacting our office directly as follows:

APENS
E1106 Park Center
Department of Physical Education
SUNY Cortland
Cortland, NY 13045
607-753-4969
APENS@cortland.edu
www.cortland.edu/APENS

Appendix D

APENS 2018 Evaluation and Review Committee Members

Last name	First name	State
Achler	Jeff	IL
Alexander	Melissa	NJ
Alverson	David	TX
Augustin	Matthew	MD
Bader	Antoinette	WA
Bakken	Laura	ND
Banes	Jessica	TX
Barnhart	Candice	OR
Begin	Jennifer	OH
Boeren	Sarah	VA
Boswell	Wendy	TX
Brevig	Gail	MT
Buchanan	Alice	AL
Butterfield	Stephen	ME
Colombo-Dougovito	Andrew	TX
Colquitt	Gavin	GA
Combs	Clarice	NC
Corson	Sean	CA
Davis	Diana	IL
Deschenes	Patricia	NJ
Dillon	Leslie	VA
Doherty	Theresa	TX
Dole	Blake	IL
Faulkner	Stephanie	TX
Fox	Brian	MA
Fujioka	Lance	HI
Garrison	Brett	NJ
Glueck	Pamela	CA
Green	Nicole	UT
Griffin	Dianna	NH

Last name	First name	State
Groff	Stephanie	UT
Halscheid	William	CT
Hanestad	Troy	AK
Hanhardt	Luke	CA
Hankey	Crista	OR
Helhoski	Gail	NJ
Hilgenbrinck	Linda	TX
Hill	Barbara	MN
Hope	Erica	MI
Hughes	Ann	NC
Hughes	Miriam	PA
Hutt	Benjamin	VA
Jackson	Dallas	PA
Johnson	Geoben	TX
Katz	Heather	TX
Kelly	Darcy	CA
Kiernan	John	CA
Koppenhaver	Sarah	NY
Laughlin	Michael	HI
Lee	Jihyun	CA
Longo	Melissa	PA
Lovings	Tacara	UT
Lucas	Matthew	VA
Martinez	David	GA
Mason-Foederer	Vicki	TX
Mazella	Janet	IL
Mazik	Teresa	MA
McDowell	Kate	MD
McManus	Melanie	MD
McNamara	Scott	MI

Last name	First name	State
McPeak	Kaky	NC
Meiners	Valerie	MA
Meleney	Barbara	NC
Mell	Sherri	TX
Menear	Kristi	AL
Mirtz	Timothy	FL
Morriss	Janice	TX
Murdock	Valerie	UT
Myrga	Wayne	MD
Neal	Lisa	CA
O'Mara	Patricia	NY
Oswald	Stacey	UT
Papaccio	Patrick	NY
Pariso	Christine	WI
Piletic	Cindy	IL
Pope	Marcia	CA
Powell	Delia	MI
Puyear	Michael	LA
Quinlan	Darcy	OH
Rawlins	Knolan	PA
Rebecca	Douglas	NY
Reder	Sam	AK
Renkoski	Rachel	CA
Rice	Kellie	OR
Rizzo-Riley	Paula	MA
Roberts	Anna	GA
Rose	Tami	KS

Last name	First name	State
Samalot-Rivera	Amaury	NY
Sato	Takahiro	OH
Schaults	Kelly	VA
Schultz	Charles	TX
Simmons	Victoria	NC
Skogstad	Pamela	AK
Slone	Christy	VA
Sorensen	Jacquelyn	RI
Stimpson	Cheryl	IL
Stratton	Christopher	WI
Streicher	Christopher	UT
Swinden	Thomas	TX
Szyman	Robert	IL
Thom	Stephen	CA
Tible	Elizabeth	NJ
Tunnicliffe	Kerri	RI
Umhoefer	Donna	TX
Vance	Mike	NY
Velasco-Huerta	Fernanda	TX
Walker	George	TN
Webbert	Linda	MD
Weiner	Brad	MD
White	Laura	CA
Wood	Matt	MI
Wyatt	Dennis	TX
Zagrodnik	James	UT
Zinn	Jody	MD

Glossary

504 plan—A plan, much like an IEP, that helps a student with a disability that substantially limits his or her ability to learn and participate in the general education classroom, but who does not qualify for an IEP to have a plan that outlines how the student's specific needs will be met with accommodations, modifications, and other services.

academic learning time (ATL)—Unit of time when an individual is engaged in activities related to class objectives.

achievement-based curriculum (ABC)—Model for integrating program planning, assessing, prescribing, teaching, and evaluating so that the physical education needs of all individuals are met.

activities of daily living (ADL)—Skills that are necessary to perform everyday functions such as walking and dressing.

adapted physical education (APE)—Programs designed to develop physical and motor fitness, fundamental motor skills and patterns, and skills in aquatics, dance, and individual and group games and sports so that the individual with a disability can ultimately participate in community-based physical activity programs to enjoy an enhanced quality of life. Diversified programs generally have the same goals and objectives as general physical education but are modified when necessary to meet the unique needs of each individual.

adaptive behavior—The collection of conceptual, social, and practical skills that all people learn in order to function in their daily lives.

adventitious—Arising from an external source; extrinsic. Occurring accidentally or spontaneously, not caused by heredity.

administrative feasibility—A number of factors such as cost, time, training, and specialized equipment required to use an assessment instrument accurately and reliably (Kelly & Melograno 2014, p. 154).

agonist—Muscle acting to cause a movement (Hall, 2012).

American Sign Language (ASL)—Primary language of the deaf; uses hand signs and finger spelling. ASL is concept-based and is grammatically and symbolically different than signed English.

ancillary skills—Skills that support the achievement of a task but are not essential to completing the task. Having good eye–hand coordination is an ancillary skill to hitting a ball with a bat.

annual goals—General statements of student outcomes, projected over the school year.

Annual Report to Congress—Short for the Annual Report to Congress on the Implementation of the Individuals with Disabilities Education Act, which is required as a part of IDEA's legal mandates and focuses on the children and youth with disabilities being served under IDEA, Part C or B, nationally and at the state level.

antagonistic—Muscle that in contracting tends to produce movement opposite to that of the agonist.

antecedent stimulus—Stimulus that occurs prior to a response.

anticipation—Ability to predict what is going to occur in the environment and when it will occur, and then perform various information-processing activities in advance of the event.

applied behavior analysis—Techniques derived from the principles of behavior that are systematically applied to meaningfully enhance socially significant behavior and demonstrate experimentally that the technique used caused the improved behavior.

assessment—Interpretation of measurements for the purpose of making decisions about placement, program planning, and performance objectives

assessment plan—Predetermined procedures and instruments for gathering, interpreting, and reporting data gathered in the assessment process.

assimilation-contrast theory—Theory that states that an individual's current belief serves as an internal reference point to which the persuasion attempt is compared. When an individual is presented with an anchor—be it an idea, message, or a view—that is credible and congruent enough with his or her own beliefs, it is assimilated and contributes to attitude adjustments, which in turn influence behavior. If the discrepancy is too significant to be assimilated, the anchor is rejected (contrasted) and fails to influence attitude or behavior.

associative learning—A learning process by which a certain stimulus comes to be associated with another stimulus or behavior, as through classical or operant conditioning.

ataxia (cerebral palsy)—Type of cerebral palsy that is characterized by hypotonia, poor coordination, and poor balance.

atlantoaxial instability—Misalignment of the first and second cervical vertebrae, which can cause permanent damage to the spinal cord during hyperflexion or hyperextension of the head or neck.

augmentative and alternative communication—Supplemental communication techniques that are used in addition to whatever naturally acquired speech and vocalization exists, to include such things as sign language and gestures.

augmented feedback—Information in addition to sensory feedback that is provided by a source external to the person making the movement.

authentic assessment—The systematic collection of physical and motor performance data while observing individuals playing games, sports, and physical activities in natural settings.

automaticity—Process to deal with information that is (1) fast; (2) not attention demanding, in that such processes do not generate significant interference with other tasks; (3) parallel, occurring together with other processing tasks; and (4) involuntary, often unavoidable (Schmidt & Lee, 2011).

automatic processes (processing)—Mode of information processing that is fast, not attention demanding, parallel, and often involuntary.

aversives—Unpleasant stimuli that induce changes in behavior. By applying an aversive stimulus immediately following a behavior, the likelihood of that behavior occurring in the future is decreased (punishment). By removing an aversive stimulus immediately following a behavior, the likelihood of that behavior occurring in the future is increased (negative reinforcement).

axis of rotation—Imaginary lines or points about which a body or a segment rotates (Kreighbaum & Barthels, 1996).

backward chaining—Teaching a desired behavior by beginning with the last behavioral link in the chain of behaviors.

baseline—Behaviors or scores collected before an intervention is implemented. Baseline data are used to set goals, establish criteria for measuring change, and determine the schedule of reinforcement.

behavior contract—An agreement, verbal or written, that details the behavioral expectations of a student and the teacher in implementing an intervention plan.

behavior intervention plan—An intervention plan, developed by using data from a functional behavior assessment, that describes inappropriate behavior(s), ideas about why the behavior is occurring, and intervention strategies and positive behavioral supports to be implemented to address the behavior.

behavior management—A process that involves both the science and art of systematically applying evidence-based prevention and intervention techniques to enhance the probability that another person or group will develop socially acceptable behaviors as well as develop self-discipline, responsibility, self-direction, and character in order to create an environment that is conducive for learning.

brittle diabetes—Insulin-dependent diabetes that is not well controlled and has increased potential for symptoms to occur at any time such as dizziness, nausea, and loss of consciousness.

calorimetry—Measurement of heat expressed in calories.

Canon Communicator—Portable tape typewriter, with a control display that contains the letters of the alphabet. The interface consists of multiple switches or keys that the user depresses as selections are made.

caregiver—Guardian of an individual with a disability who provides care. This includes parents, supervisors, or home staff.

chains—Sequencing of a series of learned behaviors presented in a fixed order to achieve a more complex terminal response (Lavay, French, & Henderson, 2016).

child kinship—Relationships between a child and significant persons in his or her life, including natural and adopted parents and other adults who assume responsibility for the child.

circuit type or station arrangement (of teaching)—Creation of discrete learning areas within the general teaching area where individuals work on activities independently and at their own rates. This technique is especially effective when a group possesses a wide range of abilities.

closed loop model—A feedback control system in which an individual is provided with error detection that is used for correction of the motor behavior.

closed skill—Movement skill where the environment is stable and predictable, allowing the performer to control what happens next. A handstand and a shot put are examples of a closed skill.

cognitive dissonance—The state of having inconsistent thoughts, beliefs, or attitudes, especially as relating to behavioral decisions and attitude change.

collaboration—Work done jointly with others to accomplish a common goal such as making decisions or implementing assessment plans and programs.

command style of teaching—Style in which the teacher makes all the decisions regarding the organization of the lesson (starting, stopping, activities to be performed, how they are performed, etc.), and the student is only required to respond to the teacher's command signals (Mosston & Ashworth, 2001).

communication—Means by which an individual relates experiences, ideas, knowledge, and feelings to another (includes speech, sign language, gestures, and writing).

communication board—Apparatus on which the alphabet, numbers, and commonly used words are represented; used when oral expression is difficult or cannot be obtained.

community-based programming—Curriculum-based programming that relates to real-life situations where the individual is involved in life experiences inside and outside the school environment.

community resources—Personnel, materials, services, and facilities available in the community for use by educators to enrich IEPs, facilitate IFSPs, and actualize transition plans for individuals with disabilities.

Congressional Record—The official record of the proceedings and debates of the U.S. Congress.

consultation—Providing support services to parents, teachers, and other professionals; adult education, which may include various forms of in-service education, parent training, and collaborative teamwork; and expert advice and contract services, such as assessment or evaluation for a school district (Sherrill, 2004).

contained choices—Limited number of choices given to an individual.

content-referenced standards—Established expectations in terms of the content of components of the task to be mastered.

contextual interference—A learning phenomenon where interference during practice is beneficial to skill learning (Magill & Anderson, 2013).

contingency—Relationship between the behavior to be changed and the events or consequences that follow that particular behavior (Lavay, French, & Henderson, 2016).

contingent observation time-out—A combination of modeling and time-out procedures in which the individual is removed from the group but is left near enough to observe peers demonstrating appropriate behavior.

continuous reinforcement—Schedule of reinforcement based on the individual being rewarded immediately each time the behavior is performed.

continuous skill—Skill in which the input or action repeats a pattern without a recognizable beginning or end (e.g., swimming and running).

continuum of placement—The offering of appropriate placements in educational programs along a continuum from least to more restrictive educational settings.

contractility—The ability of the muscle to contract or shorten.

contraindicated—Conditions, activities, or tasks that are not recommended because they may aggravate or exacerbate a condition of a disability.

cooperative games—Games designed with alternative approaches in order to effectively accommodate and include rather than exclude all participants.

cooperative learning—A learning environment in which an individual learns from others in the class by working in teams that allow those with abilities in specific areas to help others in the group. Individual accountability is fostered. The group, not the individual, reaches the goal, giving all members of the group a feeling of success. The intent is social outcomes along with content mastery.

coping and avoiding strategies—Techniques used by individuals with disabilities to avoid practicing learning the tasks being taught.

corporal punishment—A consequence to an inappropriate behavior that involves causing deliberate pain or discomfort provided with the intent of decreasing the future occurrence of that behavior.

corrective physical education—Physical education activities of a prescriptive nature that involve a body part(s), posture, or remediation, or correction of specific weaknesses.

criterion-referenced instrument—Standardized or nonstandardized instrument designed primarily to collect process measures that are then compared to established reference standards. (Kelly & Melograno, 2014, p. 149).

criterion-referenced standards—Explicit definitions of tasks or behaviors to be mastered.

cross-disciplinary approach—Any professional activity that involves two or more academic disciplines including viewing one academic discipline from the perspective of another academic discipline.

cue—See *prompt*.

culturally responsive pedagogy—A pedagogy that empowers students intellectually, socially, emotionally, and politically by using cultural referents to impart knowledge, skills, and attitudes. Culturally relevant teaching utilizes the backgrounds, knowledge, and experiences of the students to inform the teacher's lessons and methodology.

curriculum-embedded—Ongoing and continuous process of gathering performance data during the instructional phase of teaching. See also *content-referenced standards*.

data-based gymnasium—Systematic approach used to assess and teach physical education to individuals with severe disabilities developed by Dunn, Morehouse, and Fredericks (1986). The curriculum requires the use of cues, consequences, and data analyses.

demonstrations—The exhibition of the task or behavior so that the individuals may have a visual representation of the task in order to model the task appropriately. The demonstration is often accompanied by verbal cues.

developmental coordination disorder—Condition in which a child has difficulty with motor coordination. Other terms for this disorder are clumsiness, physical awkwardness, and developmental dysphasia (Clark, Betchell, Smiley-Ogen, & Whitall, 2005).

developmental delay—Discrepancy between an individual's chronological age and functional age in the cognitive, motor, or affective domains.

developmentally appropriate (activities)—Activities designed to meet the developmental needs, capabilities, and limitations of students.

differential reinforcement—Reinforcing an appropriate response in the presence of one stimulus while extinguishing an inappropriate response in the presence of another stimulus.

direct measures—Data-gathering techniques used to measure movement parameters directly through the use of instrumentation that often does not require the performance of a skill or pattern.

direct service (physical education)—Delivery of physical education services by an adapted physical educator including screening, evaluation, assessment, and implementing education programs.

discrete skill—Skill in which the action is usually brief and with a recognizable beginning and end; e.g., hitting, throwing.

discrimination reaction time—Time required to respond to a specified stimulus given multiple stimuli.

distributed practice—Practice schedule in which the amount of rest between practice trials is long relative to the trial length.

divergent or exploratory style of teaching—Teaching style in which the learner is encouraged to develop multiple responses to a single question or problem (Mosston & Ashworth, 2001).

due process—Legally defined set of procedures available to individuals with disabilities to assure that their rights are not violated. These procedures include mediation hearings and court actions.

duration recording—Recording the number of minutes (duration) the behavior occurs during a predetermined period of time. For example, the number of minutes an individual is exhibiting on-task behavior.

dynamic systems theory—The belief that a movement pattern can be created as a result of a near infinite combination of interactions of component parts and the development of these patterns is discontinuous or constantly changing (Payne & Isaacs, 2016).

Dynavox—Brand name for a variety of speech generating devices used to assist individuals in overcoming their speech, language, and learning challenges.

ecological task analysis—An analysis of the subskills and progressions needed to complete tasks and skills that are appropriate to the individual with a disability within the specific environment in which these skills will be performed (Block, 2016). Also referred to as ecological inventory.

ecological theory—Interactions between the individual and everything in the individual's environment. In teaching and learning, this suggests that environmental factors, as well as personal factors, must be considered.

economy of measurement instruments—Desirable test characteristics having minimal cost in terms of time, personnel, and equipment needed to administer. See also *administrative feasibility*.

endocrine control (system)—Collection of glands that help regulate and maintain body functions through the production and release of hormones.

endurance—Ability to continue a movement activity (McArdle, Katch, & Katch, 2014).

equilibrium—State of a system whose motion is not being changed, accelerated, or decelerated (Kreighbaum & Barthels, 1996).

equilibrium reactions—Automatic reactions that the body uses for maintaining or controlling its center of gravity.

ergometry—Technique to measure work output usually by means of a collaborated apparatus such as an arm crank ergometer.

ERIC—Educational Resources Information Center.

error detection (capability)—Learned capability to detect one's own error through analyzing response-produced feedback (Schmidt & Lee, 2014).

evaluation—The process of comparing initial assessment data with reassessment data to make informed decisions (Kelly & Melograno, 2014, p. 147).

event recording—Recording the number of times the behavior (event) occurs during a predetermined period of time.

Everyone CAN—Extensive set of elementary teaching resources for 70 physical education objectives based upon the ABC model composed of performance objectives, assessment items, instructional activities, and games.

evidence-based practice—An intervention that is based in science (with empirical evidence to support its use), as well as the disposition of a practitioner to base the selection of his or her interventions in science (adapted from Council for Exceptional Children, 2018).

executive functioning—A set of processes that all have to do with managing oneself and one's resources in order to achieve a goal. *Executive functions* is an umbrella term for the neurologically based skills involving mental control and self-regulation (from the National Joint Committee on Learning Disabilities, 2018).

extinction—The process of eliminating or reducing the occurrence of a conditioned response by not administering any form of reinforcement.

extracurricular services—Nonacademic activities that may include counseling services, athletics, transportation, health services, recreational activities, referral to agencies that provide assistance, etc.

extrinsic feedback—Feedback provided artificially over and above that received naturally from a behavior is being performed.

extrinsic reinforcers—Reinforcers provided artificially over and above that received naturally occurring in the environment in which the behavior is being performed.

facilitated communication—Method of enabling individuals with disabilities to communicate, using an alphabet board, a handheld typewriter (e.g., a Canon Communicator), or a computer.

fading—Gradual removal of a cue, prompt, or reinforcer.

Federal Register—A legal newspaper published daily by the National Archives and Records Administration containing federal agency regulations, proposed rules, and public notices.

flexibility—Range of motion of a joint (static flexibility); opposition or resistance of a joint to motion (dynamic flexibility) (McArdle, Katch, & Katch, 2014).

fluid mechanics—Effects that a fluid environment (i.e., air, water) have on the motion of a body (Kreighbaum & Barthels, 1996).

force—A push or pull acting on an object. Force is the product of mass and acceleration (Hall, 2012).

formal assessment—Data gathered that supports the conclusions made from standardized measures that have the statistics that yield scores such as percentiles, stanines, or standard scores.

formative evaluation—Measurement and evaluation of an individual's performance using a predetermined standard; parallels ongoing assessment and focuses on the process and interpreting why certain results occur, used to make short-term instructional decisions (Kelly & Melograno, 2014, p. 242).

forward chaining—Technique in which the behavior is taught starting with the first step and ending with the last step.

functionally appropriate—Motor activities or tests that have everyday relevance for an individual.

functional skills—Skills that possess everyday relevance for an individual. See also *activities of daily living*.

generalization—Process of applying what is learned to other, unpracticed tasks of the same class or in another environment.

general (regular) physical education—A physical education program that includes goals in one of the following areas: physical and motor fitness, fundamental motor skills, aquatics, dance, and individual and group games.

group contingency—Presentation of a highly desired reinforcer to a group of individuals based on the behavior of one person or the group.

group dynamics theory—A system of behaviors and psychological processes occurring within a social group (intragroup dynamics) or between social groups (intergroup dynamics).

guidance—Procedure in which the learner is physically or verbally directed through the performance to reduce errors.

guided discovery style of teaching—Teaching style in which the learning environment is arranged by the teacher to lead the individual to the learning outcome (Mosston & Ashworth, 2001).

heart rate—Number of times the heart beats per minute.

hemiplegia—Paralysis of the arm and leg on the same side of the body.

hydrocephalus—Abnormally large head caused by an accumulation of cerebrospinal fluid (Berkow, 1987).

I-CAN—Extensive set of preprimary, primary, and secondary teaching resources based upon the ABC model composed of performance objectives, assessment items, instructional activities, and games.

impulsivity—Tendency to move rapidly without carefully considering the alternatives (American Psychiatric Association, 2015).

incidental learning—Learning that is not a result of formal instruction (Schmidt & Wrisberg, 2008).

inclusion—Placement of an individual with a disability (even a severe disability) into general classes with peers in the neighborhood school. The individual is not an occasional visitor, but a viable member of the class with appropriate support services provided in the general classes.

inclusive sport opportunities—Opportunities to play sports that are the same for individuals with disabilities as for individuals without disabilities.

indirect service—Service not provided directly to a child but provided by a special education teacher or related services personnel to help the teacher who is working directly with the child.

individual family service plan—A written document that insures that special services are delivered from birth to three years of age to children with developmental delays.

individualized education program (IEP)—Written statement of instruction and services to be provided based on a multidisciplinary assessment of the needs of each child with a disability; includes goals and objectives, evaluation methods, personnel responsible, and dates for initiation and completion of services.

infant reflexes—Reflexes that appear during gestation or at birth and typically become suppressed by approximately six months of age.

informal assessment—Criterion-referenced measures or performance-based measures to gather data used to inform instruction.

integrated settings—Physical education class settings that include individuals with disabilities learning together with individuals without disabilities. See also *inclusion*.

interaction skills—Personal skills such as communication and social behavior required by individuals to enable them to successfully work with and relate to others around them.

interdisciplinary approach—Philosophical approach that facilitates a sharing of information among professionals for the purpose of increased service to individuals with disabilities.

intertrial interval—Time separating two trials of a task.

interval reinforcement—Schedule of reinforcement based on the individual being rewarded for the performance of a desired behavior over a certain period of time.

intoxicants—Chemical toxins such as alcohol and cocaine that, when ingested by a woman during pregnancy, place the developing fetus at high risk for brain-related disorders.

intrinsic feedback—Feedback naturally received from performing a movement. See also *extrinsic feedback*.

involuntary—Muscle that is not under voluntary control.

Karvonen formula—Method for determining heart rate reserve. Used to establish target heart rate for exercise programs.

Kelly-Rimmer equation—A regression equation for estimating the percent body fat of adult males with intellectual disability. The Kelly-Rimmer equation is % fat = 13.545 + 0.487 (waist circumference, cm) −0.52 (forearm circumference, cm) −0.155 (height, cm) + 0.077 (weight, kg) (from NCHPAD, n.d.).

kinematics—Area of study that is concerned with time and space factors in the motion of a system.

kinesiology—Study of human movements, performance, and function by applying the sciences of biomechanics, anatomy, physiology, psychology, and neuroscience.

kinesthesis—Sense derived from muscular contractions during purposeful movements, related to proprioception.

kinetics—Area of study that is concerned with the forces of the movement pattern produced.

knowledge of performance—Feedback related to the way in which a specific skill is performed.

knowledge of results—Feedback or verbalizable information about success in meeting the movement goal; refers to the outcome or product (i.e., goals scored, distance covered) (Kelly & Melograno, 2014, p. 192).

least restrictive environment (LRE)—Educational setting in which the individuals can safely and successfully function and meet their goals and objectives prescribed based on assessment results.

leisure counseling—Counseling involving a knowledge and understanding of leisure, the importance of leisure lifestyles, and personal concepts of leisure choices and the exploration of personal resources including skills, finances, experiences, and home and community resources.

life span—Continuous and cumulative process of development originating at birth and ending at death.

Light Talker—Augmentative device, similar to the Touch Talker, that uses a scanning device activated by a switch for individuals who cannot directly select symbols.

local education agency (LEA)—Educational agency such as a school, school district, or county, who under the law is responsible for the education of a given individual.

long-term goals—Broad general statements of student outcomes.

long-term memory—Contains information that has been collected over a lifetime; it may be essentially limitless in capacity. See also *short-term memory*.

manipulatives—Tangible objects that a child can use to learn concepts.

Maslow's theory—A theory used in developmental psychology to describe human growth. Often presented in a pyramid, it is a hierarchy of human development beginning with basic physiological needs and ending with self-actualization. The goal is to obtain self-actualization and or self-transcendence.

massed and distributed practice—Practice schedule in which the amount of rest between trials is short relative to the trial length.

mechanical—Ability of the human body for producing efficient mechanical work such as walking, running, and cycling.

medical gymnastics—System popularized by Dudley Sargent in the early 1900s in which exercise was prescribed for various physical disabilities.

mental practice—Practice procedure in which the learner imagines successful action without overt physical practice.

mercury switch—Device attached to an individual's body or clothes, which completes an electrical circuit when the individual performs the desired movement, allowing a reinforcer such as a light or music to be activated.

metabolic equivalent (MET)—Resting energy requirement, estimated to be 3.5 ml of oxygen per kilogram of body weight per minute.

metabolic rate—Energy expended by the body per unit time (Spence & Mason, 2018).

metabolism—Sum total of all chemical reactions that occur in the body during the production of energy for work.

microcephalus—Abnormally small head.

mineralization—Mineral deposits in the tissues.

modeling—A procedure in which another person demonstrates the correct performance of the task or behavior to be learned.

moral development—Process whereby humans progress from behaving in a way that receives rewards and avoids punishment to the desired stage in which unselfish concern for human rights, cognitive thought process, and moral reasoning are believed to be parallel.

motor fitness—Components of physical performance such as agility, coordination, speed, and power that contribute to success in various physical activities.

motor program—A series of subroutines organized into the correct sequence to perform a skill.

multidisciplinary—The involvement of many disciplines in the service delivery process, including separate evaluations and prescriptions to different specialists (various team members).

multidisciplinary (model) approach—Approach in which separate evaluations and prescriptions by different specialists are used to identify the individual's specific problem.

multidisciplinary team—A group of individuals from multiple disciplines who meet to pursue a common goal such as evaluating a student for placement in special education or creating an IEP for a student.

muscular endurance—Ability of a muscle or a muscle group to perform repeated contractions against a light load for an extended period of time (McArdle, Katch, & Katch, 2014).

muscular strength—Amount of force exerted or resistance overcome by a muscle for a single repetition (McArdle, Katch, & Katch, 2014).

myoelectric arm—Particular type of prosthesis for individuals who have a portion of their arm amputated. The arm, which operates by means of a small battery-driven motor, obeys signals received from electric energy produced by movement of the remaining muscle groups. This allows control of the elbow or hand.

negative reinforcement—Removal of an aversive stimulus as a consequence of a behavior in order to increase the frequency of that behavior in the future (Lavay, French, & Henderson, 2016).

negative transfer—Hindrance or interference by the experience with a previous skill with the learning of a new skill.

neurodevelopmental theory—Theory that suggests (1) delayed or abnormal motor development is the result of interference with normal brain maturation, (2) this interference is manifested as an impairment of the postural reflex mechanism, (3) abnormal reflex activity produces an abnormal degree and distribution of postural and muscle tone, and (4) righting and equilibrium reactions should be used to inhibit abnormal movements while simultaneously stimulating and facilitating normal postural responses.

nonverbal communication—Any approach designed to support, enhance, or supplement the communication of individuals who are not independent verbal communicators in all situations.

normalization—Concept that emphasizes that individuals with disabilities should live and function as closely as possible to the normal living, learning, and working conditions of people in society.

occupational therapy—Primarily concerned with the components of performance to maintain the individual's self-care, work, and leisure activities. Major components include motor, sensory integrative, and cognitive functioning.

open loop system—System where feedback is available but cannot be used because of the nature of the task.

open skill—Movement skill in which the environment is unpredictable or unstable, requiring adaptability from the performer to suit the needs of the environment; decision making is required. Passing a soccer ball in a game is an example of an open skill.

operant conditioning—A method of learning in which consequences are provided following a behavior in order to modify the future occurrence of that behavior. Reinforcement following a behavior is intended to increase the future occurrence of that behavior. Punishment following a behavior is intended to decrease the future occurrence of that behavior (Lavay, French, & Henderson, 2016).

opportunity to respond—Number of appropriate learning trials (opportunities) a student had during a lesson.

organizing centers—Focal points for the curriculum and learning; they are the frame of reference, emphasis, or theme around which the subject matter is designed (Kelly & Melograno, 2014).

orientation and mobility training specialist—Related service specialist who provides training designed to develop or relearn skills and concepts needed to travel safely and independently through environments for individuals who are blind or have visual impairments.

orthoptic vision—Activity of the six external muscles of the eye that move the eyes up, down, in, out, and in diagonal directions.

orthosis—Straightening or correction of a deformity or disability.

outcome-based goals and objectives—Goals and objectives that focus on the result or outcome of the completed task and not the way in which the task is completed.

overcorrection—Process by which a person or group is required to engage in excessive or repetitive appropriate behavior as a consequence of an inappropriate behavior in order to decrease the future occurrence of the inappropriate behavior (Lavay, French & Henderson, 2016).

overcueing—Providing more than the necessary cues to encourage a student to initiate or continue a task that he or she had previously executed.

overfat—Having a proportion of body fat that exceeds recommended limits, usually over 15 percent for men and 24 percent for women (McArdle, Katch, & Katch, 2014).

overlearning—Additional practice beyond the amount needed to achieve a performance criterion.

overload—Resistance greater than that which a muscle or muscle group normally encounters. The resistance (load) can be maximal or near maximal (McArdle, Katch, & Katch, 2014).

overselectivity—An attentional abnormality characterized by hyperattentiveness to selected stimuli in the environment and lack of attention to other relevant stimuli.

overweight—Condition in which the body weighs more than normal based on height-weight charts.

oxygen consumption—Volume of oxygen used for energy expenditure. It is usually expressed in liters per minute or in a relative term, milliliters per kilogram per minute (mL/kg/min) (McArdle, Katch, & Katch, 2014).

oxygen transport—Function of the cardiorespiratory system, which is composed of the stroke volume (SV), the heart rate (HR), and the arterial mixed venous oxygen difference (McArdle, Katch, & Katch, 2014).

pairing techniques—Matching or associating a primary reinforcer with a secondary reinforcer (that is perhaps more socially normal and acceptable) that gradually replaces the primary reinforcer.

paraplegia—Paralysis or involvement of lower extremities and trunk resulting from spinal lesion or neurological dysfunction.

paraprofessional—Individual who is not prepared to teach physical education but who can assist the physical educator in tasks such as securing materials and equipment and working in one-on-one situations with students who need more personalized attention.

pathobiomechanics—Study of the nature and cause of disease, which involves changes in structure and function of the mechanics of the human system (Kreighbaum & Barthels, 1996).

pathokinesiology—Study of the nature and cause of disease, which involves structural and functional changes in the ability of a human body to move (Kreighbaum & Barthels, 1996).

peer tutor—Student with or without a disability serving as an aid or friend in order to assist the individual with a disability.

perception—Process by which information is interpreted within the cortical areas of the brain or the process of obtaining meaning from sensation and thus having knowledge of the environment (Sherrill, 2004).

performance generalization—Ability to utilize a performance in a broad array of contexts, (e.g., balancing on one foot, balancing while moving, balancing on a beam, etc.).

performance sampling—Practice of measuring representative factors of motor performance as a means for obtaining an overview of an individual's true ability.

perseveration—Persistence or fixation on a single feature or source of stimuli, manifests in repetitive behavior such as vocalizations, hand gestures, and fixation on a task.

personality disorders—Broad category that characterizes individuals whose personality traits are inflexible and maladaptive and significantly impair social, leisure, or vocational functioning (American Psychiatric Association, 2015).

phenylketonuria—Recessive genetic disorder accompanied by an enzyme disorder interfering with food metabolism. If untreated, brain damage and intellectual disability may result.

physical activity reinforcement—Systematic procedure in which a structured time to choose among various preferred physical activities is contingent on the individual's meeting of a predetermined criterion of behavior (Lavay, French, & Henderson, 2016).

physical guidance—Most intrusive level of cueing or prompting. Physical guidance can range from the touch of a body part to the physical manipulation of the individual's limbs and body so that the individual can complete a movement sequence (Block, 2016).

physical or psychological aversive strategies—Application of a stimulus that the individual does not like that decreases the likelihood that the inappropriate behavior will be performed again.

physical restraints—Equipment or personnel used to control or reduce the freedom of movement an individual has so as to prevent them from causing injury to themselves and others.

physical therapy—Identification, prevention, remediation, and rehabilitation of acute to prolonged movement dysfunction. Treatment by physical means, evaluating patients and treating through physical therapeutic measures as opposed to medicines or surgery.

Piaget's theory of cognitive development—Theory explaining how a child develops and constructs a mental model of the world as he or she progresses through four stages of cognitive development (i.e., sensorimotor, preoperational, concrete operational, and formal operational).

positive practice overcorrection—Intervention in which an individual is required to practice an appropriate behavior for an extended period. For example, if an individual becomes angry and refuses to shake hands with another person after a contest, the individual might be required to shake hands with a number of individuals. See also *overcorrection*.

positive reinforcement—An intervention procedure in which a pleasant stimulus is provided as a consequence of a behavior in order to increase the future occurrence of that behavior.

positive specific immediate feedback—Information given to the individual immediately upon completion of the behavior that reinforces (increases the likelihood that it will be done again) a specific aspect of the behavior (Schmidt & Wrisberg, 2008).

positive transfer—Occurs when experience with a previous skill aids or facilitates the learning of a new skill.

power—Application of force and speed in relation to the quantity of work done per unit of time (Hall, 2012).

Premack principle—Use of more preferred, highly reinforcing, or valued activities (e.g.,. shooting a basketball) that are contingent on completing less preferred activities (e.g., performing basketball drills). Telling a student, "Do what I want you to do, then you can do what you want to do" would be an example of using the Premack principle. (Lavay, French, & Henderson, 2016).

present level of performance—Performance information obtained through an assessment process designed to indicate baseline performance. It is a point of reference for developing goals and objectives (Lavay, French, & Henderson, 2016).

primary reinforcers—Those reinforcers that satisfy a biological need, such as food when hungry or water when thirsty (Lavay, French, & Henderson, 2016).

prime mode of communication—Method of communication with which an individual with a disability is most comfortable and competent.

professional development—Any systematic attempt to educate school personnel.

program evaluation—Process by which program merit can be determined by measuring student outcomes, consumer satisfaction, and quality of program operations for the purpose of improvement, accountability, and enlightenment.

prompt—Cue that increases the probability of the behavioral response, usually in the form of physical guidance to initiate a proper movement (Block, 2016).

prompting hierarchy—Continuum of prompts ranging from physical assistance (most intrusive) to natural cues in the environment (least intrusive).

proprioception—Sensory information arising from within the body, resulting in the sense of position and movement, similar to kinesthesis.

proprioceptive neuromuscular facilitation (PNF)—Series of therapeutic techniques designed to enhance the neural muscular response (relaxation or contraction) of a body part, based on neuropsychological principles. PNF techniques place the muscle group to be stretched in a position that stretches the muscles and places them under tension. The individual then contracts the stretched muscle group briefly while a therapist, teacher, partner, or object applies sufficient resistance to inhibit movement.

prosthesis—Replacement of a missing body part by an artificial substitute, such as an artificial extremity.

protein—A macronutrient that is essential to building muscle mass. Proteins make up about 15 percent of a person's body weight. Chemically, protein is composed of amino acids.

proximity control—The concept that being physically near a student will improve his or her behavior and focus.

pulmonary system—System of blood vessels that carries the blood between the heart and lungs.

punishment—Intervention procedure in which a pleasurable stimulus is removed or an aversive stimulus is presented as a consequence of a behavior in order to decrease the frequency of the occurrence of that behavior in the future (Lavay, French, & Henderson, 2016).

quadriplegia—Paralysis or involvement of all four extremities in the trunk, resulting from cervical spinal lesion or neurological dysfunctions.

qualitative aspects of skills—Elements of the skill that relate to how the skill is performed rather than the outcome (quantitative) of the skill. Evaluation of the qualitative aspects of a skill is conducted using criterion-referenced tests and assessments (Roth, Zittel, Pyfer, & Auxter, 2017).

quantitative skill teaching—Skill instruction where the emphasis lies in the final product (outcome or result) of the skill and not the process (the way) in which the skill was performed. Evaluation of this kind of instruction is done using normative assessment tools and objective assessment measures (Siedentop, & Tannehill, 2001).

random practice—Practice sequence in which tasks are experienced in random order over consecutive trials.

reaction time—Interval of time from a suddenly presented, unanticipated stimulus until the beginning of the response.

reasonable accommodation—Provision that may include (1) making existing facilities used by employees readily accessible to and usable by individuals with disabilities; and (2) job restructuring, part-time or modified work schedules, reassignment to a vacant position, acquisition or modification of equipment or devices, appropriate adjustment or modifications of examinations, training materials or policies, the provision of qualified readers or interpreters, and other similar accommodations.

reasoned action theory—Theory that predicts that behavioral intent is created or caused by two factors: our attitudes and our subjective norms.

reciprocal style of teaching—Style of teaching where the teacher has the learner work with a partner. Learners receive feedback from the partner based on criteria prepared by the teacher (Mosston & Ashworth, 2001).

reflex—A response to a stimuli without conscious thought.

regular education initiative (REI)—The goal of keeping as many students as possible in the general education setting.

reinforcement—Intervention procedure in which a pleasurable stimulus is provided or an aversive stimulus is removed as a consequence of a behavior in order to increase the frequency of the occurrence of that behavior in the future (Lavay, French, & Henderson, 2016).

reinforcement event menu—A list of highly desirable reinforcers that are displayed for individuals to observe. These items can be earned by meeting a predetermined criterion of behavior.

reinforcement schedules—Set of rules or a plan that outlines the number of times or length of time a behavior must be performed before reinforcement is given to the individual performing the behavior. Used to strengthen the occurrence of a behavior.

reinforcer—Something desirable as a consequence of a behavior in order to increase the future occurrence of that behavior (Lavay, French, & Henderson, 2016).

related services—Supportive services as are required to assist an individual with a disability to benefit from special education. These include physical therapy, occupational therapy, speech therapy, etc.

remedial physical education—See *corrective physical education*.

response cost—Withdrawal of a positive reinforcer as a consequence of the occurrence of an undesirable behavior in order to decrease the frequency of occurrence of that behavior. Examples would be fines or loss of privileges (Lavay, French, & Henderson, 2016).

response programming—Organization of the motor system for the desired movement.

response selection—Decision as to what movement to make given the nature of the environment.

restitutional overcorrection—An intervention procedure in which an individual is required to rectify the situation by returning the environment to an improved state. For example, an individual who throws trash on the playground is made to pick up all of the trash on the playground (Lavay, French, & Henderson, 2016).

RPE—Ratings of perceived exertion.

rubric—A list of the criteria to accomplish a task often used as a scoring tool that explicitly represents the performance expectations for an assignment or a skill.

satiation—Elimination of the effectiveness of a reinforcer on a behavior caused by excessive application.

secondary reinforcers—Stimuli or events that have acquired reinforcing capabilities (e.g., money or tokens) through being paired.

segregated sport opportunities—Sport programs in which students with disabilities participate with other students with the same or similar disability.

Segway—A two-wheeled motorized personal vehicle consisting of a platform for the feet mounted above an axle and an upright post surmounted by handles.

self-actualization—As proposed by Maslow, the realization of one's potential. Emphasis is on internal rather than external motivation and personal responsibility.

self-efficacy—One's belief in one's ability to succeed in specific situations or accomplish a task.

self-management—Taking responsibility for one's own behavior and well-being.

self-model—A form of observational learning in which individuals observe themselves performing a behavior successfully on a video and then imitating the target behavior.

self-monitoring—Process by which a person keeps track of one's own behavior such as using self-recording.

self-stimulatory—Behaviors that are self-induced, repetitive, non–goal oriented, and provide stimulation.

sensory integration—Theory that the inability to organize sensory information for use accounts for some aspects of learning disorders; it is theorized that enhancing sensory integration will make academic learning easier.

sensory receptors—Devices sensitive to light, heat, radiation, sound, mechanical, or other physical stimuli.

service delivery—Programs, processes, and safeguards established to ensure a free, appropriate public education is provided for children with disabilities.

shaping—Reinforcing small steps or approximations of the desired behavior.

short-term memory (STM)—An individual's capacity to hold, but not manipulate, a small amount of information in one's mind in an active, easily retrievable, available state for 15 to 30 seconds. STM is limited in capacity, duration, and encoding.

short-term objectives—Statements written in measurable, behavioral terms, consisting of the following components: (1) audience, (2) performance or behavior, (3) condition (optional), and (4) criteria.

short-term sensory memory—The most peripheral aspect of memory; involves processing in the stimulus-identification stage resulting in memory of the environmental sensory events that are stored for a maximum duration of about one-fourth of a second.

shunt—Device implanted in the body to remove or drain excess cerebrospinal fluid.

social imperception—Inability to gather information from the environment to utilize in determining the appropriateness of one's actions.

social reciprocity— Social reciprocity is the back-and-forth flow of social interaction. The term reciprocity refers to how the behavior of one person influences and is influenced by the behavior of another person and vice versa. Social reciprocity is the dance of social interaction and involves partners working together on a common goal of successful interaction. (ASBC, 2018)

social reinforcers—Actions of a social nature (physical contact, standing close by, verbal praise, etc.) that reinforce the desired behavior.

social values—Rules, morals, and ethical standards that when exercised, reflect socially appropriate behavior.

spatial uncertainty—A lack of, or error in, knowledge about one's position that leads to uncertainty about the spatial relationship between the individual and surrounding objects or individuals.

special education—Specifically designed instruction at no cost to the parents, to meet the unique needs of a child with a disability including classroom instruction, instruction in physical education, home instruction, and instruction in hospitals and institutions (IDEIA, 2004).

specially designed physical education—Physical education program with modifications to allow students enrolled in a special education class to participate safely and successfully.

speed–accuracy trade-off—Tendency for accuracy to decrease as the speed or velocity of a movement increases.

standardized instruments—Tests that specifically describe procedures for administration including set of conditions, equipment, and instructions (standardized administration) to which data collection must conform in order for the data to be considered valid.

static lung volume—Lung volume measured during rest.

stimulus identification—Primarily a sensory stage that requires analyzing environmental information from a variety of sources, such as vision, hearing, touch, and kinesthesis to decide whether a stimulus has been presented and, if so, what it is.

stimulus overselectivity—Abnormally limited attentional scope, inability to select relevant cues and to see the whole.

stroke volume—Amount of blood pumped by the left ventricle of the heart in one contraction or beat (McArdle, Katch, & Katch, 2014).

structural remediation—A therapeutic approach intended to restore balance and alignment to the body through muscular stretching and fascia lengthening and repositioning.

student evaluation—The process of determining changes in learner knowledge, understanding, and physical and motor ability over time.

summative evaluation—The measurement and evaluation of an individual's performance using a predetermined standard that focuses more on the overall outcomes of instruction over time; done periodically and is designed to address larger programmatic decisions such as whether students are mastering objectives on schedule (Kelly & Melograno, 2014, p. 243).

tactile defensive—Hypersensitive to touch or pressure.

tactile signals—Signals that are provided through touch.

tangible reinforcement—An object that when provided after the performance of a behavior increases the likelihood that the behavior will again be performed.

task analysis—The breaking down of a skill into its component parts; sequenced subskills or intermediate progressions that a student must generally learn in order to complete the next or more complex subskill (Kelly & Melograno, 2014, p. 76).

task description—Approach to specifying curriculum content that describes in a step-by-step progression the elements of a task; the outcomes generated by this task analysis process is a series of descriptions that follow the progress of a given task through its various component operations.

task teaching style—Teaching style in which the teacher determines the basic framework to the lesson (e.g., what tasks will be learned, in what order they will be learned, etc.) where the students are permitted to make decisions on the pace at which they work and how the skill is to be executed (Mosston & Ashworth, 2001).

task variation—Teaching method that involves increasing a student's motivation by presenting different types of instructions and also mixing new topics with those previously mastered.

temporal uncertainty—Difficulties with the ability to prepare for future movements or to make movement decisions based on expected outcomes because of errors in predicting movement events, timing, or anticipated outcomes.

teratogenic factors—Agents that can disturb the development of the embryo or the fetus causing developmental malformations. Teratogens include radiation, maternal infections, chemicals, and drugs.

therapeutic recreation (TR)—Profession that promotes wellness and improves the quality of life through leisure activities for individuals with disabilities.

thermoregulation—Ability of the body to regulate its temperature influenced by environmental conditions (e.g., sweating).

time on task—Time spent in the lesson or task where the learner is actively involved in the assigned activity.

time-out—Removal of an individual for a period of time from a reinforcing environment. This is contingent upon the emittance of inappropriate behavior in an attempt to decrease the future occurrence of that particular behavior (Lavay, French, & Henderson, 2016).

token economy—Tokens, checkmarks, points, or chips are earned for meeting a predetermined criterion of behavior in order to increase the future occurrence of that behavior. The tokens are later exchanged for items which are reinforcing and of value to the individual (Lavay, French, & Henderson, 2016).

top-down (model)—Process for developing a curriculum based on creating goal statements that define specifically what students will be able to do when they complete the program. These goal statements are then broken down into developmental lists of objectives that are sequenced across the various grade levels in the program (Kelly & Melograno, 2014, p. 104).

total communication—Combination of communication modes (e.g., verbal, gestural, pictorial) that offers the individual with a disability an extended range of communication options.

total inclusion—This model places and instructs all students, including those with disabilities, in a general education environment regardless of the type or severity of disability. Multidisciplinary teams of professionals bring their collective skills and knowledge together to provide personal programs for each student (Kelly & Melograno, 2014, p. 14).

Touch Talker—Augmented device that allows the nonverbal student to directly select (point to) symbols (ranging from 8 to 128) to communicate his or her wants and needs.

transdisciplinary approach (model)—A model of communication that encourages a sharing of information and cooperation among team members throughout the implementation of services to the individual.

transitional procedures—Methods used to move from one activity to another.

transition planning—A formal process for helping students with IEPs figure out what they want to do after high school and how to accomplish the goals they set.

transition time—Time spent during a lesson in moving from one activity to another.

traumatic brain injury—Closed head injuries caused by concussion, contusion, or hemorrhage that result in permanent damage (Sherrill, 2004).

underweight—Body weight is lower than normal weight calculated from skeletal measurements; body weight lower than the 20th percentile by height-for-age; and percent body fat is lower than 17 percent (McArdle, Katch, & Katch, 2014).

universal design for learning (UDL)—A set of principles for curriculum development that give all individuals equal opportunities to learn. It provides a blueprint for creating instructional goals, methods, materials, and assessments that work for everyone—not a single, one-size-fits-all solution, but rather flexible approaches that can be customized and adjusted for individual needs.

utility (of measurement instruments)—Desirable test characteristic referring to the usability of the data as well as the usability of the instrument. See also *administrative feasibility*.

variable practice—A practice sequence in which individuals rehearse a task in a number of different ways.

ventilation—Movement of air into and out of the lungs (McArdle, Katch, & Katch, 2014).

verbal communication—Medium of oral communication that employs a linguistic code (language); through this medium one can express thoughts and feelings and understand those of others who employ the same code.

verbal directions—Least intrusive level of cueing or prompting that consists of the individual verbally explaining to another individual what should be done in order to respond and complete the task (Block, 2016).

vestibular—Apparatus in the inner ear that provides signals related to movement in space (Sherrill, 2004).

vocational specialist—Vocational educator who provides services to individuals with disabilities who cannot succeed in a general vocational setting. These professionals provide various services such as modified instruction, guidance counseling and testing services, employability skill training, and communication skill training.

Bibliography

American Education Research Association, American Psychological Association, and The National Council on Measurement in Education. (2014). *Standards for educational and psychological testing.* Washington, DC: American Psychological Association.

American Physical Therapy Association. (1980). *Definition and guidelines.* Rockville, MD: Author.

American Psychiatric Association. (2015). *Diagnostic and statistical manual of mental disorders—revision* (5th ed.). Washington, DC: Author.

American with Disabilities Act of 1990, PL 101-336, 2, 104 Stat. 328 (1990).

Anshel, M. H. (Ed.). (1991). *Dictionary of sport and exercise science.* Champaign, IL: Human Kinetics.

Autism Society of Baltimore-Chesapeake (ASBC). (2018). Definition of Social Reciprocity. Retrieved November 1, 2018 from https://www.baltimoreautismsociety.org/glossary/term/social-reciprocity/

Ayres, A. J. (1981). *Sensory integration and learning disorders.* Los Angeles, CA: Western Psychological Services.

Barnes, M. R., Crutchfield, C. A., & Heriza, C. B. (1979). *The neuropsychological basis of patient treatment* (Vol. 2)*: Reflexes in motor development.* Atlanta, GA: Stokesville.

Baumgartner, T. A., Jackson, A. S., Mahar, M. T., & Rowe D. A. (2006). *Measurement for evaluation in physical education and exercise science* (8th ed.). New York, NY: McGraw Hill.

Berkow, R. (Ed.). (1987). *Merck manual of diagnosis and therapy* (15th ed.). Rahway, NJ: Merck Sharp & Dohme Research Laboratories.

Bigge, J. L. (1991). *Teaching individuals with physical and multiple disabilities.* New York, NY: Macmillan.

Block, M. E. (2016). *A teacher's guide to including students with disabilities in general physical education* (4th ed.). Baltimore, MD: Paul H. Brooks.

Buck, M. M., Lund, J. L., Harrison, J. M., & Blakemore, C. L. (2007). *Instructional strategies for secondary physical education* (6th ed.). New York, NY: McGraw-Hill.

Carlson, N. R., & Birkett, M. A. (2017). *Physiology of behavior* (12th ed.). Essex, England: Pearson.

Cartwright, G. P., Cartwright, C. A., & Ward, M. F. (1989). *Educating special educators* (3rd ed.). Belmont, CA: Wadsworth.

Clark, J. E., Betchell, N., Smiley-Ogen, A. L., & Whitall, J. (2005). Developmental coordination disorder: Issues, identification, and intervention. *Journal of Physical Education, Recreation and Dance, 76*(4), 48-53.

Cooper, J. M., Adrian, M., & Glassow, R. B. (1982). *Kinesiology* (5th ed.). St. Louis, MO: C. V. Mosby.

Cooper, J. O., Heron, T. E., & Heward, W. L. (2007). *Applied behavior analysis* (2nd ed.). Upper Saddle River, NJ: Pearson; 2007.

Council for Exceptional Children. (2018). *Evidence-based practice resources.* Retrieved from www.cec.sped.org/Standards/Evidence-Based-Practice-Resources-Original

Cowden, J., & Tymeson, G. (1984). *Certification in adapted/special education: National status-update.* Dekalb, IL: Northern Illinois University.

Craft, D. (1994). Inclusion: Physical education for all. *Journal of Physical Education, Recreation and Dance, 65*(1), 22-23.

Davis, T. (2001). *A validation study of the 1997 Adapted Physical Education National Standards (APENS) certification exam* (Dissertation). University of Virginia, Charlottesville.

Davis, T. & Dillon, S. R. (2010). Psychometric properties of the 2005-2010 Adapted Physical Education National Standards certification exam. Paper presented at the 10th North American Federation of Adapted Physical Activity Symposium, Riverside, CA.

Dillman, D. (1978). *Mail and telephone surveys: The total design method.* New York, NY: John Wiley & Sons.

Dillon, S., & Davis, T. (2014).

Dreikurs, R., Cassel, P., & Ferguson E. D. (2004). *Discipline without tears* (Revised ed.). Toronto, Canada: Wiley.

Dummer, G. M., Reuschlein, P. L., Haubenstricker, J. L., Vogel, P. G., & Cavanaugh, P. L. (1993). *Evaluation of K-12 physical education programs: A self-study approach.* Dubuque, IA: Brown.

Dunn, J. M., & Leitschuh, C. A. (2014). *Special physical education* (10th ed.). Dubuque, IA: Kendall/Hunt.

Dunn, J. M., Morehouse, J. W., & Fredericks, H. D. B. (1986). *Physical education for the severely handicapped.* Austin, TX: Pro-Ed.

Education of All Handicapped Children Act of 1975 (PL 94-142, Nov. 29, 1975), *United States Statutes at Large, 89*, 773-796.

Education of the Handicapped Act Amendments of 1990, Pub. L. No. 101-476, 104 Stat. 1103, codified as amended at 20 U.S.C.A. SS 1400-1487 (West 2000 & Supp. 2006).

Eichstaedt, C. B., & Lavay, B. W. (1992). *Physical activity for individuals with mental retardation: Infancy through adulthood.* Champaign, IL: Human Kinetics.

ESSA. (2015). Every Student Succeeds Act of 2015, Pub. L. No. 114-95 § 114 Stat. 1177 (2015-2016).

Fiorentino, M. (1981). *A basis for sensorimotor development: Normal and abnormal.* Springfield, IL: Charles C. Thomas.

Fisher, A., Murray, E., & Bundy, A. (2002). *Sensory integration: Theory and practice* (2nd ed.) Philadelphia, PA: F. A. Davis.

Fox, E. L., Kirby, T. E., & Fox, A. R. (1987). *Bases of fitness.* New York, NY: Macmillan.

French, R., Lavay, B., & Henderson, H. (1985). Take a lap. *Physical Educator, 42*, 180-185.

Gabbard, C. (2018). *Lifelong motor development* (7th ed.). Philadelphia, PA: Wolters Kluwer Health.

Gagne, R. M., Wager, W. W., Golas, K. C., & Keller, J. M. (2004). *Principles of instructional design* (5th ed.) Belmont, CA: Wadsworth Publishing.

Gallahue, D. L., Ozmun, J. C., & Goodway, J. D. (2012). *Understanding motor development in children* (7th ed.). Dubuque, IA: McGraw-Hill.

Graham, G., Holt-Hale, S., & Parker, M. (2013). *Children moving* (9th ed.). New York, NY: McGraw-Hill.

Hall, S. J. (2012). *Basic biomechanics* (7th ed.). Boston, MA: McGraw-Hill.

Hay, J. G. (1993). *The biomechanics of sport techniques* (4th ed.). Englewood Cliffs, NJ: Prentice Hall.

Hellison, D. (1984). *Goals and strategies for teaching physical education*. Champaign, IL: Human Kinetics.

Hodge, S., Lieberman, L., & Murata, N. (2012). *Essentials of teaching adapted physical education: Diversity, culture and inclusion*. Scottsdale, AZ: Holcomb Hathaway Publishers.

Horvat, M., Kelly, L. E., Block, M., & Croce, R. (2018). *Developmental and adapted physical activity assessment* (2nd ed.), Champaign, IL: Human Kinetics.

Hurd, A., & Anderson, D. (2011). The park and recreation professional's handbook. Champaign, IL: Human Kinetics.

Individuals with Disabilities Education Act (IDEA) Amendments of 1990, 20 U.S.C. 1400 et seq.

Individuals with Disabilities Education Act (IDEA) Amendments of 1997, Pub. L. No. 105-17, 111 Stat. 37, codified as amended at 20 U.S.C.A. SS 1400-1487 (West 2000 & Supp. 2006).

Individuals with Disabilities Education Improvement Act (IDEIA) of 2004, Pub. L. No. 108-446, 118 Stat. 2647, codified at 20 U.S.C.A. SS 1400-1487 (West Supp. 2006).

Kelly, L. E. (1991a). [Developing outcome standards for adapted physical education]. Unpublished raw data.

Kelly, L. E. (1991b). Is there really a national need for more adapted physical educators? *Advocate, 2*(1), 7-8.

Kelly, L. E. (1991c). National standards for adapted physical education. *Advocate, 20*(1), 2-3.

Kelly, L. E. (1992). *National standards for adapted physical education* (Grant No. H029K20092). Washington, DC: United States Department of Education, Office of Special Education and Rehabilitation Services.

Kelly, L. E. (Ed.). (1995) *Adapted physical education national standards*. Champaign, IL: Human Kinetics.

Kelly, L. E. (Ed.). (2006) *Adapted physical education national standards (2nd ed.)* Champaign, IL: Human Kinetics.

Kelly, L. E. (Ed.). (2009). *APENS study guide* (2nd ed.). Cortland, NY: SUNY Cortland.

Kelly, L. E. (2011). *Designing and implementing effective adapted physical education programs*. Urbana, IL: Sagamore Publishing, LLC.

Kelly, L. E., Block, M., & Colombo-Dougovito, A. (2017). *Physical education*. In J. M. Kauffman & D. P. Hallahan (Eds.), Handbook of special education (2nd ed., pp. 586-605). New York, NY: Routledge.

Kelly, L. E., & Gansneder, B. M. (1998). Preparation and job demographics of adapted physical educators in the United States. *Adapted Physical Activity Quarterly, 15*, 141-154.

Kelly, L. E., & Melograno, V. J. (2014). *Developing the physical education curriculum: An achievement-based approach*. Long Grove, IL: Waveland Press, Inc.

Kelly, L. E., Wessel, J. A., Dummer, G., & Sampson, T. (2010). Everyone CAN: Elementary physical education curriculum and teaching resources. Champaign, IL: Human Kinetics Publishers.

Kreighbaum, E., & Barthels, K. M. (1996). *Biomechanics: A qualitative approach for studying human movement* (4th ed.). San Francisco, CA: Benjamin Cummings.

Lavay, B., French, R., & Henderson, H. (2016). *Positive behavior management in physical activity settings* (3rd ed.). Champaign, IL: Human Kinetics.

Lieberman, L. J., & Houston-Wilson, C. (2017). *Strategies for inclusion* (3rd ed.). Champaign, IL: Human Kinetics.

Magill, R. A., & Anderson, D. (2013). *Motor learning: Concepts and applications* (10th ed.). New York, NY: McGraw-Hill.

Marieb, E. N. (2015). *Essentials of human anatomy and physiology* (11th ed.). Glenview, IL: Pearson.

Marieb, E. N., & Hoehn, K. (2015). *Human anatomy and physiology* (10th ed.). Glenview, IL: Pearson.

McArdle, W. D., Katch, V. I., & Katch, V. L. (2014). *Exercise physiology: Energy, nutrition, and human performance* (8th ed.). Philadelphia, PA: Lippincott, Williams & Wilkins.

Mohram, D. E., & Heller, L. J. (2013). *Cardiovascular physiology* (8th ed.). New York, NY: McGraw-Hill.

Moon, M. S., & Bunker, L. (1987). Recreation and motor skills programming. In M. E. Snell (Ed.), *Systematic instruction of persons with severe handicaps*. Columbus, OH: Merrill.

Morris, G. S. D., & Stiehl, J. (1999). *Changing kids' games* (2nd ed.). Champaign, IL: Human Kinetics.

Mosston, M., & Ashworth, S. (2001). *Teaching physical education* (5th ed.). San Francisco, CA: Benjamin Cummings.

National Association for Sport and Physical Education. (2008). *Advanced standards for physical education*. Reston, VA: Author.

National Association of State Directors of Special Education. (1991). Physical education and sports: The unfulfilled promise for students with disabilities. *Liaison Bulletin, 17*(6), 1-10.

National Board for Professional Teaching Standards. (2014). *Physical Education Standards* (2nd ed), www.boardcertified-teachers.org.

National Consortium on Physical Education and Recreation for the Handicapped. (1991, July). Summary of the NCPERID board meeting, Arlington, VA. *Advocate, 20*(1), 4-5.

National Joint Committee on Learning Disabilities. (2018). *LD online: The educators' guide to learning disabilities and ADHD*. Retrieved from www.ldonline.org

National Resource Center for Paraprofessionals in Special Education. (1988). *A training program for paraprofessionals working in special education and related services*. New York, NY: New Centers Training Laboratory.

NCHPAD. (n.d.). *Exercise testing: Body composition*. Retrieved from www.nchpad.org/117/915/Down~Syndrome.

Nicolosi, L., Haryman, E., & Kresheck, J. (2003). *Terminology of communication disorders* (5th ed.). Philadelphia, PA: Lippincott, Williams & Wilkins.

No Child Left Behind Act of 2001, Pub. L. No. 107-110, 115 Stat. 1425, codified as amended at 20 U.S.C.A. SS 6301-7941 (West 2003 & Supp. 2006).

Obrusnikova, I., & Dillon, S. R. (2011). Challenging situations when teaching children with autism spectrum disorders in general physical education. *Adapted Physical Activity Quarterly, 28*(2), 113-131.

Orlick, T. (2006). *Cooperative games and sports* (2nd ed.). Champaign, IL: Human Kinetics.

Pangrazi, R. P., & Beighle, A. (2007). *Dynamic physical education for elementary school children* (18th ed.). San Francisco, CA: Pearson.

Payne, V. G., & Isaacs, L. D. (2016). *Human motor development: A lifespan approach* (9th ed.). New York, NY: Taylor & Francis.

Randall, L. E. (1992). *The student teacher's handbook for physical education*. Champaign, IL: Human Kinetics.

Rimmer, J. H. (1994). *Fitness and rehabilitation programs for special populations*. Dubuque, IA: Brown.

Rink, J. (2014). *Teaching physical education for learning* (7th ed.) New York, NY: McGraw-Hill.

Roth, K., Zittel, L., Pyfer, J., & Auxter, D. (2017). *Principles and methods of adapted physical education and recreation* (12th ed.). Burlington, MA: Jones & Bartlett Learning.

Sage, G. (1984). *Motor learning and control: A neuropsychological approach.* Dubuque, IA: Brown.

Schmidt, R. A. (1991). *Motor learning and performance: From principles to practice.* Champaign, IL: Human Kinetics.

Schmidt, R. A., & Lee, T. D. (2011). *Motor control and learning: A behavioral emphasis* (5th ed.). Champaign, IL: Human Kinetics.

Schmidt, R. A., & Lee, T. D. (2014). *Motor control and performance: From principles to application* (5th ed.). Champaign, IL: Human Kinetics.

Schmidt, R. A., & Wrisberg, C. A. (2008). *Motor learning and performance* (4th ed.). Champaign, IL: Human Kinetics.

Seaman, J., DePauw, K., Morton, K. E., & Omota, K. (2006). *Making connections: From theory to practice in adapted physical education* (2nd ed.). Scottsdale, AZ: Holcomb Hathaway.

Sears, C. J. (1982). The transdisciplinary approach: A process for the compliance with Public Law 94-142. *Journal of the Association for the Severely Handicapped, 6,* 22-29.

Shea, T. M., & Bauer, A. M. (2011). *Behavior management: A practical approach for educators* (10th ed.). New York, NY: Pearson.

Sherrill, C. (1988). *Leadership training in adapted physical education.* Champaign, IL: Human Kinetics.

Sherrill, C. (2004). *Adapted physical activity, recreation, and sport: Crossdisciplinary and lifespan* (6th ed.). Dubuque, IA: McGraw-Hill.

Short, F. X. (2000). Individualized education programs. In J. P. Winnick (Ed.), *Adapted physical education and sport* (pp. 47-60). Champaign, IL: Human Kinetics.

Siedentop, D., & Tannehill, D. (2001). *Developing teaching skills in physical education* (4th ed.). Dubuque, IA: McGraw-Hill.

Siedentop, D. J., Herowitz, J., & Rink, J. (1984). *Elementary physical education methods.* Englewood Cliffs, NJ: Prentice Hall.

Snell, M. E., & Grigg, N. C. (1987). Instructional assessment and curriculum development. In M. E. Snell (Ed.), *Systematic instruction of persons with severe handicaps.* Columbus, OH: Merrill.

Society of Health and Physical Educators (SHAPE). (2008). *Advanced standards.* Reston, VA.

Society of Health and Physical Educators (SHAPE). (2017). *National standards for initial physical education teacher education.* Reston, VA: Author.

Spence, A. P., & Mason, E. B., (2018). Human anatomy and physiology (4th ed.). Minnesota: West Publishing.

Teki, S., Chait, M., Kumar, S., von Kriefstein, K., & Griffiths, T. (2011). Brain bases for auditory stimulus-driven figure–ground segregation. *Journal of Neuroscience, 31*(1), 164-171.

U.S. Department of Education, Office for Civil Rights. (2013, January 25). *Dear colleague.* Washington, DC: Author.

U.S. Department of Education, Office of Elementary and Secondary Education. (2002). *No child left behind: A desktop reference.* Washington, DC: GPO.

U.S. Department of Education, Office of Special Education and Rehabilitative Services, Office of Special Education Programs. (2011). *Creating equal opportunities for children and youth with disabilities to participate in physical education and extracurricular athletics.* Washington, DC: Author.

Van Houten, R. (1980). *Learning through feedback: A systematic approach for improving academic performance.* Blaine, WA: Kluwer.

Venes, D. (Ed.). (2017). *Taber's cyclopedia medical dictionary* (23rd ed.). Philadelphia, PA: Davis.

Weeks, Z. R. (2007). *Opportunities in occupational therapy careers.* New York, NY: McGraw-Hill.

Williams, H. (1983). *Perceptual and motor development.* Englewood Cliffs, NJ: Prentice Hall.

Winnick, J. P., &Porretta, D.L. (Ed.). (2017). *Adapted physical education and sport* (6th ed.). Champaign, IL: Human Kinetics.

Winslow, R. M. (1989). Therapeutic recreation: Promoting wellness through leisure. *California Association for Health, Physical Education, Recreation & Dance Journal, 51*(6), 11-12.

Wolfgang, C. H. (2009). *Solving discipline and classroom management problems* (7th ed.). Hoboken, NJ: John Wiley & Sons, Inc.

About the Editor

Luke E. Kelly, PhD, is a certified adapted physical educator and is a professor of kinesiology, holder of the Virgil S. Ward endowed professorship, and director of the graduate programs in adapted physical education at the University of Virginia. He has 38 years of experience working with public schools in evaluating and revising their physical education curricula to meet the needs of students with disabilities. Dr. Kelly has written extensively about the achievement-based curriculum model, assessment, and the use of technology in physical education. Dr. Kelly has served as the president of the National Consortium for Physical Education for Individuals with Disabilities (NCPEID) and directed the NCPEID adapted physical education national standards project from 1992 to 1999. Dr. Kelly is a fellow in the National Academy of Kinesiology (formerly the American Academy of Kinesiology and Physical Education). He has also received the G. Lawrence Rarick Research Award and the William A. Hillman Distinguished Service Award from the NCPEID. His hobbies and interests include fly-fishing, reforestation, and building projects.